THE

FRUGAL

COOK

A.

Absolute Press

THE
FRUGAL
COOK

FIONA
BECKETT

BUY CLEVERLY. WASTE LESS. EAT WELL.

First published in Great Britain in 2008 by
Absolute Press
Scarborough House
29 James Street West
Bath BA1 2BT
Phone 44 (0) 1225 316013
Fax 44 (0) 1225 445836
E-mail info@absolutepress.co.uk
Website www.absolutepress.co.uk

This revised and updated edition published 2011

Text copyright © Fiona Beckett, 2008
This edition copyright © Absolute Press

Publisher Jon Croft
Commissioning Editor Meg Avent
Editorial Assistant Andrea O'Connor
Art Director Matt Inwood
Designer Claire Siggery
Food Photography Mike Cooper
Food Styling Genevieve Taylor
Illustrations Andy Pedler and Claire Siggery

ISBN 13: 9781906650537
Printed and bound by C&C Offset Printing,
China

A catalogue record of this book is available
from the British Library.

Note about the type
This book has been set using Gill Sans and
Century. Gill Sans was designed by the English
artist and type designer Eric Gill and issued by
Monotype in 1928 to 1930. It has a very 'British'
look to it (inspired as it was by the typeface used
to sign London's Undeground Railway in 1918,
designed by Gill's teacher, Edward Johnston).
It is a classic display typeface. The first Century
typeface was cut in 1894. In 1975 an updated
family of Century typefaces was designed by
Tony Stan for ITC.

CONTENTS

6 PREFACE TO THIS NEW EDITION 7 CHANGING THE WAY YOU THINK ABOUT FOOD
8 20 WAYS TO CUT YOUR FOOD BILLS BY 20% 12 THE ART OF USING LEFTOVERS
14 THE SKILL OF STRETCHING FOOD
16 THE BEST WAYS TO SHOP FOR AND SOURCE YOUR FOOD
22 HOW TO BAG A BARGAIN 26 THE FRUGAL STORECUPBOARD (AND FRIDGE)
28 FRUGAL KITCHEN EQUIPMENT 30 HOW TO BE MORE ENERGY-EFFICIENT
32 STORING FOOD SAFELY 36 WASTE DISPOSAL
38 PORTION CONTROL 40 THE FRUGAL DINER

43
BUDGET BREAKFASTS & BRUNCHES

59
LIGHT LUNCHES & SNACKS

85
EASY MIDWEEK SUPPERS

123
BIG WEEKEND COOK-UPS

171
THE FRUGAL HOST

203
A–Z OF INGREDIENTS & LEFTOVERS

226 INDEX 238 THE FRUGAL COOK ONLINE AND OTHER BOOKS
240 ACKNOWLEDGEMENTS

PREFACE TO THIS NEW EDITION

When I finished writing *The Frugal Cook*, roughly three years ago, I guess I imagined we'd all be out of the woods economically by now, so it's not entirely good news there's still such a need for the book. Jobs have disappeared, the cost of living's gone up, times for many are still tough – **the art of simple home cooking is more valuable than ever before**.

The danger is that we reduce the quality of the ingredients we buy at the expense of our own health and the survival of our farmers and other food producers. But I firmly believe it is possible to eat healthily – and to eat the kind of food you enjoy – on a tight budget. And to enjoy it. There's something quite David-and-Goliath-like about beating the supermarkets at their own game – working out what the real bargains are rather than just falling for the special offers. And finding that independent shops can often match them for price.

This new edition has had a bit of a makeover, with a shiny new cover and some glossy food photography. I hope they persuade you just how appetising frugal food can look; persuade you that you really can feed your friends on cheap cuts, market bargains and leftovers and they'll never know the difference... so long as you don't let on... ;-)

FIONA BECKETT
Bristol, March 2011

CHANGING THE WAY YOU THINK ABOUT FOOD

I've always been a scavenger cook. Of course, it's great having fabulous, freshly-bought ingredients but there's nothing quite as satisfying as rustling up a really good meal from leftovers or assorted odds and ends from the fridge or the storecupboard – a skill that a lot of people are finding they have to learn in a tough economic climate in which we currently find ourselves.

Of course, we've been here, before. Or, rather not us but our parents and grandparents, most notably during and after the second world war when rationing was in force. But times have changed!

Few of us can afford to be stay-at-home parents nowadays, even if we'd like to. Fewer still have the cooking skills their parents did. We can't or don't want to spend hours in the kitchen. We've got used to convenient, quick, easy-to-prepare meals.

We're more concerned about the way we look. That means we're less likely to want to fill up on inexpensive carbohydrate and fat-laden meals which we can't work off because we don't take enough physical exercise. We've travelled and developed more sophisticated tastes. We don't want to live off rissoles and Woolton Pie.

We're concerned about where our food comes from and how it is sourced. Many of us actively seek out organic, Fairtrade produce. We don't want cut-price chicken if the price to be paid is that they're kept in appallingly inhumane conditions.

In short, we can't turn the clock back. But is it possible to square the circle? Cut down what we spend on food without reliving the past? I believe it is.

It's simply a matter of changing the way you think about food. In much the same way, perhaps, as you would if you were going on a diet and trying to lose weight.

- Be more conscious of how much you're buying and what you're going to do with it. Not necessarily spending more time in the kitchen, but more time thinking about meals so that you don't end up with quantities of wasted food.

- Cut down the amount of expensive protein you eat (no bad thing anyway from a health point of view).

- Schedule cooking sessions when you have a bit more time so that you don't have to do as much when you're busy.

- Be willing to try – and get your children to try – new dishes, picking up ideas from cultures that traditionally have a frugal but often delicious diet.

It should – hopefully – open up new ways of cooking and shopping that may well be more enjoyable than your current ones. Cooking thriftily is creative, and exploring the vast array of independent and ethnic shops – with bargains that are much better than those found in your average supermarket – can be richly rewarding.

I don't mind admitting I've learnt a lot in the process of writing this book and its accompanying blog (www.thefrugalcook.blogspot.com).

I'm not only a more economical cook now but a better, more inventive one. I hope you will be too....

20 WAYS TO CUT YOUR FOOD BILLS BY 20%

Depending on how frugal you already are there are many ways to make substantial savings on your food bill. If you currently waste a lot you could save as much as a third of what you spend.

1
ONLY SHOP WHEN YOU NEED TO

This is possibly the most valuable lesson to take on board – certainly the one I've found has changed my shopping habits most. Don't buy food unless you need to. Take a look at what you've got in the fridge, freezer or storecupboard before you go to the supermarket or down to the local shops. More than likely you can make a meal from it. In fact, you could probably survive the week. Try and have at least one No Food Shopping Day a week, as I call it in the blog. A day when you think you need to go to the shops but you hold off. No stopping off for a sandwich or going to a restaurant either. Good for the soul. Better still for the purse.

2
MAKE A SHOPPING LIST

Not just off the top of your head. Check which ingredients you already have so you don't end up duplicating them.

3
AVOID IMPULSE BUYING

This is the discipline I've found it hardest to stick to. I get totally over-excited about good ingredients, especially in markets and invariably buy more than I need – or at least I used to. Supermarkets are also brilliant at making us part with our money. Just because a product is new, doesn't mean you have to try it.

4
STOP STOCKPILING

Get out of the habit of making 'just in case' purchases – food for family or friends who might drop by. They might – but you might go to their house instead and not need any of it.

5
PLAN AHEAD...

Exactly how far ahead depends on your temperament and lifestyle. If you never know where you're going to be from one day to the next, it's hard admittedly but in that case the answer, if you want to avoid wasting massive amounts of food, is only to buy fresh, perishable produce when you know you can eat it within 24 hours. This strategy may involve more visits to the shop, but you won't spend as long in there as you do for a big supermarket shop – so long as you resist impulse purchases (see above).

6
....BUT NOT TOO FAR AHEAD

Some people prefer to do a big weekly shop but I must say I'm not one of them, partly because I'm not a big fan of supermarket shopping (see page 17), but mainly because it's so easy to buy more than you need. The best way I find is to plan in two to three day blocks, shopping on a Friday or Saturday for the weekend then taking stock on Monday or Tuesday in the light of what's left over and what we're doing for the rest of the week.

7
DON'T OVER-CATER

One of the most common reasons for wasting food is over-catering, especially when you're entertaining. Cheese is a classic example. You go out and buy four or five different kinds to fill a cheese board. Half of that – if you're lucky – gets eaten on the night. The leftover Cheddar and maybe the Brie gets used over the next few days. The rest lurks in the back of the fridge for a couple of weeks until you discover it mouldering away. Instead, buy one really great cheese – one that you can use up during the week if any is left over – and you'll find the whole lot goes (see also Cheese, page 209).

8
EXERCISE PORTION CONTROL

Adjust your idea of portion size by checking out pages 38–39, or the very useful calculator published by **lovefoodhatewaste.com**. We all tend to eat too much protein. The standard recommendation for chicken, for example is 140g per person for an adult and 100g for children. That doesn't take into account whether the meat is on or off the bone or what age and size the children are (teenage boys have an awesome capacity to put away food) but it's a useful reality check.

9
SET LEFTOVERS ASIDE

The only way to limit how much food gets eaten and whether you have any left over is to serve it out yourself, firmly putting aside any you need for the following day before it even reaches the table (an essential strategy in the case of a Sunday roast). That may mean denying your family second helpings but they'll be mollified if you offer them a pudding instead (which is exactly how families used to eat 30 or 40 years ago).

10
BAN FRIDGE-RAIDING

Of course, there's no point in creating loads of lovely leftovers if everyone picks at them freely throughout the day – or night. It may sound draconian but you need to issue an edict against fridge-raiding – or at least create a 'no go' shelf from which the family – including you – are strictly banned.

11
FEED EVERYONE
THE SAME FOOD

And while we're on the subject of changing family habits how many different meals do you serve in one night? If you're making more than two – and even that's only justifiable if there's a vegetarian in the house – it's too many. I can't claim to have got this right over the years – we did occasionally let our ultra-fussy youngest, (inevitably the youngest), opt out of the family meal. And what's the result? An ultra-fussy – though very sweet, of course – adult. More to the point, it's expensive and time-consuming. Even with a vegetarian in the house it's possible for the whole family to eat the same meal at least two or three nights a week.

12
DON'T FOLLOW RECIPES
SLAVISHLY

Yes, even these ones! They're only there as a guide. Too often we rush to the shops simply because we think we're lacking what we imagine is a vital ingredient in a recipe (and pick up a whole load of other stuff while we're there). But there's often a substitute. To take some common examples you can get an onion flavour from onions, shallots, spring onions, chives and leeks, a tomato one from fresh tomatoes, tinned tomatoes, passata and tomato paste and give a spicy kick to a recipe with fresh chillies, chilli powder, chilli sauce, hot paprika or pimenton and cayenne pepper. A blue cheese like Stilton can easily be substituted for Gorgonzola in a pasta recipe (see page 110). Who cares if it's British rather than Italian? Necessity is the mother of invention.

13
HAVE A GOOD BASIC
STORECUPBOARD
– AND FREEZER STOCKS

A supply of basics such as pasta, rice and pulses, some tinned tomatoes and a range of herbs and spices (see pages 26–27) will make rustling up a scratch meal a lot easier. So will a well-stocked – but not over-filled – freezer.

14
LEARN TO SPOT A BARGAIN...

Many people miss out on bargains because they're not aware that they exist or fail to realise just what good value they are. A great example is a ham hock, a brilliantly frugal buy that will stretch to 8–10 helpings (see pages 73, 79 and 146). Another is Quark, a low-cost, low-fat cheese which is mysteriously cheaper than any comparable product simply, I suspect, because it's German and has a funny name.

15
...AND SOMETIMES
WALK AWAY FROM ONE

A bargain is not a bargain if you can't eat or cook it before it goes off. Example: a couple of kilos of bananas for a $1 may sound like a fantastic buy but what are you going to do with them? Live off smoothies for a week? Bake ten banana breads? Probably not.

16
AVOID OVERPRICED INGREDIENTS

Which means carrying around in your head what things should cost. There comes a point when even healthy ingredients like a red pepper – recently spotted at over £1 each – are simply not worth buying (frozen vegetables like peas, peppers and spinach and fruits such as raspberries can be cheaper than fresh and are just as, if not more, nutritious). Prime cuts of meat such as steak and chicken breasts are always going to cost more than their less glamourous counterparts (see more examples on page 23).

17
CUT DOWN ON CONVENIENCE FOODS

I say cut down rather than cut out because sometimes convenience foods can save money – when you're cooking just for one, for example. But in general, if someone else saves you time in the kitchen, you pay. Bagged salad leaves, pre-prepared fruit, ready-grated cheese, pasta sauces and salad dressings... just add it up.

18
BUY PRODUCE IN SEASON (AS A GENERAL RULE)...

'As a general rule' because so efficient are distribution systems nowadays that it can, depressingly, be cheaper to buy in season produce like asparagus and tomatoes from another country (usually Spain) than to buy it home-grown. Of course, it doesn't taste as good but if frugality is the only object it's hard to be patriotic. Nevertheless, you will generally find that root vegetables and citrus are cheaper in winter and salad vegetables such as cucumber, tomatoes and lettuce and berry fruits like strawberries and raspberries are cheaper in the summer.

19
...AND BUY IT LOOSE

It's not simply that pre-packed fruit and vegetables are significantly more expensive than their loose counterparts – they also encourage you to buy more than you need, particularly if you're shopping for one. Particular culprits on cost grounds are pre-packed fresh herbs (much cheaper by the bunch from Middle-Eastern or Asian grocers) and nuts, dried pulses and cereals (all cheaper from the bins in health food shops).

20
MAKE AND TAKE YOUR OWN LUNCH

I suspect part of the reason we all go out and buy sandwiches at lunchtime is to get out of the office. But making and taking your own packed lunch can save a significant amount every week. Take a walk in the park, go for a swim or find some other displacement activity. Or have your lunch at work and just go out for a coffee rather than for food.

The very word 'leftover' has a dreary sound to it, conjuring up visions of drab, reheated meals, odd dun-coloured soups and tired-looking salads. But it doesn't have to be like that. With a little imagination your leftovers can not only be turned into delicious meals for you and your family, but feasts for your friends. To achieve that you need to recognise what type of leftover you're dealing with and whether it's planned or unplanned.

UNPLANNED LEFTOVERS

Food that remains uneaten at the end of a meal or ingredients that don't get used up. Examples of the former – leftover vegetables like peas, broccoli or mashed potatoes, leftover pasta and rice, even a bit of leftover stew. The latter might be half a pepper, half a tin of tomatoes, half a pot of pesto, a small piece of cheese, a spoonful or two of yoghurt or cream.

Being uncooked, the latter are more easy to deal with than the former. Once food is cooked, especially if it's well seasoned, it can be quite unappetising. Your best bet is to deal with it straightaway. Rice and potatoes for example absorb a dressing much better while they're still warm so if you want to make a salad with them dress them as soon as possible after you've cooked them. Pasta becomes gluey and sticks together if left too long. Toss it in any leftover sauce and it'll reheat perfectly well. If you want to make fishcakes or a topping for a shepherd's pie with leftover mash do so as soon as it's cool.

The way you present leftovers also makes a big difference. Cooked foods tend to lose their colour so you need to liven them up with fresh herbs or accompany them with a colourful salad or vegetable. If you're making soups from leftover vegetables try and avoid blitzing them into a uniform sludge colour. Arrange salads artistically on a plate or platter and no-one will know you've salvaged the ingredients from the fridge.

PLANNED LEFTOVERS

Another strategy is consciously to cook more than you need to create leftovers for a meal the next day – or days. A Sunday roast is a classic example of this but if it's not to get scrumped before you get round to using it you need to cordon it off in the fridge (see pages 33–34). It's almost always worth cooking extra potatoes, pasta, rice and couscous to form the basis of a hash or sauté, pasta bake, egg-fried rice or rice or couscous salad. To repeat, if the ingredient in question is not being cooked again, as with a rice salad, make it up as soon as possible after the meal so that it retains its texture and has a chance to absorb the accompanying flavours.

If you want to get maximum shelf life out of a valuable ingredient like a roast chicken or other joint it's important to cool it and refrigerate it as soon as possible and to wrap it thoroughly. You'll find tips on the best way to store different foods on pages 31–35.

BATCH COOKING

The main argument people put forward against frugal eating is that it takes too much time. I don't agree – it's simply a matter of using time more cleverly. It takes roughly the same time to make a stew or a batch of mince for 8 as it does for four – certainly a lot less than it would to start two smaller batches from scratch. You put in the work at the weekend. You reap the benefit during the week when all you have to do is heat it up. You also save fuel by doing a whole batch of cooking at once.

Batch cooking is useful for entertaining too as you can get well ahead which means less last minute hassle. Obviously it helps to have a freezer which I do think is a good investment for the frugal cook (page 29). So long as you don't stuff it with food you never get round to cooking or eating....

You just have to look at the past or think about the structure of meals in communities where money is, or traditionally has been, scarce to find out the best way of making expensive ingredients stretch. Our grandparents had the knack of making the best use of what they had.

THE SKILL OF STRETCHING FOOD

In Italy, the antipasti and pasta courses were there to take the edge off hungry appetites before the expensive meat course was served. In France, supper would always start with a vegetable soup before going on to more expensive cold meats or cheese. Croûtons would be added to make it more substantial.

In the English kitchen, a roast would be stretched by an accompanying stuffing or forcemeat balls and a stew padded out with dumplings. Any leftovers could be put in a pie while a simple bread or milk pudding would fill up children who were still hungry.

Sauces and gravy weren't just there to make food taste more appetising but to make it more filling. A boiled cauliflower isn't much of a meal. Cauliflower cheese is. Some of the most delicious meals are born out of thrift. Take meatloaf (page 140) and meatballs (page 138), for example.

Over the last few decades we've got out of this habit, working more, spending less time in the kitchen, becoming more concerned about healthy eating (not least because we're physically less active). None of us would want to turn the clock back completely but if you do want to cut back your spending it's worth taking a few of these lessons to heart.

It is perfectly possible to do that without spending hours in the kitchen and still maintaining a healthy lifestyle. Simply increasing the number of vegetables you serve will make a Sunday roast go a lot further, for example. So will adding more vegetables to a Bolognese sauce or ragu which typically involves a very small amount of meat in Italy. Get into the French habit of eating a salad after your main course. You might think leaves aren't that sustaining but they do help to fill you up. Fruit-based puddings and pies are quite simple to make with in-season fruit and can also use up leftovers. Eating a mid-morning and mid-afternoon snack, as many people used to do, makes it less likely that you'll fall ravenously on whatever's on offer when the main meal comes. There was a practical payoff in 'elevenses' and afternoon tea.

There are small tricks I find quite useful – like extending a salad dressing by whisking in a spoonful of water once it has emulsified, (which also makes the dressing lighter and healthier). Or adding a splash of water to the eggs for an omelette or a spoonful of milk or cream to scrambled eggs. You can also stretch a more expensive ingredient with a cheaper one such as mixing fresh fruit with canned or frozen fruit as I've done with the Strawberry and Apricot Fruit Salad with Orange and Mint on page 52. Or sneak a couple of chopped lamb hearts into a lamb tagine (see page 190).

Finally, bring a touch of psychology to bear. It's not so much what you eat as the amount of satisfaction you get from eating it. It can be simply a matter of the way you arrange the food on your plate – and how big that plate is (see pages 38–39).

Grating, shredding or slicing your ingredients thinly creates the impression – and reality – of volume. Compare for example 25g of grated cheese with the same cheese cut into cubes or a finely sliced fennel salad (see page 100) with a roughly chopped one. It's well worth honing your knife skills.

There's no totally perfect solution to where to shop. No one store or outlet has a monopoly of bargains, despite what the supermarkets would like you to think. It also depends where you live – shopping in the country is a very different proposition to shopping in town. But here are a few useful pointers.

THE BIG SUPERMARKETS

The obvious and most convenient one stop shop for most of us but also where the greatest number of pitfalls await the unwary. Supermarkets offer a dazzling range of special offers, not all of which are quite as special as they appear. I've noticed recently that supermarkets have become more than usually flagrant about pricing fresh produce well over the going rate then claiming dramatic reductions when they bring the price down to what everyone else is charging (and still more than many market stalls). And you can be sure that what they're offering on one line they're compensating for on another so watch the cost of those staples you buy without thinking such as bananas, cucumbers and olive oil.

Now that you can buy online you're not tied quite so much to your local supermarket and can even compare what different supermarkets charge for the items you buy most often, on sites such as **www.moneysupermarket.co.uk**. You're also less likely to be tempted by impulse purchases if you're not actually wandering the aisles. And you can shop after supper when you're not feeling ravenously hungry.

Best for... Own brands, particularly the basic 'value' or 'basics' ranges which can be perfectly good quality. Frozen and canned foods – often cheaper than fresh for fish, vegetables and fruit. Staples such as tea, coffee, oil and vinegar. Pizza (cheaper than a takeaway). Reduced fresh produce (look for bargains at the end of the trading day, especially after the weekend). Money-off tokens (it's worth picking up the supermarket magazine just to get them).

Worst for... Fresh fruit, vegetables and herbs, especially when pre-packed. Other 'convenience' products such as bagged salads and grated cheese.

Fashionable ingredients that are featured by TV chefs such as Mascarpone, 'vine-ripened tomatoes' and extra virgin olive oil. Bacon (almost always watery). Bread. Dried herbs and spices.

Coping strategies... Make a list before you shop. Be aware of what different foods cost so you can assess special offers. Buy fresh ingredients loose. Look on lower shelves – cheaper lines are often located there rather than at eye level. Pause before you go through the checkout. Do you actually need every item you've bought? If not you could always put it back....

DISCOUNTERS (SUCH AS ALDI, LIDL AND NETTO)

Making rapid inroads on the UK grocery market, often substantially undercutting the big four. Good for basics though more restricted in choice. Quality of fresh produce, meat in particular, can be less than impressive, though it is improving all the time. Unlikely to meet all your shopping needs but worth stocking up on what they do well and checking their websites for special offers. The same caveats apply as above but if you've never walked through their doors you should definitely try them.

INDEPENDENT SHOPS

BUTCHERS

A dying breed, sadly, but a good source of bargains if you happen to have one near you particularly if you're prepared to buy less popular cuts such as offal and meat on the bone (see page 23). Generally know their meat better and hang and cut it more skilfully than market traders and farmers. If you're a regular customer some will throw in the odd extra or give you free chicken carcasses for stock.

Best for Bacon, cheaper cuts, old-fashioned specialities like ham hocks and meat pies, well-hung tasty meat and game.

Worst for Ready-marinaded meats and sausages – with one or two honourable exceptions (most butchers are not chefs).

FISHMONGERS

Rare as hens' teeth, particularly the good ones. In general, better to buy from a reliable market stall, online or, better still, direct from a boat.

Best for Whole fish, smoked fish.

Worst for Good fishmongers aren't cheap these days.

GREENGROCERS

A particularly good option if you live in the country where the proportion of locally sourced produce will be greater.

Best for Local, in-season produce. Buying the exact amount you need.

Worst for Can be inconsistent. Quality and freshness is sometimes not all it might be.

CHEESE SHOPS AND DELIS

Certainly the nicest place to shop for cheese, giving you the opportunity to try before you buy. But pricey.

Best for Quality artisanal cheese.

Worst for Cheese that will keep. Many are full matured and need to be eaten within a couple of days. Delis are generally off-limits for frugal cooks.

BAKERS

Many have been given a new lease of life by Polish bakers. Far, far better in quality than supermarket bread.

Best for Substantial bread with good keeping properties, old fashioned buns.

Worst for Yukky cakes (far better to bake your own).

HEALTH FOOD SHOPS

Have the best deals on products such as nuts and dried fruits (turnover is usually good). If they have bins you can also buy exactly the amount of any ingredient you need.

Best for Nuts, pulses and cereals, especially from the bins. Soy products and other products that form part of a special diet.

Worst for Vegetables not always as fresh as they might be and bread and cheese can be expensive.

ETHNIC SHOPS

Towns with large ethnic communities tend to have a wealth of shops and supermarkets that offer incredibly reasonable prices. The best place by far to buy spices, and specialist herbs and vegetables.

Best for Spices, cheap rice and pulses, flatbreads such as pitta bread and naan, fresh herbs such as mint and coriander. In the case of Chinese and Asian supermarkets, cheap soy sauce, fish sauce and other ingredients you need for Chinese, Japanese, Thai or Vietnamese cooking.

Worst for Well known brands. Don't be tempted to pick up the rest of your shopping at the same time.

MARKETS

Shopping in markets is a pleasure for anyone who loves food but it's easy to get carried away and buy more than you need. Of course, there are markets and there are markets, ranging from old-fashioned street market to upscale farmers' markets which, it pains me to say, are sometimes not particularly good and very expensive. Women's Institute Country Markets often offer more keenly priced home-grown produce as well as reasonably priced cakes, pies and preserves.

Best for Fresh seasonal fruit and veg direct from the producer, especially salad leaves. Fish and sometimes meat, though butchery standards can leave a lot to be desired. Good for cheese and, in the case of WI markets, preserves.

Worst for Buying fruit and vegetables you can't get through before they deteriorate.

BUYING DIRECT FROM THE PRODUCER

Can be a source of outstanding bargains though the more sophisticated the operation the less likely that is to be the case. Many farmshops have similar prices to smart delis these days. Producer websites can be even dearer, plus there's the cost of transport to build in. If you do have a producer nearby, it's well worth the effort to see what's available at the farm gate.

Pick your own can be a good option if you have the energy and facilities to freeze or otherwise process your harvest before it deteriorates. Always travel with a coolbag!

Best for Fresh meat (although again butchering can be clumsy). Bacon. Fish and shellfish (a good option if you live near the coast).

Worst for Readymade dishes such as ready meals, pies and cakes can be far from cheap.

VEG BOXES

Having experimented with several veg boxes I've come to the conclusion they don't work for me though I know many (including my eldest daughter) who swear by them. I dislike the inflexibility and the fact that there never seems to be the right amount of any vegetable. They're also hard to use up unless your diet is vegetable based. Possibly the answer is to have one a fortnight but I'm still not convinced. I'd rather see what I'm buying.

Best for Vegetarians

Worst for Workaholics. If you don't have time to cook the contents it's bound to go to waste.

FOOD SHOPPING ON HOLIDAY

If you're taking a car to France or elsewhere on the continent there are certainly foods – and drink – on which you can make a substantial saving. Wine, obviously but also, in the case of France, the country I know best, mustard, coffee, tinned and bottled vegetables, tinned fish and pâté and strings of garlic. Don't bother with olive oil. It reacts badly to heat and light and is generally no cheaper than it is at home.

GROWING YOUR OWN

Anyone can grow one or two vegetables but it takes real commitment to embark on a proper vegetable garden or allotment, let alone be self sufficient. Unless you're also prepared to spend time processing the fruits of your labours, you're likely to be left with a surplus that will simply go to rot. I'm ashamed to say I never managed to store the apples from the four trees we inherited at our previous house – or even to give them away. Anyone who was interested was generally in a similar position.

Growing herbs is a different matter. There are many herbs of which you need such a small quantity that it makes far more sense to grow your own than to buy an expensive pack. Examples are rosemary, sage and thyme. And there are others such as parsley, basil, chives and coriander which it's a boon to have constantly to hand – if you have sufficiently green fingers. You stand a much better chance of success if you buy them from a nursery or garden centre than by the pot from a supermarket. You might also try sprouting seeds which make a cheap, nutritious and tasty addition to salads. If you have room and feel slightly more ambitious you could cut your salad bills by growing rocket and other salad greens or attempting easy-to-grow crops such as spinach and courgettes. And possibly runner beans which for some reason I can never fathom are ridiculously expensive even in season and lose all their taste and texture when frozen.

FORAGING

There's plenty of free food out there if you have a mind to turn yourself into a hunter-gatherer. No, I'm not talking about poaching or, heaven forbid, roadkill, but the wild herbs and plants you can find in the hedgerows. Assuming you live within striking distance of any. Here's the sort of produce to look for:

Spring
Wild garlic, sorrel, young nettles, dandelion leaves.

Summer
Elderflowers, nasturtium flowers and leaves, wild berries, samphire.

Autumn
Blackberries, elderberries, sloes, crab apples, mushrooms (with the aid of a qualified mycologist, I suggest) rowan berries and rosehips.

Google 'foraging' for more detailed guidance or invest in Richard Mabey's *Food for Free* (Collins).

FREE GOODS AND BARTER

The barter economy is definitely booming with organisations such as Freecycle – **freecycle.org** – now making it possible to find people locally who want to give unwanted possessions away. Of course you can organise this on a more informal basis with family, friends and neighbours. Maybe they'd give you some produce from their allotment in return for your preserving some into jams and chutneys for them. Or perhaps you can bake bread for them in return for a batch of meals for your freezer. It's worth sharing delivery costs on any online items too.

One of the reasons many of us spend so much on food is that years of comparative prosperity have accustomed us to base our shopping decisions on convenience rather than price. If you look at most of the 'dinner under 30 minutes' recipes in the food magazines, they're mainly based on prime products such as chicken breasts, salmon fillets and fashionable salad veg like rocket. Simple and speedy to prepare, of course, but not by any means cheap.

To make real savings you need to develop – or redevelop – a nose for a bargain. Here's a reminder of the best buys out there:

MEAT

It wasn't until I'd written several recipes for this book that I realised how many involved meat on the bone, especially lamb. Apart from offal, it was the main way to continue to afford to shop at my local organic butcher. Bargains included scrag end and breast of lamb, beef short ribs and pork ribs and chicken wings and thighs – and even, memorably, an organic chicken from a batch of extra large birds they decided to sell off at half price (I got 10 helpings out of that plus some really fabulous stock!).

By contrast, budget favourite mince isn't necessarily that cheap, particularly the extra-lean varieties. It's better to buy cheaper mince and fry off and discard the fat. Best to look out for special offers.

PORK... BEST BUYS
Belly pork, shoulder chops, pork mince (often cheaper than beef mince). Sausages – buy the mid-priced lines rather than the cheapest ones, which tend to have a very low meat content (chipolatas also stretch further). Streaky bacon, ham and gammon hocks, pig's liver.

BEEF... BEST BUYS
Brisket (a good joint for pot roasting), gelatinous leg of beef is brilliant for braising, skirt (for cheap steak dishes, see pages 86 and 90), mince, oxtail, ox kidneys and ox liver (sometimes as good as calves' liver). Tinned corned beef is a good buy too.

LAMB... BEST BUYS
Breast, shoulder, stewing lamb (like scrag end), liver and kidneys. Fashionable lamb shanks, formerly frugal, have become quite expensive but look out for lamb knuckles.

CHICKEN... BEST BUYS
Whole chickens (though initially expensive will stretch a long way – see pages 124–125), wings, thighs (cheaper on the bone), drumsticks and chicken legs, chicken livers.

DUCK... BEST BUYS
Duck legs.

GUINEA FOWL... BEST BUYS
Whole birds – sometimes not much more expensive than chicken.

GAME... BEST BUYS
Whole game birds such as pheasant and pigeon. Rabbit. Mixed game (for casseroles).

SEAFOOD

Fresh fish and shellfish has become really pricey but there are still bargains to be had especially if, as with meat, you're prepared to buy it on the bone. Otherwise frozen fish is often considerably cheaper and may well be fresher. And don't overlook tinned fish, especially from France and Spain if you're on holiday there.

FRESH... BEST BUYS
Lesser known varieties such as dabs, coley, whiting and pollack (though the latter has become expensive since chefs discovered it was sustainable); cod cheeks, if you can find them, fish on the bone such as trout, mackerel and sardines, crab if you're in a seaside area, salmon if it's on special offer.

FROZEN... BEST BUYS
White fish, mackerel fillets, fish 'steaks', small North Atlantic prawns.

TINNED, SMOKED, PICKLED/BRINED... BEST BUYS
Tinned: mackerel and sardines and tuna.
Smoked: mackerel and kippers.
Pickled: herrings.
In brine: prawns, crayfish and cockles.

CHEESE

The best strategy with cheese, depressing though it may sound, is to buy and eat slightly less of it. A cheeseboard is a particularly expensive way of enjoying it – it's much more economical to buy one good cheese and serve it with accompaniments that will really set it off. Strong cheeses are also better value than milder ones as you need to use less of them.

Surprisingly, some of the best known British cheeses are also some of the best value – Stilton, for example, and crumbly white cheeses such as Caerphilly and Wensleydale which tend to be better value than fashionable Feta. Avoid flavoured and ready grated or sliced cheeses if you want to save money.

BEST BUYS...
Stilton, Cheddar and other British regional cheeses (see above), Brie, Grana Padano and Pecorino (cheaper than Parmesan), Quark (an inexpensive German low-fat cheese). It's also worth trying basic supermarket ranges which are often quite similar in quality to the standard ones.

FRUIT AND VEG

Always buy loose rather than pre-packed and don't overlook frozen and canned veg. Frozen peas, broad beans and spinach and tinned tomatoes are particularly good value.

BEST BUYS IN WINTER...
Root veg, especially potatoes, onions and carrots, cabbage and other greens, cauliflower, leeks, citrus fruit (oranges, grapefruit and lemons), apples, pears.

BEST BUYS IN SUMMER...
Lettuce, cucumber, spring onions, tomatoes, peppers, aubergines, courgettes, strawberries, raspberries, melon, grapes. Fresh herbs.

BREAD

It's worth buying loaves with some texture and keeping quality as they'll stay fresh for longer and can always be used for breadcrumbs and other recipes that are based on stale bread (see pages 207–208). You can also freeze them if you find them reduced at the end of the day.

BEST BUYS...
Traditional rustic loaves (Polish ones are very good value), pitta bread and other flatbreads, crumpets, baguettes or French 'sticks' (cheaper than Italian ciabatta). Give up expensive flavoured breads (cheaper to make yourself) and wraps.

OTHER FOOD BARGAINS

- Pearl barley instead of risotto rice.
- Canned pulses such as chickpeas, cannelini beans and lentils.
- Porridge oats/oatmeal (can be used for baking as well as porridge, see pages 165 and 167).
- Cocoa powder (an inexpensive substitute for chocolate).
- Large cartons of plain yoghurt (more versatile than flavoured ones).
- Buttermilk spreads for baking (easier to beat and cheaper than butter, better flavoured than old-style margarine).

THE FRUGAL STORECUPBOARD (AND FRIDGE)

You might actually wonder why anyone needs a storecupboard these days when shops are open 24/7. If you live miles from the shops maybe, but otherwise why bother unless you buy into the more apocalyptic websites' view that the world is about to end.

The three very persuasive reasons are that it stops you spending more on food than you need, wasting food that you have and making the food you buy taste better. Obviously everyone's tastes are different but here's what I think are useful ingredients and seasonings to have to hand.

THE RESOURCES TO MAKE A SCRATCH MEAL

Milk, eggs and flour are the holy trinity of the frugal kitchen, enabling you to create simple sauces, batters, pancakes, cakes, biscuits and bread. Other obvious candidates are bread, bacon, pasta, Parmesan or Grana Padano cheese, tomato sauce, garlic, cans of chickpeas and other beans, rice, a couple of onions and a bag of frozen peas. Plus spices and seasonings as listed below.

STORES OF THINGS THAT ARE CHEAP OR LEFTOVER

It's well worth buying non-perishable ingredients such as pasta or tinned tuna you use regularly when you find them at a good price. And, if you have a freezer and enough room in it, perishable ingredients such as bacon and sausages too. Bread and other bread products such as pitta bread and crumpets also freeze well.

It's also a good idea to freeze leftovers straightaway if you don't anticipate being able to use them up for a day or two. Stock and leftover liquid from stews can be frozen in ice-cube trays then transferred into plastic bags so you can take out by the cube as needed. Chicken carcasses can be frozen until you have enough to make a batch of stock. Small amounts of fresh meat and fish freeze perfectly well as do many fresh fruits and vegetables, providing you freeze them while they're still in peak condition. The key thing is not to leave them until they're past it.

HERBS, SPICES AND SEASONINGS TO MAKE YOUR FOOD TASTE GOOD

If you're basing your meal on inexpensive ingredients it pays to have a basic store of herbs, spices and seasonings that will make it taste delicious. However, it's easy to let this get out of hand. You try a new recipe and acquire a new spice. How often do you then use it?

Two solutions. One is not to take recipes literally. There are often, as I've already remarked (see page 10) substitutions that can be made. If you don't have herbes de Provence for example you can use oregano or rosemary. If you haven't got dried chillies you could use chilli sauce.

The other is not to treat a new recipe as a one-off. It's better to resolve to get into a certain type of cooking such as Thai food or baking or breadmaking and have a real go at it over a few weeks. If you enjoy it then those ingredients can become part of your storecupboard. If you tire of it then at least you'll have used them up.

HERE ARE MY 'MUST-HAVE' STORECUPBOARD SEASONINGS

Extra-virgin olive oil
for dressings and drizzling, not cooking.
Cooking oil
sunflower for preference.
Vinegar
wine or cider – can be substituted for red wine
Dried thyme
Dried oregano
Cumin
Smoked pimenton or sweet paprika
Moroccan-style Spice Mix
which I find goes with all kinds of dishes, especially baked fish and vegetables. My own blend consists of 10g of ground cumin, 10g of ground coriander, 5g of ground turmeric and 2g of hot pimenton (or chilli powder or hot paprika). Mix them all together thoroughly and store in an airtight jar. Use 2–3 teaspoons at a time.
A good medium-hot curry paste
Fine sea salt
Black peppercorns
I also like cheaper ground white pepper for some dishes.
Dijon Mustard
(far, far cheaper to buy it in France, if you're over there).
Light soy sauce
buy in large bottles from Asian supermarkets.
Marigold vegetable bouillon powder
better than almost any stock cubes I've come across
Honey
good for sweetening fruit and baking as well as spreading.
Yeast extract
(such as Marmite) good basis for stock and gravy.

Tomato ketchup
oddly useful for rounding out sauces.
Worcestershire sauce
adds zip to stews and gravies and lasts for ages.
Wine
not special 'cooking wine' but leftovers from drinking (assuming there are any!) – don't let them get vinegary though.

AND IN THE FRIDGE

Butter
Cheddar or another hard cheese
Plain yoghurt
more versatile than fruit-flavoured ones because you can use it with savoury dishes.
A fresh lemon or bottled lemon juice
Fresh parsley
A tube of tomato paste
cheap way of boosting tomato flavour.

Just as there's no need to overstock your cupboards with food and ingredients, you might also believe there's no need to clutter your kitchen with equipment you only use once or twice a year. Unfortunately, if you're a gadget junkie like I am, it can be hard to resist temptation, especially when electrical appliances have become so cheap. But as with the storecupboard, it is worth thinking about what equipment you really do and don't need.

BIG EQUIPMENT

Changing your cooker or fridge – even if it still appears to be functioning reasonably well – could help you save significantly on running costs if you can invest in a new energy-efficient model. If you haven't yet got a fan-assisted oven, for example, you would find that cheaper than a conventional one because it works on lower temperatures and you don't have to preheat it. Electric hotplates tend to be more expensive to run than gas ones because they need to heat up before you can use them. For a small household it might be worth buying a mini-oven rather than using the main oven to roast or bake small quantities of food. And a microwave costs less to run than any of these (though whether you like the texture of microwaved food is another matter).

The main pitfall to avoid when buying a freezer is to buy too large a model as you will then be tempted to fill it with food you never get round to eating! Or run it half empty, which can be costly. A fridge-freezer should allow you to take advantage of well-priced special offers and store portions of meals you've cooked in batches (see pages 136–137).

SMALL APPLIANCES

A kettle and a toaster are a must (kettles can be energy efficient too these days). My other essentials include some kind of food processor or blender, without which it's hard to make homemade soups or purées, and a hand-held electric whisk so that you can whisk up cream and egg whites. There's an argument for a juicer if you have access to an inexpensive source of fruit or grow your own, and a bread machine if you have a family to feed and are baking your own. Slow cookers are economical to run and can also be useful if you are working and want to come back to a hot meal, though only you know whether you're up for preparing a casserole at 8 o'clock in the morning. Pressure cookers are not an appliance close to my heart – unless you live off dried legumes.

The problem with most appliances is that you don't know if you're going to find a use for them until you've had an opportunity to try them. Ideally, try to borrow one from a friend or relative for a weekend when they're away or while they're on holiday. Or at the very least, pick one up cheap off eBay or from a car boot sale rather than buying one at full cost (though you obviously have to be careful about second hand electrical appliances). Amazon now sells appliances at substantial discounts too.

PANS, TINS, BOWLS AND KNIVES

What you need in the way of kitchen equipment obviously depends on the way you cook. If you bake your own bread, cakes and biscuits you'll need baking tins and sheets. If you do a lot of Oriental cooking, you will need a wok and a steamer. But just like ingredients, equipment is interchangeable. If you've got a wok you don't necessarily need a large frying pan. If you've got a metal steamer you don't need a colander to strain your pasta.

Many basics such as mixing bowls and baking dishes can be bought for next to nothing in charity shops. The only thing you're unlikely to find there is good quality sharp knives (though these you can pick up cheaply in the sales or discount stores like TK Maxx). I'd also recommend sales as a good way to buy pans and baking tins. Cheap ones tend to scratch and buckle and an uneven base can waste energy.

You might also consider buying a mandolin simply because they can cut food so much more finely than even the sharpest knife (unless you're a Japanese sushi-master). And the thinner you cut foods the further they stretch....

HOW TO BE MORE ENERGY-EFFICIENT

Compared to the cost of heating and hot water the amount we spend on cooking food – and keeping it cool – is comparatively modest. But there are savings you can make which, if added up, could save quite a bit.

OVENS, HOBS AND OTHER COOKING APPLIANCES

- When you make a coffee or tea don't boil more water than you need. Kettles apparently use around a third of the energy we use for cooking.

- Don't switch on the oven to cook just one small dish. It may be worth it if there are two of you having an additional smaller oven or oven and microwave combined. When you do use the oven try and cook some other dishes to make maximum use of it.

- Many recipes start with an instruction to switch on the oven even before the food is prepared but actually you don't need to pre-heat it except where the initial temperature is critical (e.g. for bread, cakes or pastry).

- Use the heat of the oven while it heats up, and the residual heat as it cools down, to warm through and refresh bread and nuts or toast oatmeal.

- Don't keep opening the oven door to check how things are going. The temperature immediately drops by about 15°C, extending the cooking time.

- Microwaves are much more energy-efficient than hobs and ovens, so if you have one make use of it for foods it suits such as fish and vegetables.

- Don't boil water (e.g. for pasta) in uncovered pans. It takes far longer and uses more energy.

- Use the smallest ring you can for the size of the pan you're using – i.e. don't put a small pan on a big ring or you'll waste heat round the sides.

- Don't cook with flimsy pans with bases that don't heat evenly. And don't let too much oil or grease accumulate on the bottom of the pan (or around the burner) which will make them harder to heat.

- Turn off electric rings a few minutes before the end of the cooking time and the food will finish off in the residual heat.

- Cook a big batch of dishes such as pasta sauces and stews so that you just have to reheat them the next day rather than start cooking again from scratch. It saves time too, obviously. See pages 136–137.

FRIDGES AND FREEZERS

- Don't cram too much food in the fridge and leave enough space for air to circulate round the contents.

- Don't put warm food in the fridge. (A health hazard too as it raises the temperature of the other food in there.)

- Don't place the fridge next to a radiator

- Defrost your fridge and freezer regularly so they don't have to labour through a heavy ice build-up to keep the contents cold or frozen.

- Thaw frozen food in the fridge rather than in a microwave or oven. It will help keep the fridge temperature down and won't use up any extra energy.

- Don't keep a large chest – or upright – freezer if you haven't much to fill it. Half-empty freezers cost more to run than full ones. On the other hand it's not worth stocking up with a whole lot of food you may not eat....

WHICH DISHES COOK AT A SIMILAR TEMPERATURE

If you are assembling an oven-load here's a simple guide to the kind of dishes that cook at a similar temperature. The simplest strategy is obviously to cook two – or more – dishes of the same type (e.g. two loaves, quiches or casseroles).

VERY LOW
110–140°C/110–130°C Fan/Gas $\frac{1}{2}$–1
Slow roasts and braises, meringues, large fruit cakes, rice pudding.

LOW
150–160°C/140–150°C Fan/Gas 2–3
Cakes, teabreads and casseroles (e.g. chicken casseroles) that don't need quite such a long cooking time.

MODERATE
160–190°C/150–160°C Fan/Gas 3–5
Pot roasts, vegetable bakes and gratins, roast vegetables, quiches, sponge cakes, muffins.

HIGH
200–220°C/170–180°C Fan/Gas 6–7
Quick roasts. Baked and roast potatoes. Crumbles.

VERY HIGH
230–240°C/190–200°C Fan/Gas 8–9
Bread, pizza.

Some dishes of course start at a high temperature and can then be turned down.

I titled the food safety section of my student cookbook, *Beyond Baked Beans* as 'How Not to Poison Your Friends' ...but I'm assuming you've mastered the rudiments of food hygiene.

More relevant to this book is how long different foods keep and how to store them so that you get the longest possible use out of them. I've touched elsewhere on the advantages of having a freezer (page 26) but making sure your fridge is operating properly is even more crucial. That means – at the risk of stating the obvious – not overcrowding it, putting things in the right section (models vary so you'll need to consult the manufacturer's handbook) and never putting food in it until it has completely cooled down (which should be done as quickly as possible). There's also a lot to be said for having a fridge thermometer to check it's running at the right temperature.

Having some kind of orderly system for where you store different foods is also an advantage when it comes to finding and retrieving leftovers and other ingredients for a scratch meal. It's also well worth having a collection of different sized containers in which to store cooked foods. You can buy these quite inexpensively at shops such as Woolworths, IKEA and discount supermarkets such as Aldi and Lidl. I would also buy some labels so you can keep track of what food you've put in what identical-looking box.

Even ingredients that come pre-wrapped need to be re-wrapped carefully, if you don't use them all in one go. Cheese for example needs to be re-wrapped every couple of days – preferably in waxed or greaseproof paper or foil rather than clingfilm. A washed lettuce will need to be kept in a different plastic bag from the one it originally came in.

HOW LONG THINGS KEEP IN THE FRIDGE

Obviously it depends when and where you bought them and how quickly you got them home. Produce bought loose, especially from small shops will generally need to be eaten sooner than pre-packed produce which has been chilled, though it also depends on the 'sell by' date. If you buy things cheap because they've reached or are nearing the end of their shelf life you should generally eat them the same day.

WITHIN 24 HOURS
High-risk foods such as shellfish and other fresh fish, mince, offal, pre-prepared salads, stir-fries and beansprouts, cooked rice.

WITHIN 1–3 DAYS
Chicken and other meat, sausages (if wrapped), mushrooms, soft fruit such as strawberries, other leftovers.

WITHIN 4–6 DAYS
Soft cheese, yoghurt, milk and fresh salad veg, stone fruit such as peaches and apricots.

A WEEK TO 10 DAYS
Bacon and ham (though consume within a couple of days once you open the pack) hard cheese, eggs, lemons and limes.

A MONTH OR MORE
Butter and spreads (check the use-by date).
Frozen foods (but ice cream should never be refrozen once thawed).

NB: Many products such as mayonnaise and cook-in sauces need to be kept in the fridge once opened. Check the recommended 'use-by' time on the label.

FRESH PRODUCE THAT'S BEST STORED OUTSIDE THE FRIDGE

POTATOES AND OTHER ROOT VEGETABLES
Best stored at cool room temperature – an outside room such as a garage is ideal. They'll keep longer if unwashed. Don't put garlic or onions in the fridge – they'll taint the other food you've got stored there, especially butter.

BANANAS AND AVOCADOS
Go black and soggy, if refrigerated.

FRESH BASIL
Can blacken if refrigerated. Best to grow as a plant.

TOMATOES
Will carry on ripening if left in a bowl though they will deteriorate more quickly.

SHELVES AND CUPBOARDS

Outside the fridge it's principally a question of wrapping foods thoroughly so they don't stale or deteriorate as the result of any dust or grease particles in the air:

BREAD
Best in a purpose-designed bin or crock where it should keep for 2–5 days (a day for a baguette) but can be transferred to the fridge or freezer before then (see page 26).

BISCUITS AND CAKES
Best stored in airtight tin (unless they contain cream). It's worth buying those biscuit assortments at Christmas just for the tins. Highly perishable baked goods which deteriorate quickly such as muffins are best frozen as soon as cool. Sponge cakes will keep for a day or two. Fruit cakes or teabreads for up to a week.

COFFEE AND TEA
Ground coffee is best kept in the fridge once opened. Tea should be kept in an airtight caddy.

FLOUR, NUTS
Comparatively short shelf life. Aim to use within a month of opening the pack. Nuts can be refreshed in the oven.

OIL, VINEGAR, MUSTARD, RELISHES
Good oil needs to be kept away from the light and should be used within two months of opening. Nut oils have a short shelf life (about a month after opening). Vinegars and mustards typically deteriorate after 2–3 months. Many chutneys and relishes are best refrigerated once open.

SPICES AND HERBS

Keep well-sealed away from light. Herbs last 6 months, ground spices about nine months and whole spices a year though some types such as cloves, nutmeg and cardamom last longer than this.

PASTA, RICE AND PULSES

Once opened, unused contents can be kept in their original bags so long as carefully sealed or secured with a rubber band or bulldog clip. Pasta and white rice should keep in good condition for 6–9 months. Brown rice should be eaten within six.

CANNED FRUIT, PULSES AND VEGETABLES

2–3 years but even canned foods don't last forever. Transfer the contents to another container once opened and keep in the fridge, as open tins can corrode.

For more information about storage look at the Food Standards Authority website **www.eatwell.gov.uk** and **www.lovefoodhatewaste.com**.

Finally it's always worth having a quick check through the fridge and cupboards before you go shopping and having a more comprehensive check through your cupboards and freezer every few weeks.

Even assuming you're fantastically efficient at using up leftovers there are bound to be some things you have to chuck out, like egg shells and banana skins. So rather than chuck it in the bin is there anything useful you can do with it.

Certain councils, such as the one where I live in Bristol, now have schemes to enable you to get rid of food waste which accounts for 30% of the waste we throw away. In fact its website – **www.bristol.gov.uk** – is a mine of information on recycling.

Food they can process include dairy foods such as cheese, fish bones, fruit and vegetable peelings, bread, meat and bones, tea leaves and coffee grounds. All of which can apparently be composted by being heated and turned for 3 weeks in an incinerator then left in a compost heap for three months. This reduces the need for landfill and avoids the creation of methane gas.

If you're recycling food yourself you obviously don't want to include foods like raw meat and fish and dairy produce that will go off and attract predators such as rats and foxes, so stick to fruit and vegetable skins and peelings, egg shells (which should be crushed), coffee grounds and used teabags and leaves. There's an insane amount about composting on the internet including a dedicated website run by the Composting Association – **http://compost.org.uk** – and various composting blogs. Your approach will need to vary depending on whether you want a cool heap or a hot heap, as you'll see if you visit the Garden Organic site – **www.gardenorganic.org.uk**.

WHAT ABOUT WORMERIES?

Or vermiculture, as it's accurately called. Basically this is a fast-track compost heap using worms to accelerate the breakdown of leftover food. Not the normal earthworms but a small red worm called a Tiger or Brandling worm which has a voracious appetite and can eat its own weight in food in a single day, I discovered this from an exemplary Australian book called *Leftover Food* which encourages Australian kids to be good citizens. From everything I read, the technique is undoubtedly effective. It just depends how squeamish you are about the idea of having a compost bin full of worms at the bottom of the garden, or extracting the resulting, squirming worm-ridden mulch. For more information check out sites such as **www.originalorganics.co.uk**.

FEED IT TO THE BIRDS

Another possibility is to feed appropriate scraps of food waste to birds and farm animals such as pigs. But the foods that can be used in this way are quite limited – stale bread, biscuits, cake or cereal, fresh (not rancid) bacon fat and windfall apples (pigs can eat rather more but should obviously not be fed meat or decomposing food that has gone off). But again you need to take care that this does not attract pests.

PORTION CONTROL

One of the trickiest things to get right – and the reason we all tend to waste so much – is how much food to prepare. In other words what is a portion?

Recipes – including mine – indicate a number of servings, but I don't know you or your family. Maybe you have small children who will eat less than adults. Or a teenage boy who consumes vast amounts of food, as one of my boys did (but not both of them, interestingly). Maybe you have an elderly parent in your household with a very small appetite. All these variations need to be taken into account.

Women tend to – and should – eat less than men but because we get given the same amount of food in restaurants often expect the same at home. It suddenly dawned on me when I was researching this book that the reason weight had been creeping on over the years is that I'd got into the habit of serving myself a similar sized portion to my husband.

Individual appetites aside, the majority of us tend to eat more than we need, especially expensive sources of protein such as meat and fish. A recommended serving, according to the website www.lovefoodhatewaste.com is 140g or 5oz. A small fish fillet or a good slice of roast beef. A standard portion of cheese is just 40g.

A serving of pasta is 100g – a fifth of a standard 500g pack. You need even less rice – 75g but how often do you just tip the pack in boiling water till it looks 'about right'. And how often do you have loads left over? We've all done it.

Most of the time, it's not that you're hungry, it's just that the food's tasty and it's there. If you seriously want to keep your spending under control you need to take a leaf out of the dieter's book and cut down the amount you eat without being conscious of it.

• Weigh the ingredients you're going to use, especially ingredients such as pasta and rice.

• Serve your food on smaller plates which makes you feel you have a more generous portion in front of you.

• Sit down at a table and eat slowly, savouring each mouthful. I wouldn't go so far as to suggest you count the number of times you chew, Madonna-style, but just focus on and enjoy the food you're eating. Don't shovel it down while you're watching TV.

• Drink a glass of water before you eat. Often when we think we're hungry we're actually thirsty.

• Stop when you're full (blindingly obvious but how often do we do it?).

• Put aside any leftovers or, better still, if you're serving a dish you know will feed more than the number you have round the table, remove a proportion of the food for a subsequent meal.

HOW MANY CALORIES
DO YOU NEED?

These are the figures given by the 'Dietary Reference Values for Food Energy and Nutrients for the UK' but age is not an infallible guide. It obviously depends on your height, your build and how active you are, assuming reasonable levels of activity.

CALORIE REQUIREMENTS

Children aged 0–3 years
Males 545–1230 per day.
Females 515–1165 increasing with age.

Children aged 3–10 years
Males 1230–1970 per day.
Females 1165–1740 increasing with age.

Children and adolescents 10–18 years
Males 1970–2755 per day.
Females 1740–2110 per day increasing with age.

Adults aged 19–59 years
Males 2550 per day.
Females 1940, reducing, after 50 years, to 1900 per day in the case of a non-active or light level of activity.

Adults aged 60 and over
Males 2380–2100 per day (decreasing with age).
Females 1900–1810 per day (decreasing with age).

For more information on portion sizes visit
www.lovefoodhatewaste.com and
www.5aday.nhs.uk.

Even frugal cooks – well, especially frugal cooks – deserve an evening off but there's no point in blowing the week's savings on a profligate meal. Here are seven simple ways to trim your restaurant bill.

ORDER TWO STARTERS OR A STARTER AND A DESSERT
RATHER THAN A STARTER AND A MAIN COURSE.

•

JUST HAVE ONE COURSE. I THINK PEOPLE ARE SOMETIMES
EMBARRASSED TO DO THAT BUT IT'S A PERFECTLY REASONABLE
THING TO DO. THINK OF THE FRENCH *PLAT DU JOUR*.

•

GO SOMEWHERE YOU CAN GRAZE OR SNACK, LIKE A
TAPAS BAR, RATHER THAN HAVING A FULL MEAL AND
DON'T SPEND ALL EVENING THERE. THE LONGER YOU STAY,
THE MORE YOU'RE LIKELY TO SPEND.

•

HAVE A DRINK BEFORE YOU GO OUT TO AVOID RATCHETING
UP A COSTLY BOOZE BILL. POST-DINNER COFFEE AND TEA
TOO ARE CHEAPER AT HOME.

•

IF YOU WANT TO GO TO A SMART RESTAURANT GO AT
LUNCHTIME MIDWEEK RATHER THAN IN THE EVENING
– NOT OFTEN POSSIBLE WHEN YOU'RE WORKING,
ADMITTEDLY, BUT WORTH IT WHEN YOU CAN.

•

TAKE THE SET MENU, ESPECIALLY IF YOU'RE IN A GROUP.
ENCOURAGES EVERYONE ELSE TO FOLLOW SUIT.

•

DRINK TAP WATER RATHER THAN MINERAL WATER
– AND BEER RATHER THAN WINE OR COCKTAILS.

BUDGET
BREAKFASTS
AND
BRUNCHES

BREAKFAST LIKE A KING, LUNCH LIKE A PRINCE AND DINE
LIKE A PAUPER GOES THE OLD SAYING WHICH SUGGESTS
THAT THE FIRST MEAL OF THE DAY IS THE LAST ONE ON
WHICH YOU SHOULD MAKE ECONOMIES. BUT IF IT'S
SUBSTANTIAL ENOUGH IT MAY MEAN YOU DON'T NEED
SUCH AN EXTENSIVE – OR EXPENSIVE – LUNCH. AND
BESIDES, MANY BREAKFAST TREATS ARE NOT THAT PRICEY.

REAL PORRIDGE

If you've never tasted porridge made with real oatmeal you haven't experienced the real thing. And it only takes a fraction longer than porridge oats. Because you make it with water rather than milk it's good for dairy-intolerant members of the family or friends (you can serve it with soy milk).

SERVES 2

50g coarse oatmeal
a small pinch of salt
Demerara sugar
whole creamy milk or soy milk

Bring 280ml of water to the boil and pour in the oatmeal in a steady stream, whisking as you go. Simmer for 10 minutes, stirring occasionally. Add a pinch of salt and spoon into two small bowls. Sprinkle with Demerara sugar.

VARIATIONS

For a deluxe version replace the sugar and milk with honey and single – or double – cream.

THRIFTY TIP

Demerara sugar is often better value than the more fashionable soft brown sugars.

APPLE AND CINNAMON PORRIDGE

A way of ringing the changes on basic rolled oats.

SERVES 2–3

50g porridge oats
200ml semi-skimmed milk
a small apple, peeled and finely sliced
2 tbsp soft brown sugar or Demerara sugar
a small pinch (about $^1/_4$ tsp) cinnamon

Put the oats, milk, chopped apple, sugar and cinnamon in a small (preferably non-stick) saucepan together with 200ml water and bring slowly to the boil, stirring occasionally. Turn the heat down and simmer for 5 minutes. Serve with a little extra milk and sugar to taste.

FRESH FRUIT MUESLI WITH YOGHURT

As part of the research for this book I investigated whether it was cheaper to make your own muesli than to buy it readymade. I'm sure muesli-enthusiasts would clamour to prove me wrong but I couldn't make the sums work unless you opt for a quite spartan muesli with no nuts, seeds or fruit. You can cut the cost (see Thrifty tip below) but as with most foods it's more a question of moderating the quantity. This is a particularly nice way to eat it.

SERVES 2

4 heaped tbsp muesli
about 75ml apple juice or semi-skimmed or soy
  milk
2 heaped tbsp of plain or soy yoghurt
fresh fruit – a chopped apple, pear or peach; a
  couple of apricots or plums; some strawberries,
  raspberries, blackberries or blueberries; or a
  mixture of these, depending on what you have
  available
a teaspoon of clear honey (indulgent but nice)

Soak the muesli in the apple juice or milk for at least 15 minutes or overnight in the fridge. Stir in the yoghurt without wholly mixing it in and fold in the fruit leaving a little to top the muesli. Spoon into glass bowls and top with the remaining fruit. Drizzle over a little honey.

VARIATIONS

Frozen berries are a good substitute for fresh ones out of season. Canned pears and apricots in natural juice are fine. Or you can stir in a couple of spoonfuls of Fruit Compôte (see pages 47 and 55).

THRIFTY TIP

Buy your muesli loose from the bins in your local health food shop. It's quite a bit cheaper than buying it pre-packed.

WINTER RASPBERRY COMPÔTE WITH YOGHURT AND TOASTED OATMEAL

This recipe stemmed from a mistake, as many do. I found a pack of thawed frozen raspberries at the bottom of the fridge, heated them through with some sugar minutes later, and stirred them into yoghurt. They made a wonderful breakfast compôte on a winter's morning when we were berry-starved. Incidentally, they were organic – and Scottish – which may have accounted for the taste.

SERVES 4

250g raspberries or frozen mixed berries
2 tbsp unrefined caster sugar
200g plain or Greek yoghurt
40g toasted oatmeal (see page 166)

Tip the fruit into a saucepan, add the sugar, bring to the boil and simmer for two minutes. Take the pan off the heat, cool for 10 minutes then mix roughly with yoghurt to create a streaky, marbled effect. Spoon into tumblers or glass dishes and sprinkle with toasted oatmeal.

VARIATIONS

If you have some raspberry jam handy use that instead of the sugar for an even more intense raspberry flavour. (You can do the same with other fruits such as apricots).

LEFTOVERS

If you have a spoonful or two of compôte leftover you can use it like jam.

THRIFTY TIP

For most of the year (apart from mid-July to mid-September) frozen raspberries are cheaper and taste better than fresh ones.

SPRING VEGETABLE FRITTATA

A frittata is a great way of using up the previous night's veg – and any other bits and pieces in the fridge. You can either make a deep one and cut it into wedges or make it thinner, more like an omelette, and use it to stuff a pitta bread or roll.

SERVES 2–3

1 tbsp olive oil
half a bunch of spring onions, trimmed and finely sliced or a small onion, peeled and finely chopped, or a trimmed and finely chopped leek
175g cooked new potatoes cut into small cubes
60g cooked or thawed frozen peas or podded and skinned broad beans
60g lightly steamed purple sprouting broccoli or broccoli
5 large fresh free range eggs
1 heaped tbsp finely chopped parsley (optional)
salt and freshly ground black pepper

Preheat a grill on medium heat. Heat the oil in a small (20 cm) frying pan and fry the chopped onion gently for a minute or two until softened. Add the cubed potatoes, peas and broccoli, stir and heat through without browning for another 3–4 minutes. Beat the eggs and season with salt and pepper. Turn the heat up under the vegetables for a minute then pour in the egg mixture. Using a palette knife or round bladed knife lift the sides of the frittata so the liquid egg falls back underneath. Cook for about 3–4 minutes until the underside of the frittata is nicely browned then pop the pan under the grill for another 4 minutes or so until the remaining liquid egg has puffed up and browned and the top is firm. Cool for 10 minutes then serve warm or cool and refrigerate.

VARIATIONS

You could add a roughly chopped thick slice of ham or some crisply fried and crumbled bacon rashers. Mix a couple of heaped tablespoons of Parmesan cheese with the beaten eggs. Alternatives to broccoli could be a small chopped courgette, some peeled and chopped up asparagus stalks or up the amount of herbs. Make a 'cheat's' tortilla by frying together a small onion and red pepper with 50g of diced chorizo and a couple of diced cooked potatoes then follow the recipe as above.

LEFTOVERS

Make a great light lunch or packed lunch (a bit like a crustless quiche).

THRIFTY TIP

If you've got the energy it's worth whipping this up after an evening meal so you've got an easy lunch for the next day.

SMOKED HADDOCK, PARMESAN AND CHIVE OMELETTE

A version of a scrumptious omelette called Omelette Arnold Bennett. Making it as an open rather than a folded omelette cuts down the number of eggs you need to use though you can obviously fold it if you prefer. This amount of fish would fill two to three standard omelettes.

SERVES 2–3

1 portion Smoked Haddock in Cream Sauce (see page 223)
2 tbsp milk
3 large eggs (4 if you're making it for 3)
2 heaped tbsp finely snipped chives plus a few extra chives for decoration
about 10g butter
grated Parmesan (about 2 tbsp)

Preheat the grill. Tip the smoked haddock into a saucepan with the milk, stir and heat through gently. Beat the eggs lightly, mix in 2 tbsp of chopped chives and season with salt and pepper. Heat a medium sized frying pan over the heat and add a small knob of butter. Once the butter foams up, add the beaten eggs and swirl them around the pan, lifting up the cooked edges with a fork to allow the liquid egg to run through. Cook for a minute more then take off the heat and spoon over the hot smoked haddock. Sprinkle with Parmesan and place the pan under the grill for a couple of minutes until lightly browned. Sprinkle with a few roughly cut chives and serve, cut into wedges. Good with a dark green salad such as watercress or spinach.

VARIATIONS

You could substitute finely sliced spring onion tops for the chives and leftover salmon in a creamy sauce for the haddock.

THRIFTY TIP

It's worth growing chives yourself so you always have them to hand.

STRAWBERRY AND APRICOT FRUIT SALAD WITH ORANGE AND MINT

This summery recipe is delicious in its own right but it's also an economical way to stretch a punnet of strawberries.

SERVES 4

250g fresh strawberries, hulled
1 tsp caster sugar
1 x 400g apricot halves in apple juice
1 orange
4–6 mint leaves (optional)

Slice the strawberries into a glass bowl and sprinkle over the sugar, stir and leave for 5 minutes. Drain the apricots, reserving the juice for another use (like a smoothie).

Halve the apricot halves and add them to the bowl. Squeeze the orange juice and strain over the fruit and gently mix together. Chill for an hour if possible. Tear or shred the mint leaves and scatter them over the salad.

VARIATIONS

You could add a peeled sliced kiwi fruit to make it even more colourful.

THRIFTY TIP

Tinned fruit such as apricots are fantastic value but buy them canned in fruit juice rather than syrup.

FRENCH TOAST WITH POLISH CHERRIES

This is one of those deceptively simple recipes that is actually quite hard to get right. You want your bread impregnated with lovely eggy vanilla-y flavours but you don't want it to go soggy. Part of the trick is having the right kind of bread – a rustic loaf with real texture that is almost on the verge of going stale (i.e. 3–4 days old). Polish bread fits the bill perfectly.

SERVES 2

2 tbsp unrefined caster sugar
150g sour Polish cherries in juice
I large egg, lightly beaten or 2 egg yolks
2 tbsp double cream or I tbsp crème fraîche and
 I tbsp milk
I tbsp unrefined caster sugar
a few drops of vanilla extract or essence
25g butter (ideally French butter which has a
 lower water content)
2 thick slices of 3–4-day-old country bread or
 brioche

Put 2 tablespoons of sugar in a small pan with 2 tablespoons of the cherry juice, heat until boiling then simmer for a minute or two until thick. Add the cherries, heat through and set aside. Lightly beat the egg in a shallow dish then add the cream, sugar and a few drops of vanilla extract or essence (the mixture should be roughly the consistency of beaten egg). Dip the bread slices into the egg mixture, making sure that the liquid is thoroughly absorbed. Heat a medium frying pan for a few seconds then slice the butter into the pan so that it foams up. Lay the two bread slices in the pan and cook over a moderate heat for 2–3 minutes each side until puffed up and golden. Put a slice on each plate and top with the warm cherries.

VARIATIONS

You can use other types of fruit for this such as lightly cooked fresh berries, apricots or apples. You could season the egg mixture with a little nutmeg or cinnamon (good with apples). You could use brioche rather than ordinary bread.

THRIFTY TIP

If you have some leftover bread and no time to make French toast with it, slice it thickly and freeze it. Thaw before you use it for this recipe.

DRIED FRUIT COMPÔTE WITH REDBUSH TEA, CINNAMON AND HONEY

I always have South African redbush (Rooibos) tea in the cupboard. It makes a great caffeine-free alternative to ordinary tea. You can also use it to make this delicious fruit compôte.

SERVES 6

3 redbush teabags
400g mixed dried fruit e.g. apricots, pears, apples, prunes (Holland & Barrett often have it on special offer)
1–2 tbsp runny honey
1 stick of cinnamon or $1/2$ tsp ground cinnamon
4 cloves (optional)
1 thinly pared slice of orange rind
50g whole unsalted almonds (optional)
Greek yoghurt or homemade yoghurt, to serve

Put the teabags in a jug, pour in 700ml of boiling water, leave to infuse for 4 minutes then remove the teabags. Put the dried fruit in a saucepan and pour over the tea. Add 1 tbsp of the honey, cinnamon, cloves if using and orange rind, stir and bring to the boil. Simmer the fruit for 5 minutes then turn off the heat and check for sweetness, adding the remaining honey if you think it needs it. Cover the pan and leave to cool. Remove the cinnamon stick, cloves and orange rind and add the almonds, if using. Refrigerate for at least 2 hours. Spoon into individual glass bowls or dishes and top with a dollop of yoghurt.

VARIATIONS

If you already have some opened packs of dried fruits you can obviously use those, though small fruit like raisins and currants don't look too great so only use a small proportion of them.

THRIFTY TIP

It's cheaper to buy almonds in their skins and skin them (by pouring boiling water over them) than buying them ready-skinned.

INA PINKNEY'S BUTTERMILK PANCAKES

The best pancakes I've ever eaten were at a Chicago diner called Ina's. She isn't called The Breakfast Queen for nothing!

MAKES 6 LARGE PANCAKES

10g butter and another small slice for greasing the pan
90g plain flour
$\frac{1}{2}$ tsp bicarbonate of soda
1 tsp caster sugar
$\frac{1}{4}$ tsp salt
1 large egg
150ml buttermilk
50ml whole milk (i.e. not semi-skimmed)
a few drops of vanilla extract (optional)
2 tbsp oil
fresh fruit and honey, to serve

You'll need a medium sized pancake pan or griddle

Set the oven on to its lowest setting or turn on your plate warmer.

Heat the butter in a small pan until melted and set aside. Sift the flour, bicarbonate of soda, caster sugar and salt onto a plate. Lightly beat the egg in a medium-sized bowl and gently mix in the buttermilk, milk, cooled butter and vanilla extract if using. Sift the dry ingredients into the batter and fold in with a metal spoon – just enough to incorporate any pockets of flour but still leaving it looking alarmingly lumpy. (Don't worry, it's supposed to be like this).

Heat the oil and the remaining butter in a small pan and set aside. Heat a medium frying pan or pancake pan until moderately hot. Scrunch up a piece of kitchen towel, dip it in the oil/butter mixture and rub it round the pan. Scoop out a coffee cup or small ladle of batter and pour it into the pan, tilting the pan so it spreads out to give you a pancake about 12cm wide. Cook for a minute until the surface is covered with tiny bubbles (about 1–11/2 minutes) then flip the pancake over and cook the other side. When both sides are lightly browned transfer to a warm plate in the oven and repeat with the remaining batter, greasing the pan lightly between each pancake. Serve warm with fresh fruit such as blueberries or strawberries and drizzle with honey or, less frugally, maple syrup.

VARIATIONS

You could flavour the pancakes with a little ground ginger, mixed spice or cinnamon or serve them with a fruit compôte rather than fresh fruit.

THRIFTY TIP

Honey is easier to drizzle if you dip your spoon in a cup of boiling water first.

LIGHT LUNCHES AND SNACKS

WHETHER YOU'RE TAKING A PACKED LUNCH OR EATING AT HOME, LUNCHTIME IS A GOOD TIME TO USE UP LEFTOVERS. AND THAT DOESN'T MEAN DREARY FOOD. ONCE YOU GET THE HANG OF USING ODD BITS AND PIECES CREATIVELY YOU'LL FEEL JUST AS SATISFIED WITH WHAT YOU'VE RUSTLED UP AS YOU DO WITH MEALS YOU'VE MADE FROM SCRATCH. MORE SO, IF ANYTHING!

GARLIC MUSHROOMS ON TOAST

One of the simplest, most delicious ways to eat mushrooms.

SERVES 2

200g button mushrooms
1 tbsp olive oil
20g butter
1 small clove garlic, crushed or finely chopped
1 tbsp double cream or crème fraîche (optional)
salt, pepper and lemon juice to taste

Wipe or rinse the mushrooms under cold water, removing any dirt and slice roughly. Heat a small frying pan over a moderate heat, add the oil, then the butter. Once the butter melts tip in the mushrooms, stir them around and leave them to cook on a low heat, stirring occasionally. Once they begin to brown stir in the garlic and cook for a further couple of minutes. Stir in the cream if using and season with salt and pepper and a little lemon juice if you've added cream. Serve on wholemeal toast.

VARIATIONS

You could stir in some tarragon, parsley or dill, if you have some.

THRIFTY TIP

Ordinary button mushrooms are perfectly good for this recipe. Don't feel you have to buy a more expensive variety.

SARDINE 'RILLETTES' WITH LEMON AND PARSLEY

Part of the trick of getting away with budget ingredients is making them sound interesting. And it can be simply a question of giving it a sexy name. This is basically jazzed-up sardines on toast (very good for you – lots of calcium and Omega 3) with a little finely grated lemon rind.

SERVES 1

1 can of sardines
grated rind of half a small lemon (preferably unwaxed)
1 tsp chopped capers and/or 1–2 small gherkins
2 tbsp chopped parsley
freshly ground black pepper
1 large or 2 smaller slices of granary or wholemeal bread
a little olive oil

Drain the sardines, put them in a bowl and mash them roughly. Add the lemon rind, capers and/or gherkins and parsley (saving a little for decoration) and season well with freshly ground black pepper. Toast the bread, trickle over a little olive oil and pile the mashed sardines on top of the toast. Sprinkle over the rest of the parsley.

VARIATIONS

If you have any preserved lemons around you could replace the lemon rind with a little finely chopped up preserved lemon peel. This recipe would also work well with a small can of tuna or try it with a can of mackerel in tomato sauce. Drain the fish well, flake it, add a crushed clove of garlic and a few drops of wine vinegar then mix in the capers and parsley.

THRIFTY TIP

It's cheaper to buy tinned sardines and flavour them yourself than buy them ready-flavoured.

GRILLED TOMATOES ON TOAST

This is one of my favourite lunches. The ideal pan to use is one of those ridged grill pans but you can use an ordinary frying pan.

SERVES 2

2 slices of sourdough or rustic country bread
olive oil
1 clove of garlic, peeled and halved
6–8 small to medium fresh tomatoes, halved
some torn basil or roughly chopped parsley
salt and freshly ground black pepper
balsamic vinegar (optional)

Heat the pan for a couple of minutes till hot. Spray or drizzle the bread both sides with olive oil, put it face down in the pan and grill/fry it on both sides until nicely charred. Remove from the pan and rub the cut garlic over the surface. Rub the cut surfaces of the tomato with olive oil and season with salt and pepper. Place them cut side down in the hot pan and leave them for about 4–5 minutes until charred then flip them over and cook for another 2–3 minutes on the other side. Pile them on top of the toast, scatter over some chopped parsley, if you have some, and trickle over a little more olive oil and balsamic vinegar, if using.

VARIATIONS

You can crumble or shave a bit of fresh goat or sheep's cheese on top of this. Alternatively, just chop some fresh ripe tomatoes, add a couple of tablespoons of olive oil, a dash of wine vinegar or balsamic vinegar, toss together and pile on top of your toast or charred bread. Sprinkle with herbs and/or add cheese as above.

LEFTOVERS

In the unlikely event you have any grilled tomatoes left over you could chop them and add them to a salad or pasta sauce.

THRIFTY TIP

Put some olive oil in a plastic spray bottle and add half as much water. Shake well and use to spray toast and crostini.

PRAWN AND EGG OPEN SANDWICH

MAKES 4 OPEN SANDWICHES

3 large eggs at room temperature
1 unwaxed lemon
2 tablespoons mayonnaise
1 tbsp finely chopped chives or dill plus a few
   sprigs for garnish
200g small cooked prawns
2 medium-sized ripe tomatoes
4 thin slices rye bread

Bring a saucepan of water to the boil and lower in the eggs. Boil for 10 minutes then drain and refresh under cold running water. Cool for 10 minutes then remove the shells. Grate a little rind off the lemon, cut it in half and juice one half. Put the mayonnaise in a bowl, add the lemon rind and about a teaspoon of the lemon juice and season to taste with salt and pepper. Drain any excess liquid from the prawns and fold into the mayonnaise. Slice the egg and tomato. Top each slice of bread with a few slices of egg, a couple of slices of tomato and a heaped tablespoon of the prawn mixture. Sprinkle over a little dill or parsley. Slice the remaining lemon in half thinly and use to decorate.

VARIATIONS

You can make open sandwiches from pretty much anything you would put in a closed one but if you want to add a bit of authentic Scandanavian style to your sandwiches think in terms of pickled herrings, smoked salmon (or gravadlax) and rare roast beef with horseradish sauce.

THRIFTY TIP

Rye bread isn't so great for toast so it's worth keeping a sliced loaf in the freezer just for sandwiches.

CHICKEN AND CELERY SANDWICH FILLING

Once you've used up the breast from a chicken the remainder isn't quite as aesthetically pleasing so chop it up fine into this American-style sandwich filling.

about 175g cold chicken, skinned and finely chopped
1 stick of celery, trimmed and finely sliced
1 heaped tbsp finely chopped onion or chives or spring onions
1 heaped tbsp finely chopped sweet-sour pickled cucumber
1 heaped tbsp French-style or homemade mayonnaise (page 188)
1 tbsp plain yoghurt
salt, pepper and lemon juice to taste
crisp lettuce e.g. Cos (sweet Romaine) or Webb's Wonder

Simply mix the chicken, celery, chopped onion, mayo and yoghurt together and season to taste with salt, pepper and a little lemon juice. Use to fill a wholemeal sandwich or bap and top with some finely shredded lettuce.

VARIATIONS

This works equally well with tuna though you might also want to add a little lemon rind if you're using that. You could also use the mixture to top an open sandwich.

THRIFTY TIP

Supermarket own brand French-style mayonnaise is perfectly good and a lot cheaper than the big brands.

THE ART OF SANDWICH MAKING

Although it might sound pretentious to say so, there's an art to making a good sandwich or filled roll. It needs to be generous, it needs to be colourful, it needs to have both flavour and texture. It can also be a great way of using up leftovers.

A FEW TIPS:
• Keep butter in a cool place rather than in the fridge – it's easier to spread and you don't have to use as much of it.
• For Mediterranean-type ingredients such as grilled vegetables or continental meats like salami, olive oil is a better base than butter.

• Slice meats and cheeses thinly and layer them up rather than cutting them into thick slabs. (It's worth getting a cheese slicer)
• Always have something to lubricate and add flavour to dry ingredients such as chutney, pesto, tapénade, goat's cheese or mayo (which you can lighten by mixing in a spoonful of plain yoghurt).
• Include something with a bit of crunch – the bread or roll (if the filling is soft), otherwise add some cucumber, celery, sprouts or seeds.

GOAT'S CHEESE, BEETROOT AND ASPARAGUS SALAD

A fresh spring-like salad, making the best of in-season veg.

SERVES 4

1 bunch of fresh beetroot, trimmed and scrubbed
    clean
about 200g podded or frozen broad beans
150g podded or frozen peas
100g asparagus
a generous slice from a goat's cheese log (about
    200g)
about 80g mixed salad leaves – rocket, watercress,
    baby spinach, mustard leaves – whatever is
    available
a small handful of seasonal soft herbs – such as
    parsley, dill, chives, chervil or tarragon
2 tbsp white wine or tarragon vinegar
5 tbsp extra virgin olive oil
50g broken walnuts (optional)
salt and pepper

Heat the oven to 200C/400F/Gas 6. Wrap the beets loosely in foil, place on a baking tray and roast for 50 minutes to an hour, or until tender. When cool enough to handle, peel off their skins and cut into quarters or smaller wedges.

Meanwhile cook the beans and peas in boiling water for about 5 minutes until just cooked. When cool enough to handle pop the beans out of their skins. Cut the tips of the asparagus off about a third of the way down the spear (saving the rest of the stalk) and steam or microwave for about 3 minutes until tender. Set aside and cool.

Whisk together the ingredients for the dressing. Use half to lightly dress the beetroot. Divide the leaves between 4 plates and drizzle with a little of the remaining dressing. Arrange the beets over the leaves and top with roughly torn chunks of goat's cheese, broad beans and peas. Scatter over the herbs and walnuts, if using, trickle over the remaining dressing and grind a little black pepper over the top. Serve with new potatoes or a crusty loaf of bread.

VARIATIONS

If you want to cut down preparation time you could use vac-packed cooked beetroot and frozen broad beans and peas.

THRIFTY TIP

If you're only using asparagus tips in a recipe save the middle of the spear to use in a pasta sauce, risotto or soup.

WARM CAULIFLOWER, EGG AND ANCHOVY SALAD

This was inspired by a week's veg box experiment – an unusual but good use for cauliflower.

SERVES 2

2 large eggs
1 medium-sized cauliflower, trimmed and cut into florets
3 tbsp olive oil
$\frac{1}{2}$ bunch of spring onions, trimmed and finely sliced or a small onion, peeled and chopped
1 x 50g tin of anchovy fillets
1 tbsp capers, rinsed and chopped
2 tbsp finely chopped parsley and a little extra for decoration
1 tbsp red or white wine vinegar
salt and pepper

Hard boil the eggs for 10 minutes, drain and leave in their shells in cold water. Steam or microwave the cauliflower until just tender (about 7–8 minutes). Heat the olive oil in a frying pan over a low to moderate heat and fry the spring onions for a couple of minutes until softened. Take off the heat and mix in roughly half the steamed cauliflower (saving the rest for another recipe). Drain the anchovies, reserving the oil, and chop half the fillets finely. Shell and chop one of the eggs. Tip the anchovies, eggs, capers and parsley into the cauliflower together with the vinegar, toss together and season lightly with salt and pepper (go easy on the salt because of the anchovies). Tip the salad onto a serving plate or divide between two plates. Shell and quarter the remaining egg and arrange over the salad along with the remaining anchovies. Scatter over a little more parsley and serve with some crusty bread or new potatoes.

VARIATIONS

If you don't like anchovies or not quite as much as I like them you could save the other half of the tin for topping a pizza or adding to a pasta sauce.

LEFTOVERS

The leftover cauliflower will make a good base for a curry – as would any leftover potatoes.

THRIFTY TIP

Save the oil from anchovy tins for drizzling over pizzas (non-vegetarian ones, obviously).

AVOCADO SALSA SALAD
TO GO WITH TUNA OR MACKEREL

Another way of making salads look more appealing is to cut all the ingredients up small and serve them in a bowl. Psychologically it feels so much better than just chucking a few salad veg on a plate – you feel you've had a proper meal. I call them salsa salads or big bowl salads (if I'm making them for a crowd). There's a lot in a name.

SERVES 2–3

5–6 cherry tomatoes, halved
$1/2$ a green or red pepper, pith removed and diced
$1/4$ cucumber, peeled, de-seeded and diced
1 shallot or half an onion, finely chopped or
    1–2 spring onions, finely sliced
1 mild chilli or $1/2$ a larger one, de-seeded and
    finely chopped (optional)
1 avocado, peeled and chopped
1 $1/2$ tbsp lemon or lime juice
3 tbsp olive oil (or, even better, basil-flavoured
    olive oil)
2 tbsp finely chopped parsley or coriander or a
    few torn basil leaves
salt and freshly ground black pepper

Simply put all the vegetables in a bowl, cutting the avocado up last so it doesn't discolour. Pour over the lemon juice and olive oil, season with salt and pepper and add the chopped herbs. Mix lightly but thoroughly.

VARIATIONS

You could add a few thawed frozen prawns to the salad. Another good combination is apple, orange, celery or chicory, cheese or ham and walnuts (add a tablespoon of cream to the dressing) or try tuna, onion, red pepper and black-eye beans.

THRIFTY TIP

It's always better to use up an avocado because they discolour badly if you leave them any length of time.

MACKEREL, OLIVE AND ORANGE SALAD

Tinned mackerel is much underrated but needs some punchy flavours to counteract its slight oiliness.

SERVES 2

2 oranges
2 small or 1 large head of chicory
10–12 pitted green or black olives with herbs, chopped
2 tbsp olive oil (if no decent oil with the olives)
1 x 200g tin mackerel, drained and flaked
2 tbsp chopped parsley
salt and pepper

Cut one of the oranges in half and juice it. Remove as much rind and pith from the remaining orange as possible* and cut into chunks. Trim and slice the chicory into rounds. Put the orange and chicory into a bowl with the chopped pitted olives and orange juice. Add 2 tablespoons of oil from the olive jar if it's decent oil. If not add two tablespoons of olive oil and toss together. Add the flaked mackerel and parsley and carefully mix without breaking up the fish too much. Season to taste with salt and black pepper and mix again.

* An easy way to do this is to score round the skin of the orange as if dividing it into quarters, put it in a bowl, pour boiling water over it and leave it for a minute or two. The pith will then come away cleanly.

VARIATIONS

You could make this with tuna rather than mackerel or substitute a bunch of watercress for the chicory.

THRIFTY TIP

For some weird reason chicory is about four times as expensive in the UK as it is in France so bring some back with you if you're on a day trip. (Its season is winter to spring).

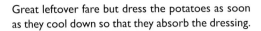

SAUSAGE, POTATO AND GHERKIN SALAD

Great leftover fare but dress the potatoes as soon as they cool down so that they absorb the dressing.

SERVES 1

1 tsp Dijon mustard
1 tbsp white wine vinegar
3 tbsp olive oil
2–3 leftover freshly cooked potatoes
$^1/_2$ a small onion, finely chopped
2 finely chopped gherkins, cornichons or a larger pickled cucumber
2–3 cooked sausages, thickly sliced
1 tbsp parsley, finely chopped

Spoon the mustard into a medium-sized bowl. Add the vinegar and a little salt and pepper then whisk in the oil. Add a tablespoon of water and whisk that in too. Roughly slice the potatoes into the dressing. (At this point you can leave them overnight in the fridge but bring them and the sausages to room temperature before completing the salad) Add the finely chopped onion, gherkins and sliced sausages and parsley and toss together, adding a little more oil or vinegar if necessary.

VARIATIONS

You can make this with sliced garlic sausage rather than leftover sausages.

THRIFTY TIP

Gherkins and pickled cucumbers are useful ingredients to have to hand to zip up cold meats.

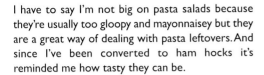

HAM, BROAD BEAN AND HERB PASTA SALAD

I have to say I'm not big on pasta salads because they're usually too gloopy and mayonnaisey but they are a great way of dealing with pasta leftovers. And since I've been converted to ham hocks it's reminded me how tasty they can be.

SERVES 1–2

200g freshly cooked pasta shapes (i.e. 100g uncooked weight).
1 tbsp olive oil
1 heaped tbsp mayonnaise
1 heaped tbsp yoghurt or sour cream
75–100g diced cooked ham, preferably from a ham hock or other ham cut off the bone
50g cooked, skinned* broad beans or peas
2 tbsp finely chopped chives
1 tbsp parsley (optional)

If you're making this with leftover pasta toss the pasta in a tablespoon of oil as soon as you can to stop it sticking, (you could then refrigerate it at this point). Mix the yoghurt or sour cream in a bowl, add the pasta, diced ham and broad beans, half the chives and the parsley. Season with salt and freshly ground pepper and toss together. Sprinkle over the remaining chives.

* You obviously don't have to skin the broad beans but they do look better. To skin them cook them for two minutes then as soon as they're cool enough to handle just pinch the outer skin and the bright green bean inside will pop out.

VARIATIONS

You can also rustle up a pasta salad with a little cooked tomato sauce then add grilled or roasted vegetables such as peppers, onions and courgettes and some slivers of Parmesan or torn basil.

THRIFTY TIP

If you're saving vegetables like peas to make a salad it's better not to add butter to them. Actually, the health police would say it's better not to add butter anyway!

SWEET POTATO AND CHICKEN HASH

An irresistibly spicy hash – a bit like a samosa filling.

SERVES 1

3 tbsp vegetable oil

1 medium onion, peeled and roughly chopped or half a bunch of spring onions, trimmed and finely sliced

1 clove of garlic, peeled and crushed or finely chopped

1 small green chilli, de-seeded and finely chopped (optional)

$1/_2$ tsp mild curry paste or 1 tsp Moroccan spice mix (see page 27) plus $1/_4$ tsp turmeric if you have some

about 125g diced, cooked chicken, turkey or duck

2 cooked sweet potatoes or ordinary cooked potatoes cut into cubes

2 tbsp finely chopped fresh coriander or parsley

salt

Heat the oil in a frying pan. Add the onion and fry over a moderate heat for about 5 minutes until beginning to brown. Turn the heat down and stir in the garlic and chillies and cumin seeds if using, then add the curry paste or Moroccan spice mix and turmeric. Cook for a minute, add the chicken and potatoes and turn them over in the spices. Cook, stirring for another 3–4 minutes until the chicken is thoroughly heated through then take off the heat, stir in the fresh coriander and season to taste with salt. Serve with onion or cucumber raita or just a dollop of plain yoghurt.

VARIATIONS

If you don't have any leftover chicken available you could substitute half a mugful of frozen peas or add some chopped spinach.

LEFTOVERS

Very tasty cold!

THRIFTY TIP

Curry paste is a useful storecupboard ingredient that can be used as the base for quick curry sauces.

SALMON, LEEK AND DILL HASH

This is quite an upmarket hash which you can make from a leftover salmon fillet or a bit of a whole, poached salmon.

SERVES 2–3

250g–300g cooked boneless, skinless salmon fillet
  or a pack of salmon flakes
2 medium leeks (cleaned and chopped) or a bunch
  of spring onions, trimmed and finely sliced
450–500g cooked, preferably new potatoes
1 tbsp olive oil
A slice of butter (about 25g)
3 tbsp finely chopped dill (or parsley)
1–1 $^1/_2$ tbsp lemon juice
salt and freshly ground black pepper
a small carton of sour cream (optional)

Heat a large frying pan or wok over a moderate heat then add the oil and the butter. Gently cook the sliced leeks for about 5 minutes until beginning to soften but still green. Slice the potatoes thickly and add to the pan. Fry with the leeks for about 5 minutes until beginning to brown. Add the salmon and heat through turning the mixture carefully so as not to break it up too much. Sprinkle half the dill over the hash and season it to taste with lemon juice, salt and black pepper. Divide the hash between 2–3 plates, spoon a little sour cream over the top of each serving and sprinkle with the remaining dill.

VARIATIONS

Unlimited. You can make a simple hash with fried up bacon, onions and potatoes (add frozen peas or parsley for colour), or a Spanish style one with onions, peppers, potato and chorizo. Or an American style corned beef hash. If you're a real hash fanatic you could cook the potatoes freshly just so that you can make it.

THRIFTY TIP

Buy dill, like other herbs, loose from a greengrocer or ethnic shop rather than a supermarket.

TWO VEGETABLE MINESTRONE

A make-do-and-mend recipe from fridge leftovers which proves minestrone doesn't have to have a zillion different veg.

SERVES 2–4

2 tbsp olive oil and extra for serving

about 75g chopped streaky bacon, lardons or pancetta

a large leek or some outer leek leaves, washed and sliced

half a bunch of celery, preferably with leaves, sliced

a pinch of dried thyme or oregano

1 x 400g tin of flageolet or cannellini beans, drained and rinsed

600ml stock made with 2 tsp vegetable bouillon powder

2 fresh tomatoes, skinned and roughly chopped or half a 400g can tomatoes or 2–3 tbsp passata

grated Parmesan or Grana Padano (optional)

Heat the oil, add the bacon pieces and fry for a few minutes until beginning to colour, then add the chopped leeks and celery and a pinch of dried thyme and cook them slowly with the lid on the pan for about 7 or 8 minutes. Add the beans, stock and chopped tomatoes and cook for another 7–8 minutes until the vegetables are tender. Add the chopped tomatoes and celery leaves if you have some and simmer for another 5 minutes. Season to taste with plenty of freshly ground pepper and serve with a drizzle of olive oil and/or some grated Parmesan or Grana Padano.

VARIATIONS

You can substitute an onion for the leek, and courgettes for the celery. You could stir in a handful of spinach or other greens at the end instead of celery leaves. You could use chopped Serrano ham instead of bacon. You could add some pasta shapes to it instead of beans.

THRIFTY TIP

If you have some Parmesan rind left over add that to the soup.

STALKY SPINACH, PEA AND MINT SOUP

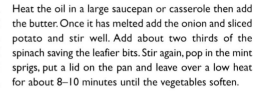

This is a frugal recipe *par excellence*, made with a couple of bunches of spinach stalks, some thawed frozen peas (which had been inadvertently left out) and the leftovers from a packet of mint. You could make something similar with broccoli or broccoli and cauliflower stalks. And with fresh young pea pods instead of peas if you sieve the soup before serving it.

SERVES 4–6

1 tbsp olive oil
15g butter
1 medium onion, peeled and roughly chopped or half a bunch of spring onions
1 medium potato, peeled and finely sliced
stalks and a few leaves from a couple of bunches of spinach or, obviously, leaves as well if you've grown it yourself and have a spinach glut
a couple of sprigs of mint
750ml vegetable or chicken stock (homemade or an organic cube)
200–240g frozen or thawed frozen peas
salt, pepper and a good squeeze or squirt of lemon juice
some finely chopped parsley, if you have some

Heat the oil in a large saucepan or casserole then add the butter. Once it has melted add the onion and sliced potato and stir well. Add about two thirds of the spinach saving the leafier bits. Stir again, pop in the mint sprigs, put a lid on the pan and leave over a low heat for about 8–10 minutes until the vegetables soften.

Add 500ml of the stock, bring to the boil and simmer until the potatoes are soft (about 15 minutes). Chuck in the remaining chopped spinach and the peas, bring to the boil and cook for 4–5 minutes. Remove the woody mint stalks and liquidise the soup in two to three batches, depending on the size of your blender, pouring the finished soup into another saucepan. Pour the remaining stock into the blender and whizz to pick up the remains of the soup. Add to the soup and reheat gently. Season to taste with salt, freshly ground black pepper and a good squeeze of lemon juice. Sprinkle over a little chopped parsley before serving.

VARIATIONS

If you don't have a potato you could thicken the soup with a spoonful or two of instant potato flakes (much nicer than instant potato powder). For a slightly posher soup you could sieve the soup before serving it with a dash of cream.

THRIFTY TIP

When you're liquidising a soup save some of the stock to whizz up the last traces of soup from the blender goblet.

PEA AND HAM SOUP

The perfect way to finish off a ham hock or use the stock from cooking a gammon or bacon joint.

SERVES 4

1 tbsp light olive oil or other cooking oil
15g butter
1 medium-large onion, peeled and roughly chopped
2 medium carrots, peeled and sliced
2 sticks of celery, trimmed and sliced (if you have some)
a ham hock bone plus some extra ham
225g green split peas
a bay leaf or a sprig of thyme
salt and pepper
a handful of fresh parsley

Heat the olive oil in a heavy saucepan or casserole, add the butter then, once it's melted, tip in the chopped and sliced vegetables and give them a stir. Cover the pan and cook on a low heat for about 10 minutes until the vegetables are beginning to soften. Add the ham bone, the split peas and bay leaf then pour in enough water to cover the bone (about 750ml). Bring to the boil and skim, then simmer the soup for about an hour until the peas are soft and mushy. Remove the bone and add a little extra water or stock. Season well with salt and freshly ground black pepper. Chop up the ham and parsley, add to the soup and reheat. Check seasoning and serve.

VARIATIONS

A good soup for using up the tail end of a veg box. Also works well with turnips and swede.

THRIFTY TIP

For some reason split peas are significantly cheaper than other pulses – one of the best food bargains around.

SPICED PARSNIP SOUP WITH GARLIC RAITA

Since not everyone likes roast parsnips there's a fair chance you'll find yourself with some left over. Here's what to do with them.

SERVES 4

3 tbsp light olive oil or sunflower oil
1 medium to large onion, peeled and chopped
1 medium carrot, peeled and finely sliced
1–2 sticks of celery (optional)
1–1 1/2 tsp ground cumin
1 tsp ground coriander
1/4 tsp paprika
500ml vegetable stock made with 2 tsp vegetable bouillon powder or an organic vegetable stock cube
300–350g boiled or leftover roast parsnips (see Variations note)
salt and freshly ground black pepper
freshly chopped coriander or roasted cumin seeds to garnish (optional)
wholemeal pitta bread, chapattis or naan, to serve

For the raita
2 heaped tbsp plain or soy yoghurt
1 small clove of garlic, peeled, chopped and crushed with 1/4 tsp salt or 1 tsp garlic paste

Heat the oil in a saucepan over a moderate heat. Add the chopped onion, stir and cook for a couple of minutes then add the carrot and celery if using. Stir, lower the temperature, cover the pan and cook for about 6–7 minutes until beginning to soften. Stir in the cumin, coriander and paprika, stir then add enough water to cover and cook the vegetables till soft. Put the cooked parsnips in a blender with a little of the stock and whizz until smooth.

Tip into a saucepan. Tip the onion and carrot mix into the blender with a little more stock, whizz that and add to the parsnip purée.

Pour the rest of the stock into the blender to pick up the remaining puréed vegetables and pour into the mix. Stir well, bring to the boil and season to taste with salt, pepper and a little more cumin if you think it needs it. Mix the yoghurt with the crushed garlic or fresh garlic paste. Ladle the soup into warm bowls, add a swirl of garlic raita and garnish with chopped coriander or roasted cumin seeds. Serve with wholemeal pitta bread, chapattis or naan.

VARIATIONS

You can, of course, make this with fresh parsnips. Just peel and chop them and add them to the other vegetables when you cook them, adding extra stock to cover. You could also use a teaspoon of mild to medium hot curry paste instead of the ground cumin and coriander.

THRIFTY TIP

Serve soup in small bowls so that it looks more generous.

JUST-LIKE-TUNA PÂTÉ

Whizzing or chopping up leftover cheese, meat or fish into tasty spreads which can also be used for an after-school snack is a useful skill to acquire. Here's a simple way of sneaking in a can of sardines.

ENOUGH TO FILL 2–3 SANDWICHES OR BAPS

1 can of sardines in sunflower or olive oil
75g Quark or low-fat curd cheese
grated rind of half a small lemon
freshly ground black pepper

Drain the sardines, split them lengthways and remove the backbone – yes, I know it's healthy but there's nothing more offputting to kids than coming across crunchy bits of bone! Put the sardines in a blender with the Quark and lemon rind. Whizz, taste and season with pepper.

VARIATIONS

You could add some chopped chives if your child doesn't mind 'green bits'.

LEFTOVERS

Can be used as a spread for crackers.

THRIFTY TIP

Quark is much cheaper than comparable creamy cheeses.

TORTILLA CHIPS AND SALSA

This quick recipe is great for an after school snack and it's much healthier and more delicious than shop-bought salsa.

SERVES 3–4

400g ripe tomatoes
$1/_2$ medium onion, finely chopped
1 mild green chilli, cut lengthways, seeds removed and finely chopped
3 tbsp lime juice
1 heaped tbsp finely chopped fresh coriander
salt
tortilla chips, to serve

Remove the tomato skins by making a small cut in the top of each tomato, placing them in a bowl and pouring boiling water over them. After a minute, drain off the water and plunge them into cold water. The skins should come away easily. Finely chop the tomato flesh and seeds and place in a bowl with the chopped onion, chilli and lime juice. Season with salt and stir in the fresh coriander. Serve with tortilla chips.

VARIATIONS

You could replace the chilli with some finely chopped green or red pepper for kids who don't like their food too hot.

THRIFTY TIP

Own brand tortilla chips are much, much cheaper than the well-known brands.

EASY
MIDWEEK
SUPPERS

JUST BECAUSE YOU'RE TRYING TO EAT FRUGALLY DOESN'T
MEAN YOU HAVE TO SPEND HOURS IN THE KITCHEN. HERE
ARE SOME TASTY MIDWEEK RECIPES THAT ARE EASY TO MAKE
AFTER WORK.

THAI BEEF SALAD

A great way of stretching a steak you might normally think of serving for two to four. There are quite a few other ingredients, admittedly, but if you're into Thai flavours you should be able to find good use for them.

SERVES 4

1 tbsp Thai jasmine rice or basmati
$^1/_2$tsp crushed chillies or $^1/_4$ tsp hot smoked pimenton
a thick slice of lean rump steak (about 400g), trimmed of any fat
1 tbsp sunflower or light olive oil
$1^1/_2$ –2 tsp golden or white caster sugar
the juice of 2 limes, preferably unwaxed (3–4 tbsp)
2–3 tbsp nam pla (fish sauce)
1 large clove of garlic, crushed
4 small shallots, peeled and very finely sliced or 3–4 spring onions, finely sliced
1–2 small fresh red chillies, deseeded and finely sliced
3 heaped tbsp fresh coriander leaves, chopped
2 heaped tbsp fresh mint leaves, chopped
125g cherry tomatoes, quartered
rocket or mixed salad leaves, to serve

Heat a ridged grill pan over a moderate heat, add the rice and dry fry, stirring occasionally until golden and fragrant (about 5 minutes). Take off the heat, allow to cool a couple of minutes then grind with a mortar and pestle or the end of a rolling pin. Toast the crushed chillies, if using, the same way for about a minute and set aside. Wipe the pan, turn up the heat then, when the pan is almost smoking, rub the steak with a little oil and cook for about $1^1/_2$ minutes each side until charred but still rare. Set aside to cool while you make the dressing. Dissolve the sugar in the lime juice, add 2 tablespoons of the fish sauce, 2 tbsp of water and half the roasted chillies or pimenton and taste. Add more fish sauce and chillies if you think the dressing needs it. Finely slice the steak with a sharp knife. Tip the steak strips and any juices in a bowl with the dressing and add the sliced shallots, fresh chillies, chopped coriander, mint and cherry tomatoes and toss together. Scatter a large handful of mixed salad leaves or shredded iceberg lettuce over a large platter and top with the beef salad. Sprinkle with toasted rice.

VARIATIONS

You can adapt this technique to other meats such as lamb. Try seasoning some lamb steaks with cumin and other Moroccan spices (page 27), searing them as above, then serving them with a couscous salad with herbs (see page 192).

THRIFTY TIP

Your limes will yield more juice if they're at room temperature. If you take them straight from the fridge warm them on a low setting in the microwave.

SCHNITZEL

Next to roast chicken, possibly the most perfect children's meal ever. I've not come across one that doesn't love it (unless they're vegetarian, of course). Or any adult come to that. Pure comfort food.

SERVES 4

2 skinless, boneless chicken breasts, finely sliced into escalopes
30g plain flour, seasoned with salt and pepper
I large egg, lightly beaten with I tbsp milk
50–75g natural dried breadcrumbs (see Thrifty tip below)
6–7 tbsp light olive oil
50g butter
I lemon, quartered
watercress for garnish (optional)

Place the chicken escalopes between two sheets of greaseproof paper and beat out flat with a rolling pin. Put the flour, egg and dried breadcrumbs in 3 separate shallow bowls. Dip each escalope in seasoned flour, then in the beaten egg mixture shaking off any excess then finally in the dried breadcrumbs, making sure it is evenly coated. Heat a frying pan, add 2 tablespoons of the oil then, when that has heated, about 20g of butter. Once the butter has melted lay the fillets in the pan and fry briefly for about a minute each side until nicely browned. Set aside on a warm plate. Repeat with the remaining escalopes adding more oil and butter as you need it. For kids you can serve the escalopes pretty much as they are with a lemon wedge, a simple salad and some new potatoes or spaghetti with a simple tomato sauce. For more adult tastes accompany them *Sound-of-Music*-style with some buttered noodles (schnitzel with noodles – remember?).

VARIATIONS

Lots. You could make these with turkey, pork or veal escalopes. You could top them with salsa verde or with chopped capers, anchovies and an egg (in which case it would become chicken Holstein) or chopped fresh tomato and basil, bruschetta-style. They're good with grated courgettes too.

LEFTOVERS

Fatally delicious cold. Good lunchbox fare.

THRIFTY TIP

Buy your dried breadcrumbs from an Italian deli – Italians use them all the time so they're cheap and freshly made.

PORK AND PRUNES

You might need convincing about this combination (and the unconventional, I admit, addition of tea and tomato ketchup) but it's a natural. Pork works really well with fruit. Another recipe where a small amount of meat stretches a surprisingly long way.

SERVES 2

1 teabag (ordinary breakfast tea or Rooibos)
75g prunes
250g pork fillet
1 tbsp seasoned flour
1 tbsp oil
15g butter
2 tbsp medium-dry montilla, sherry, Madeira, marsala or tawny port
1 level tbsp tomato ketchup
3 tbsp double cream or 2 heaped tbsp crème fraîche
$1/4$ tsp balsamic vinegar (optional)
salt and freshly ground black pepper

Put the teabag in a mug, pour over boiling water and leave to infuse for 5 minutes. Remove the teabag and add the prunes and let them steep for half an hour. Drain off and retain the liquid. Cut the pork fillet vertically into thin medallions then lay them on a chopping board, cover with a piece of greaseproof paper and flatten with a meat mallet or a rolling pin. Put the seasoned flour in a shallow dish and lightly dip the pork pieces in it. Heat the oil in a frying pan then add the butter. Once it stops foaming fry the pork medallions for a minute each side then lift out of the pan and set aside. Deglaze the pan with the montilla, sherry or Madeira then add the reserved tea used for soaking the prunes. Bubble up and reduce by two thirds until there are about 3–4 tablespoons of liquid left in the pan. Off the heat, stir in the tomato ketchup then mix in the cream and reheat gently without boiling. Return the meat and any juices to the pan and heat through.

Season with salt and pepper and a few drops of balsamic vinegar if you have some. Add a little hot water if the sauce has become too thick. Good with boiled new potatoes and a green salad.

VARIATIONS

You could also cook pork escalopes with onions, apples and cider or make a goulash-type sauce using paprika, tomato paste, stock and sour cream.

THRIFTY TIP

It's worth having a bottle of some kind of fortified wine in the kitchen. Montilla, which comes from outside the officially recognised area for sherry, is by far the best value.

BAVETTE AUX ECHALOTES

Bavette or skirt is one of the most popular French bistro cuts, especially cooked this way with vinegar. It needs to be cut on the cross and cooked quickly otherwise it can be tough – but it's really flavourful.

SERVES 2

2 tbsp olive oil
25g soft butter
250g evenly sized small shallots, peeled and
    quartered – or small onions, at a pinch
$^1/_3$ cup red wine vinegar
300g thinly sliced bavette (skirt steak)
75ml beef stock (see also Thrifty tip below)
salt, freshly ground pepper and tomato ketchup, to
    taste

Heat a medium-sized frying pan over a moderate heat and add a tablespoon of oil and half the butter. Tip in the shallots and fry over a medium high heat for about 6–7minutes until well browned. Pour in the vinegar and bubble up until almost evaporated then set aside. Heat a ridged grill pan or cast iron frying pan for 2–3 minutes until almost smoking. Rub the remaining oil onto both sides of the steaks and season lightly with salt and pepper. Fry the meat about $1^1/_2$ minutes each side, pressing the pieces firmly down into the pan with a wooden spatula. Transfer to a warm plate, cover lightly with foil and rest for 5 minutes. Put the onions back on the heat, whisk in the remaining butter and any juices from the meat and heat through. Check the seasoning adding salt and pepper to taste and a few drops of tomato ketchup if the sauce is too sharp – an old chefs' trick! Serve the meat with the shallots spooned over. Great with chips. Pretty good with mash or a baked potato.

VARIATIONS
You could make this with minute steak.

THRIFTY TIP

If you've any braising liquid left over from making a stew stashed away in the freezer add that instead of the stock.

WINTER SAUSAGES WITH STOEMP

Stoemp is the Belgian version of bubble and squeak and very tasty it is too. Here's how to make it from scratch but you could equally well rustle it up from leftovers.

SERVES 4

2 tbsp sunflower or other frying oil
800g plump pork sausages, dried with kitchen towel (to help them brown)
mustard to serve

For the stoemp
650g potatoes, peeled and quartered
250g turnips, peeled and cubed
1 tbsp sunflower or light olive oil
15g butter
1 large or 2 medium leeks, cleaned and sliced
1 tbsp crème fraîche or double cream (optional)
salt and freshly ground black pepper

Put the potatoes in a saucepan with the turnips, cover with cold water, bring to the boil and cook until tender (about 15–20 minutes – the turnips may take slightly longer than the potatoes so cut them slightly smaller). Meanwhile heat the oil in a frying pan, put in the sausages and fry slowly, turning them regularly until brown and sticky. Drain the vegetables thoroughly, return to the pan and mash with a potato masher and/or fork until smooth. Heat the oil in a frying pan, add the butter then once it has melted add the leeks and stir-fry over a moderate heat until beginning to brown (about 4–5 minutes). Tip the leeks and butter into the mash along with the crème fraîche, if using, mix in well and season to taste with salt and freshly ground black pepper. Serve the sausages with the stoemp and a good mustard.

VARIATIONS

You could use onion instead of leek, swede or carrot – or both – instead of turnip and/or stir in some cooked greens.

THRIFTY TIP

There's no need to use expensive olive oil for a traditional Northern European dish like this.

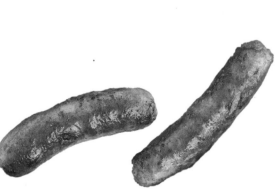

SUMMER SAUSAGES WITH PEPPERS AND BUTTERBEAN MASH

Apart from barbecues, sausages always seem more like winter fare. Here's a lighter, more summery treatment.

SERVES 2–3

4 tbsp sunflower or light olive oil
450g sausages dried with kitchen towel (to help them brown)
1 large onion, peeled and finely sliced
2 red or 1 red and 1 yellow pepper, pith removed and finely sliced
salt and freshly ground black pepper

For the butterbean mash

2 tbsp olive oil
$^1/_2$ bunch of spring onions, trimmed and finely sliced
1 large clove of garlic, peeled and crushed
1 tsp chopped fresh thyme or marjoram leaves or a pinch of dried thyme, marjoram or oregano
1 x 400g can butterbeans, drained and rinsed or 300g cooked butterbeans
1 heaped tbsp finely chopped parsley

Heat 2 tablespoons of oil in a frying pan, add the sausages and brown lightly then turn the heat down and fry over a low heat, turning them regularly until well browned and sticky. In the meantime make the butterbean mash. Put 2 tablespoons of oil in a small saucepan, add the spring onions and garlic and fry over a low heat for a couple of minutes until soft but not coloured. Tip in the thyme or marjoram, the drained, rinsed butter beans and a couple of tablespoons of water and cook over a low heat stirring from time to time so that the beans break up into a rough purée. Keep adding a spoonful or two of water to give a slightly sloppy consistency.

Heat the remaining 2 tablespoons of oil in a frying pan or wok, add the sliced onions, stir and fry for a couple of minutes, then add the sliced peppers and stir-fry over a moderate heat for about 5–6 minutes until softened and beginning to char. Season the peppers and the mash to taste with salt and freshly ground black pepper. Stir the parsley into the mash and serve with the sausages, fried peppers and onions.

VARIATIONS

Grill or barbecue the peppers. Add a sliced courgette and/or a couple of skinned, chopped tomatoes to the onion and pepper mixture. Make the mash with other beans such as cannelini or flageolet beans.

LEFTOVERS

The onion and pepper mix makes a good topping for cold meats in a sandwich. Like a sort of chutney.

THRIFTY TIP

The middle range of sausages in supermarkets is usually very competitively priced and generally has a reasonable meat content (see page 23).

FEGATO CON BALSAMICO

The Italians regard liver as a delicacy and so it is prepared this way. Get any accompanying vegetables ready first because the recipe only takes a couple of minutes.

SERVES 1

1 tbsp sunflower oil or light olive oil
3 thin slices of lambs' liver (about 140g in total)
1 tbsp balsamic vinegar
1 level tbsp tomato ketchup
salt and pepper

Heat a ridged grill pan or frying pan over a moderate to high heat for about a minute and a half. Pour a little oil in the pan then pour it away. Put the pan back on the hob, lay the liver slices in the pan and cook until you see the blood begin to rise to the surface – about a minute. Turn the liver over and cook for a minute the other side. Take the pan off the heat. Mix the balsamic vinegar with the ketchup and 3 tablespoons of water and pour in the pan. It will bubble up and reduce to about a spoonful. Serve the liver with the sauce spooned over with a dark leafy salad or some broccoli or spinach for an ultra-healthy meal or with mash for a rather more filling one.

VARIATIONS

Sometimes ox liver is tender enough to cook this way and can be even cheaper.

THRIFTY TIP

Tomato ketchup is a surprisingly good way of rounding out a sauce and giving it a touch of sweetness. Even chefs use it!

KEBDA WITH WARM RED PEPPER SALAD

This is a recipe I put in my first student cookbook, *Beyond Baked Beans* (Absolute Press), and which still remains a favourite way of cooking liver. Cook the red peppers first.

SERVES 2

For the red pepper salad
2 red peppers
2 tbsp olive oil
2 cloves of garlic
salt and pepper

2 tsp flour
2 tsp ground cumin (or 2 tsp cumin seeds, crushed with a mortar and pestle)
1 tsp sweet pimenton or paprika (or $^1/_2$ tsp hot paprika)
$^1/_4$ tsp salt
250–300g sliced lambs liver
2 tbsp oil
2 tbsp lemon juice (about $^1/_2$ a lemon)
2 tbsp plain, unsweetened yoghurt
2 tbsp roughly chopped coriander

Quarter the peppers and cut away the stalk and all the white pith inside. Peel the garlic and cut into thin slices. Heat a frying pan or wok, add the oil and stir-fry the peppers over a medium heat until beginning to soften. Turn the heat right down and chuck in the garlic. Cook stirring occasionally until the peppers are completely soft. Season and set aside.

Mix the flour, cumin, pimenton or paprika and salt in a shallow dish and dip the liver in it making sure each bit is thoroughly coated. Heat a large frying pan over a medium heat and add the oil. When the oil is hot lay the slices of liver in the pan. Cook for about 1 minute till you see blood appear on the surface then turn over and cook the other side for another minute or two. Divide the liver between two warm plates and add the lemon juice to the pan. Let it bubble up and pour it over the liver. Top with a spoonful of yoghurt and some chopped coriander and serve with some flatbread and the red pepper salad.

VARIATIONS

Instead of the warm red pepper salad you could serve the liver with a Middle Eastern-style salad of chopped tomatoes, peppers, cucumber, onion and fresh herbs.

LEFTOVERS

The liver is quite nice served cold as a nibble with other Middle Eastern mezze.

THRIFTY TIP

Watch out for prices on red peppers in supermarkets. As a popular ingredient they tend to be heavily marked up.

KIDNEYS WITH MUSTARD

An unbelievably simple and delicious recipe – if you like kidneys, obviously.

SERVES 2

4 lamb's kidneys, preferably still in their suet
3 tbsp sunflower or light olive oil
1 tbsp seasoned flour
2 thick slices sourdough or other country bread
15g butter
4 tbsp chicken stock or other light stock
1 level tbsp wholegrain or Dijon mustard
2 tbsp double cream or 1 heaped tbsp crème fraîche
1 tbsp finely chopped parsley
salt, pepper and lemon juice, to taste
watercress or rocket, to serve

Remove any suet from the kidneys. Cut in half lengthways, cut away the white core and slip off the skin then cut each piece into three. Toss the pieces in the seasoned flour. Put about $1^{1}/_{2}$ tbsp of oil in a hot pan, briefly dip each side of the bread in the oil then fry over a moderate heat until lightly browned and crisp. Set on one side. Pour the remaining oil in the pan, add the butter and fry the kidneys for about 2 minutes each side until just cooked. Remove from the pan with a slotted spoon. Pour the stock into the pan, let it bubble up for a minute then take the pan off the heat and stir in the mustard. Stir in the cream. Return the kidneys to the pan and gently reheat without boiling. Stir in the parsley and season to taste with salt, pepper and a squeeze of lemon juice. Pile the kidneys on top of the fried bread and serve with some lightly dressed watercress or rocket leaves.

VARIATIONS

You could add a dash of sherry or Madeira before you add the stock or add Worcestershire sauce instead of mustard and cream. The kidneys would also go well with a pastry base.

THRIFTY TIP

It's worth freezing good quality stock in an ice tray and storing the cubes in the freezer so you can bring out a small amount for a dish like this.

LAMB'S KIDNEYS AND MUSHROOMS IN SHERRY

A classic Spanish recipe which you could serve on its own or as part of a selection of tapas.

SERVES 2

4–6 lamb's kidneys, depending on size
1 tbsp seasoned flour
2–3 tbsp olive oil
2 shallots or a small onion, peeled and finely chopped
1 large clove of garlic
4–6 mushrooms, wiped clean and sliced
$1/_2$tsp sweet pimenton
$1/_2$ tsp dried oregano
2 tbsp passata or 1 tbsp tomato paste
75ml amontillado sherry
75ml beef or chicken stock
2 tbsp finely chopped parsley

Cut the kidneys in half horizontally, removing the skin and cut away the white core. Cut each half into three and toss in seasoned flour. Heat a frying pan, add 2 tbsp of olive oil and fry the kidneys on all sides until lightly browned (about 2 minutes). Remove from the pan and set aside. Add a little more oil to the pan, add the onion and sauté for about 3–4 minutes until beginning to soften. Add the crushed garlic and mushrooms, stir and cook for another 3 minutes or so until the mushrooms begin to colour then stir in the pimenton and oregano. Cook for a minute then add the passata or tomato paste, amontillado sherry and stock. Bring to the boil and cook for a couple of minutes then tip the kidneys back into the pan and heat through, adding a little water if the sauce is too thick. Sprinkle with parsley and serve hot with rice or toast.

VARIATIONS

If you can get hold of some ajvar, an amazing red pepper paste you can find in Middle-Eastern grocers, substitute it for the passata.

LEFTOVERS

Serve one day on rice, the next day on toast.

THRIFTY TIP

Try and buy kidneys that are still encased in suet. They have a much better texture. (You need to remove the suet – and the skin – before cooking them).

SEARED SALMON WITH CREAMED LEEKS AND CHIVES

There was a time when salmon was regarded as a luxury ingredient. Not any more. Someone, somewhere always has it on special offer though it's always worth paying a little extra for fish that isn't too fatty and oily.

SERVES 2

1 tbsp olive oil
two evenly sized boneless salmon fillets (about 150–175g) with their skin left on

For the leeks
1 tbsp olive oil
25g butter
2–3 leeks (about 350g) trimmed, washed and finely sliced
1 heaped tbsp crème fraîche
1 heaped tbsp finely chopped chives plus a few snipped chives for decoration
salt, pepper and a squeeze of lemon juice

Start the leeks first. Heat a frying pan, add the olive oil, then add the butter. Tip in the leeks and stir-fry over a low heat until soft, about 5 minutes, then take the pan off the heat. Season the salmon with salt and freshly ground black pepper. Heat another frying pan until quite hot. Add a tablespoon of olive oil and place the fillets in the pan skin side down. Fry for 4–5 minutes until you see the salmon flesh change colour half way up the fillet then turn the fillets over and cook for a further minute on the other side. Turn off the heat and leave for a further couple of minutes. Put the pan of leeks back over a low heat and add the chives and crème fraîche. Heat through without boiling then season with salt, pepper and lemon juice to taste. Serve the salmon on warm plates with the creamed leeks alongside. Scatter over a few more chives.

VARIATIONS

You can serve different vegetables with this such as grated courgettes with dill or mint (see page 212).

THRIFTY TIP

Salmon freezes well so it can be worth buying a pack of individual fillets when they're on special offer.

SEARED TUNA WITH FENNEL, MINT AND CHILLI SALAD

This is based on a salad they serve in our local fish restaurant FishWorks. It's a great partner for grilled fish and for seafood like prawns. The only downside is that you need a mandolin – or a lot of patience and a sharp knife – to make it.

SERVES 2

1 small to medium-sized fennel bulb, preferably still with its leaves
1 small red chilli, de-seeded and finely chopped
1 tbsp finely chopped mint leaves
juice of half a medium lemon (about 1 1/2 tbsp)
4–5 tbsp extra virgin olive oil
2 x 100g tuna steaks
salt and freshly ground black pepper

Trim the stalks and leaves off the fennel bulb and set aside. Finely slice the fennel with a mandolin or very sharp knife. Tip into a bowl and add the chilli and mint leaves. Add the lemon juice and 2 tbsp of the olive oil and toss together. Season to taste with salt, adding more oil or lemon if needed.

Rub each side of the tuna steaks lightly with olive oil and season with salt and pepper. Heat a ridged grill pan or frying pan for a couple of minutes until really hot and sear the steaks for a minute to a minute and a half each side depending how thick they are and how well done you like them. Set aside and rest on a warm plate for 5 minutes. Serve the tuna with the salad, drizzling over a little extra olive oil.

VARIATIONS
You could also serve the tuna with a tomato and bean salad or with a stir-fry. The fennel salad can also be served separately with a few small, cooked, peeled prawns.

THRIFTY TIP

You could make this with thawed, frozen tuna steaks – cheaper than using fresh.

ROAST POLLACK WITH TOMATOES, OLIVES AND CAPERS

Pollack isn't an enormously flavourful dish but because it's sustainable it's become wildly popular. Here are some gutsy flavours that will bring it to life.

SERVES 4

2 tbsp extra virgin olive oil
2 large cloves of garlic, peeled and crushed
1 x 400g tin peeled plum tomatoes
75g small black olives, pitted for preference
25g capers, drained and rinsed
2 tbsp finely chopped parsley
4 x chunky pollack, cod or haddock fillets (about 150g–175g each)
salt and freshly ground black pepper

Preheat the oven to 200°C/400°F/Gas 6. Heat 1 tablespoon of oil very gently in a medium sized frying pan and fry the crushed garlic for a minute without colouring. Tip in the tomatoes and break them up with a wooden spoon. Simmer for 8–10 minutes until thick and jammy. Add the olives and capers and half the parsley and season with salt and pepper. Place the pollack fillets skin side downwards in an ovenproof baking dish and pour the tomato sauce evenly over the fish. Bake for 15 minutes until you can flake the fish easily. Divide the fish between four plates sprinkling each portion with the remaining parsley. Serve with sautéed courgettes or some steamed broccoli and boiled basmati rice.

VARIATIONS

Instead of the olives and capers you could spice the sauce with 2 teaspoons of Moroccan spice mix (page 27) or zip up the sauce with some hot paprika or chilli sauce.

THRIFTY TIP

You could even use those rather unappealing rectangular cod or coley steaks for this recipe. They'll be disguised by the sauce and taste perfectly good.

NEWSPAPER-WRAPPED TROUT WITH LEMON BUTTER

My neighbour told me that her mother always used to wrap trout in old newspaper to bake it and that seemed such a brilliantly frugal thing to do I couldn't resist it. When you unwrap it the skin comes away in one piece leaving you with fabulous, pink succulent flesh.

SERVES 2

2 medium sized trout, gutted
2 x lemons, one whole, one juiced
fresh parsley
25g butter
2 large sheets of newspaper – a full spread of a tabloid, 2 pages of a broadsheet

Pre-heat the oven to 180°C/350°F/Gas 4.

Soak the newspaper sheets in water and lay them out flat. Rinse the trout, pat dry and place on one of the double sheets. Slice one of the lemons and stuff the cavity with lemon slices and parsley. Wrap the newspaper neatly around the trout so the whole fish is covered, place on a baking sheet and bake for 25 minutes. Have some warm plates ready. As you unwrap the fish the skin will come away with the newspaper leaving you with a perfectly skinned trout. Heat the butter and add lemon juice to taste. Plate up the fish, pour over the butter and serve with new potatoes and peas.

VARIATIONS

You could put other flavourings in the trout such as fennel or dill. Or if you have any flavoured butter, top the trout with a couple of slices rather than use melted butter.

LEFTOVERS

In the unlikely event that there's any trout left over, carefully remove any bones, flake it and mix it with a little mayo and finely snipped chives or onion. Season with salt, pepper and a squeeze of lemon and use for a sandwich filling along with some finely sliced cucumber.

THRIFTY TIP

While you've got the oven on bake some crostini (page 196), roast some vegetables or bake a quiche (page 146).

POLLACK, BACON AND SWEETCORN CHOWDER

A chowder is a filling and satisfying way to use up less glamourous fish such as pollack or whiting or some frozen cod or haddock fillets, part-thawed and cut into cubes.

SERVES 2

2 tbsp olive, sunflower or vegetable oil
4 rashers streaky bacon, rind removed and cut into small pieces or 75g lardons, pancetta or trimmed bacon bits
1 medium onion, peeled and roughly chopped
1 stick of celery, cleaned and sliced (optional)
1 medium to large potato, peeled and cut into smallish cubes
1 tbsp Thai or Vietnamese fish sauce (optional)
250ml whole milk (i.e. not skimmed or semi-skimmed) or soy milk
250g pollack, whiting, cod or haddock, skinned and cubed
150g fresh or frozen sweetcorn kernels
1 tsp cornflour (optional)
salt and freshly ground black pepper
2 tbsp fresh parsley

Heat a large saucepan, add the oil and tip in the bacon and onion. Fry for about 3 minutes until beginning to soften then add the celery, potato, fish sauce mixed with 250ml water (or just plain water) and milk. Bring to the boil then turn the heat down and simmer for about 15 minutes until the potato is almost cooked. Add the cubed fish and sweetcorn, stir, bring back to the boil then leave over a very low heat for 5 minutes. If the soup seems a bit thin or has separated, stir in a teaspoon of cornflour mixed with a tablespoon of water and bring back up to boiling point. Season with pepper and a little salt if you think it needs it and stir in the parsley.

VARIATIONS

Ritz this up with a little shellfish like frozen North Sea prawns or queen scallops. Leave out the sweetcorn if you're a sweetcorn-hater.

THRIFTY TIP

Thai or Vietnamese fish sauce diluted with water is an inexpensive substitute for fish stock.

FISH COUSCOUS

Fish couscous is a speciality of the west coast of Sicily and basically uses whatever fish is available and cheap.

SERVES 4

2 tbsp olive oil
1 medium onion, peeled and finely chopped
1 large clove of garlic, peeled and crushed
1 1/2 tsp Moroccan spice mix (page 27)
1 tbsp tomato paste
350g ripe tomatoes, skinned and roughly chopped
150g small frozen (or chilled) prawns
250g skinned fish fillets such as pollack, whiting, haddock or cod, cut into small chunks
100g cooked mussels or frozen mixed seafood (optional)
2 tbsp finely chopped fresh coriander or parsley or a mixture of the two
250g instant couscous
vegetable stock
salt and pepper

Heat a large frying pan over a moderate heat, add the oil and fry the onion for a few minutes until soft. Add the crushed garlic and spice mix, stir and cook for a minute, then stir in the tomato paste. Tip in the tomatoes and half a small wine glass of water then simmer over a low heat for about 10 minutes until the sauce has thickened, mashing the tomatoes with a fork as they soften to break them down. Meanwhile make up the couscous following the instructions on the pack but using vegetable stock instead of water. Add the prawns, fish and mussels or seafood, if using, to the tomato sauce, mix lightly and heat through until cooked (about 5 minutes). Season and stir in the coriander and/or parsley, adding a little more water if needed – you want quite a wet, soupy consistency. Fluff up the couscous with a fork and serve with the fish.

VARIATIONS

Vary the fish depending on what's available. You could also serve this fish stew with rice.

LEFTOVERS

Reheat and serve with rice or pasta. Make a couscous salad with any leftover couscous (see page 192).

THRIFTY TIP

Cooked mussels or frozen mixed seafood are a thrifty buy – dull on their own, but great in a punchy sauce like this.

A SOOTHING CHICKEN CURRY

Having said this is good for leftovers (it is), I like it best made from scratch, so do try this way too. Note the non-dairy alternatives which make the recipe OK for the dairy-intolerant.

SERVES 2

2–3 tbsp light cooking oil
2 skinless, boneless chicken thighs (about 300g in total) or 250–300g cooked chicken cut into thick strips
$\frac{1}{2}$ a bunch of spring onions, trimmed and sliced into roughly 2cm lengths
1–2 cloves of garlic, crushed
1 tsp freshly grated ginger or ginger paste
$\frac{1}{2}$ tsp ground turmeric (optional)
2 tbsp korma paste or other mild curry paste
3 tbsp double cream or – even better if you have some – coconut cream
3 tbsp plain yoghurt or soy yoghurt
2 tbsp roughly chopped coriander
salt and lemon juice, to taste

Heat 2 tablespoons of the oil in a deep frying pan or wok and lightly brown the chicken strips (if uncooked). If the chicken is cooked, add it later. Add the spring onions, stir and cook for a minute then stir in the crushed garlic, ginger and turmeric if using. Stir, then add the curry paste and 125ml of water then return the chicken to the pan. Spoon over the sauce, turn the heat down, cover the pan and simmer gently for about 15 minutes until the chicken is cooked (simmer the sauce for 10 minutes before adding the chicken if you're using cooked chicken, which only needs 4–5 minutes). Add the double cream or coconut cream and yoghurt, and heat through. Season to taste with salt and a squeeze of lemon and stir in the chopped coriander or parsley. Serve with boiled rice or naan.

VARIATIONS

Add some leftover veg such as steamed broccoli or peas to the curry. If you have some cardamom pods you could add a few finely crushed cardamom seeds along with the garlic and ginger to make the curry more aromatic. You can also employ the same approach to a lamb or beef curry, using a Rogan Josh curry paste and some creamed tomatoes or passata.

THRIFTY TIP

You can freeze fresh ginger and grate it straight from the freezer as you need it.

ASIAN-STYLE CHICKEN BROTH WITH CORIANDER AND NOODLES

Much as I love chicken soup there are times when I feel like something punchier and more invigorating. This is it.

SERVES 1–2

350ml homemade chicken stock (or, in extremis, stock made from a good chicken stock cube such as Telma)

1 large clove of garlic, peeled and very finely sliced

a small chunk of fresh ginger, peeled and very finely sliced

a fresh red or green chilli, de-seeded and finely sliced (or add a dash of chilli paste or chilli sauce at the end)

a few crushed coriander stalks and/or a couple of roots, well washed and roughly chopped

about 125g–150g shredded cooked chicken meat – whatever you have

a handful of finely shredded pak choi or spinach

light soy sauce and lime or lemon juice, to taste

50g rice noodles, cooked following the instructions on the pack

1–2 heaped tbsp coriander leaves

Put the chicken stock in a saucepan and add the garlic, ginger, chilli and coriander stalks if using. Bring to the boil, then leave over a very low heat for 20–30 minutes. Strain the stock then return to the saucepan with the chicken meat and shredded pak choi or spinach, bring back to the boil and simmer for 2 minutes. Season to taste with the soy sauce and lemon juice adding a dash of hot chilli sauce if you haven't used a chilli. Put the cooked noodles in a large, deep bowl (or half the noodles in a smaller bowl) and pour over the hot stock. Sprinkle over some fresh coriander leaves.

VARIATIONS

This is also good with prawns instead of chicken, in which case add a few drops of nam pla instead of the soy sauce.

THRIFTY TIP

Coriander stalks, a traditional ingredient of Thai curry pastes, are worth keeping as they have more flavour than the leaves. They can be added to any soup, stew or curry which you would finish with coriander leaves and simply be removed at the end of the cooking period.

LINGUINE WITH STILTON AND ONION

A scratch meal from the fridge that worked out surprisingly well. I know Stilton doesn't sound quite as sexy as Gorgonzola but it tastes just as good and it's quite a bit cheaper.

SERVES I

1 1/2 tbsp olive oil or butter
1 medium onion, peeled and chopped
100g linguine or spaghetti
40g Stilton or other blue cheese, crumbled
1 tbsp double or whipping cream, crème fraîche
   or Greek yoghurt
2 heaped tbsp finely chopped parsley
salt and freshly ground black pepper
grated Grana Padano or Parmesan to serve

Heat a frying pan, add the oil or butter then once it's melted tip in the onion, stir and leave over a low heat to fry. Pour a kettle of boiling water into a large saucepan, bring back to the boil, add salt, then add the pasta, stir and cook for the time recommended on the pack. Before you drain the linguine set aside 5 tbsp of the water you've been cooking it in. Add 3 tbsp to the onion and tip in the crumbled cheese. Leave over a low heat to melt then stir in the cream or yoghurt. Drain the pasta and add to the pan along with the parsley and toss together well. Season generously with black pepper and sprinkle over some grated Grana Padano or Parmesan.

VARIATIONS

If you're a garlic fan you could fry a crushed clove of garlic with the onions or fry up a couple of rashers of bacon or lardons to make the dish more substantial. You could also sprinkle the finished dish with finely chopped walnuts instead of Grana Padano or Parmesan.

THRIFTY TIP

It's always tempting to use more pasta than this but 100g is the recommended portion for an adult – and the size of helping an Italian would eat!

SPAGHETTI WITH ZUCCHINI AND GARLIC AND LEMON BREADCRUMBS

Tossing pasta with crisp fried breadcrumbs is a popular way of serving it in Italy and I thought it might combine rather well with sautéed courgettes.

SERVES 2

4 tbsp extra virgin olive oil
225g courgettes,
    trimmed and cut
    into small dice
1–2 cloves of garlic, peeled
3 tbsp finely chopped parsley
grated rind of half a lemon
15g butter
40g fresh breadcrumbs
175g spaghetti
salt and freshly ground black pepper
2 wedges of lemon, to serve

Heat 3 tablespoons of the oil in a medium-sized frying pan and fry the courgettes for about 7–8 minutes until soft and lightly browned. Meanwhile, finely chop the garlic, add the parsley and lemon rind to the chopping board and chop them together so that the three ingredients are evenly distributed. Put the pasta on to cook, following the instructions on the pack. Once the courgettes are cooked, tip them and their oil into a bowl, add the remaining oil to the frying pan then add the butter. When the butter has melted, add the breadcrumbs and fry, stirring, until crisp. Take the pan off the heat, stir the chopped parsley, garlic and lemon into the crumbs and season with salt and pepper. Drain the pasta, tip in the sautéed courgettes and oil and two thirds of the seasoned crumbs and toss together lightly. Check the seasoning, adding more salt and pepper if needed and divide the pasta between two large warm bowls or plates. Sprinkle the remaining crumbs over the top. Serve with a lemon wedge so you can squeeze over a little lemon juice.

VARIATIONS

You could add finely chopped anchovies, olives and/or capers to the crumbs or replace some of the parsley with some chopped mint. The recipe also obviously works with pasta shapes such as penne or fusilli.

THRIFTY TIP

It's worth buying authentic Italian pasta if you find it on special offer. Because it generally takes longer to cook it seems to absorb slightly more water than cheap own brand pasta which gives it a greater volume.

CHICKEN AND MUSHROOM PASTA BAKE

A good way to use up the leftover brown meat from a chicken – or turkey.

SERVES 3–4

40g butter
250g button mushrooms, wiped clean and sliced
I tsp finely chopped fresh thyme or tarragon or $^1/_2$ tsp dried thyme
I $^1/_2$ tbsp plain flour
300ml whole or semi-skimmed milk
250g dried pasta quills or other shapes
about 300g cooked chicken meat, skin removed and chopped small
40g grated Gruyère or 20g finely grated Parmesan (or 40g Cheddar if you have neither)
10g fresh or frozen breadcrumbs (optional)
salt and freshly ground black pepper

Melt the butter in a large non-stick saucepan or deep frying pan and add the sliced mushrooms. Fry over a moderate heat until any liquid has disappeared, then stir in the thyme or tarragon. Stir in the flour, cook for a minute, then stir in the milk. Bring to the boil then turn the heat down and simmer for 3–4 minutes until the sauce thickens. Meanwhile, put the pasta on to cook for the time recommended on the pack. Add the chopped chicken or turkey to the sauce and simmer for 5 minutes. Turn on the grill. Drain the pasta and tip into the sauce together with half the cheese. Season with salt and pepper and tip into an ovenproof dish. Mix the remaining cheese with the breadcrumbs if using and place the dish under (but not too close to) the grill and leave till the top is nicely browned and bubbling.

VARIATIONS

Add some chopped ham as well as the chicken. Use leeks as a base instead of mushrooms and add fresh spring vegetables such as chopped asparagus stalks, peas and peeled, podded broad beans. Or make a more luxurious version of this dish by adding a tablespoon of Madeira or amontillado sherry to the mushrooms as you cook them, adding a few soaked, finely chopped dried mushrooms or a spoonful of double or whipping cream to the sauce. You could also use the sauce as a filling for a pie or vol-au-vent or with rice.

THRIFTY TIP

Save any bones from the chicken for stock.

SPINACH AND RICOTTA PASTA BAKE

Spinach and ricotta is often combined with pasta but usually in a lasagne or cannelloni. Here is a simpler but no less delicious way of serving it which takes about half the time to make.

SERVES 2–3

50g butter
1 bunch of spring onions, trimmed and finely sliced
1 small clove of garlic (optional)
250g frozen spinach, thawed or 250g cooked fresh spinach (about 300g–400g before cooking – see below)
200g penne or fusilli pasta
30g freshly grated Parmesan or Grana Padano plus extra for serving if you like
1 heaped tbsp finely chopped dill, tarragon or chervil (optional)
250g Ricotta mixed with 2 tbsp milk
salt, freshly ground pepper and nutmeg to taste

Heat 40g of the butter in a large saucepan, add the spring onions and cook over a low heat for a couple of minutes until soft. Add the garlic if using and cook a minute more. Squeeze any excess water out of the spinach, chop roughly and add to the pan. Leave over a low heat to absorb the butter. Put the pasta on to cook for the time indicated on the pack. Season the spinach with salt and pepper and a pinch of nutmeg. Add 20g of the Parmesan and herbs if using. Drain the pasta and tip into the spinach. Add the Ricotta and toss together without over-mixing. Heat the grill. Tip the pasta, spinach and Ricotta into a lightly greased ovenproof dish. Sprinkle over the remaining Parmesan. Melt the remaining butter and trickle over the surface of the bake then place the dish under the grill and heat until crisp and bubbling. Serve with extra Parmesan if you like.

* If you're making this with fresh spinach, wash the leaves and tear off any tough stalks. Leave in a lidded pan over a low heat without any extra water until the spinach has wilted. Drain thoroughly then use as above.

VARIATIONS

For a more substantial dish you could mix in some fried sliced mushrooms. If you can't find any Ricotta you could mix the spinach with a light cheese sauce. You could also use the spinach and Ricotta mixture as a filling for pancakes.

THRIFTY TIP

Unless you grow your own – or have an inexpensive source of it – frozen spinach is often cheaper than fresh and fine for a recipe like this.

CHICKPEAS AND CHORIZO

Chorizo is one of my favourite ingredients. It's not cheap but you only need a small amount of it to flavour a dish and make it feel more substantial and meaty than it is. (You need the preserved salami-like kind rather than fresh chorizo).

SERVES 2

2 tbsp olive oil
1 small onion, peeled and finely chopped
a small chunk of chorizo (about 60g), skinned, halved lengthways and thinly sliced into half moon shapes
1 small red pepper or half a larger one, deseeded and cut into short strips
1 clove of garlic, peeled and crushed
1 tbsp tomato paste (only needed if you're using fresh tomatoes and they're not very ripe)
4–5 medium-sized ripe tomatoes, skinned and roughly chopped or half a 400g tin of tomatoes
1 x 400g can of chickpeas
salt and freshly ground black pepper
1 heaped tbsp chopped fresh parsley

Put a large frying pan or wok over a medium heat, add the oil, heat for 30 seconds then add the onion, chorizo and pepper. Fry for 7–8 minutes until soft, then stir in the garlic and tomato paste if using. Fry for another minute, then add the tomatoes and their juice, breaking them up with a wooden spoon or spatula and simmer for 8–10 minutes until the tomatoes have broken down and the sauce is thick. Rinse and drain the chickpeas, tip them into the sauce and heat through (about 3 minutes). Season to taste with salt and pepper, stir in the parsley if you have some, then serve in large soup bowls.

VARIATIONS

Lots! Use bacon or bacon bits instead of chorizo and add a teaspoon of hot paprika or pimenton. Make it veggie and substitute aubergine or courgettes for the chorizo. Leave it as it is, but add some rinsed capers and/or olives. Serve the sauce with pasta rather than chickpeas or spoon it over fried eggs.

THRIFTY TIP

Don't feel the need to de-seed tomatoes before adding them. If you do discard the seeds, save them to add to a salsa (page 83) or a soup.

SPICED LENTILS WITH TOMATO AND CREAM

A creamy dhal-style dish which for me constitutes perfect comfort food.

SERVES 2 AS A MAIN, 4 AS A SIDE

2 tbsp sunflower or vegetable oil
I medium onion, peeled and finely sliced
I clove of garlic, crushed
I tsp grated fresh ginger or ginger paste
I $\frac{1}{2}$ tsp garam masala
a small tin or $\frac{1}{2}$ a 400g tin of whole or chopped tomatoes or half a 500g carton of creamed tomatoes or passata
400g can of brown or green lentils, drained and rinsed
25g butter at room temperature
2 tbsp double cream
salt to taste

Heat a small pan for a couple of minutes over a moderate heat then add the oil. Fry the onion quite fast for 5–6 minutes, stirring occasionally until the edges start to blacken. Add the garlic, ginger and the garam masala, stir and cook for a minute then add in the tomatoes or passata, breaking down the tomatoes with a wooden spoon if whole. Tip in the lentils, add 100ml of water, bring to the boil and simmer for about 10 minutes, stirring occasionally until the lentils become smooth and creamy. Stir in the butter and cream and season to taste with salt. Serve on its own with some chapattis, naan or pitta bread or with pilau or boiled rice. It's also very good with an Indian-style spinach-based side dish like a sag aloo.

VARIATIONS

You could change the spicing depending on what you have available but I quite like the warm flavour of garam masala with this dish.

THRIFTY TIP

Look out for bulk buy offers on pulses. You often find three cans offered for a pound.

SPICED GAME PILAF

A pilaf is a great way to use up leftover scraps of meat but needs plenty of spice and texture to make it more than a dumping ground for leftovers. This is a master recipe you can vary in any number of ways depending on what you have in your storecupboard.

SERVES 2–3

2 tbsp oil
1 onion
1 tsp each ground cumin and coriander
1 clove of garlic, peeled and crushed
6 medium sized mushrooms (about 175g) wiped clean and chopped small
75–100g chopped dried fruit such as apricots, figs or prunes (optional)
100ml basmati rice, measured in a jug
200ml good flavoured stock, preferably made from the carcass of the bird in question
a small handful nuts and/or seeds e.g. chopped cashews, almonds or brazil nuts (optional)
about 250g lean cooked game – pheasant, partridge or duck – or even turkey
2 tbsp finely chopped green herbs such as coriander, parsley and/or mint
wedges of orange or lemon (seville oranges are great in season)

Heat the oil and fry the chopped onion over a moderately high heat until the edges are beginning to turn brown (about 5–6 minutes). Stir in the spices, cook for a few seconds then add the garlic and the mushrooms and dried fruit if using. Cook for a couple of minutes then add the rice, stir and pour over the stock. Bring to the boil, cover and turn the heat down and cook until the stock is absorbed. Turn the heat off and leave the rice to rest for 5 minutes. Dry fry the nuts and/or seeds if using in a small frying pan until lightly browned and beginning to release their fragrance. Tip onto a plate and set aside. Add a tablespoon of oil to the pan and fry the chopped game until slightly crispy. Fork the seeds, fried game and herbs through the pilaf and serve with wedges of orange or lemon for squeezing over the dish.

VARIATIONS

You can make a more spring-like pilaf based on chicken and spring vegetables such as peas, broad beans, broccoli and asparagus garnished with lighter nuts like almonds and pistachios.

THRIFTY TIP

Look out for 'bin ends' in your local health food store. It's a cheap way to buy small amounts of nuts and seeds.

SPICY CASHEW AND MUSHROOM RICE

A slight adaptation of a wonderfully simple rice recipe from cookery writer Vicky Bhogal, author of a great book called *Cooking Like Mummyji* (Simon & Schuster). You can vary it – and Vicky does – depending on what you have available. Here's my vegan version.

SERVES 2–3

2 tablespoons oil
75g cashew nuts
I tsp cumin seeds
$^1/_2$ onion, peeled and thinly sliced or half a bunch of spring onions, trimmed and sliced
$^1/_2$ tsp dried red chilli flakes or $^1/_4$ tsp chilli powder or hot sauce
$^1/_4$ tsp salt
$^1/_2$ tsp ground coriander
250g button mushrooms, wiped or rinsed clean and sliced
2 fresh tomatoes, skinned* and diced
a small handful of fresh coriander leaves, roughly chopped
$^1/_2$ a mug (150ml) basmati rice

Heat the oil in a medium sized saucepan or frying pan, tip in the cashew nuts and stir-fry for a minute until beginning to brown. Remove from the pan with a slotted spoon or tablespoon, draining the oil back into the pan. Return the pan to the heat and add the cumin seeds. Once they start sizzling, add the onion and fry until translucent (about 2–3 minutes). Stir in the chilli flakes or chilli powder, salt and ground coriander then add the sliced mushrooms, chopped tomatoes and fresh coriander. Cook for 30 seconds then return the cashews to the pan, add the rice, stir and cook for 30 seconds then pour in about $^2/_3$ of a mug of boiling water. Bring to the boil, put a lid on the pan, turn the heat right down and cook for about 15 minutes until all the liquid is absorbed. (If you find it absorbs more quickly add a little extra water but be careful as the mushrooms give off quite a lot of liquid). Turn the heat off and let the rice stand for 5 minutes. Serve with onion raita (below) and mango chutney or another Indian chutney.

* To skin tomatoes, make a small cut in the skin just by the stalk and put them into a bowl. Pour over boiling water and leave for a minute then drain off the water and cover with cold water. Peel off the skin which should come away easily.

VARIATIONS

You could make a non-veggie version with prawns. Add them at the same time as the tomato.

THRIFTY TIP

The best way to buy coriander is by the bunch with the roots still intact. Put the bunch in a jam jar or tumbler of cold water, cover with a plastic bag and secure with a rubber band. Place in the fridge. It should keep for 5–6 days if you change the water every couple of days. Wash the coriander before you use it.

ACCOMPANY WITH A SIMPLE ONION RAITA
Take 3 tablespoons of soy or plain yoghurt and spoon into a bowl. Peel a small onion and finely grate about 1 tablespoon into the yoghurt. Season with salt and serve.

ASPARAGUS AND BARLEY RISOTTO

An economical way of making risotto on two counts. You use pearl barley instead of Arborio or Carnaroli rice and the thin, stalky asparagus called sprue which is less good for show-off recipes.

SERVES 2 AS A MAIN COURSE, 3 AS A STARTER.

200g sprue or thin asparagus (about half a large bunch)
600–700ml good quality chicken, guinea fowl or vegetable stock
40g butter
$1/2$ a bunch of spring onions, trimmed and sliced or a small onion, peeled and finely chopped
150g pearl barley
$1/2$ a glass (about 75ml) dry white wine
25g Parmesan or Pecorino cheese plus a few fine shavings
2 tbsp chopped parsley (optional)
1 tbsp double cream, crème fraîche or Mascarpone
salt and pepper

Wash the asparagus thoroughly in a basinful of cold water. Snap off the tough woody ends of the stalks (if they are woody) and cut the tips off the spears a few centimetres down. Roughly chop the rest of the stalks. Heat the stock until boiling then leave over a low heat. Melt the butter over a medium heat in a large saucepan, add the chopped spring onions and cook for a minute. Add the pearl barley, stir and cook for 2–3 minutes then stir in the chopped asparagus stalks and cook for a further minute. Add the wine, stir and let it bubble up and evaporate. Then start adding ladlefuls of hot stock, stirring regularly until the stock is absorbed before adding the next ladle of stock. Continue until the stock has been used up and the pearl barley is tender (about 25 minutes). Turn the heat off then add the grated Parmesan or Pecorino, chopped parsley and a tablespoon of crème fraîche or double cream. Cover the pan and let the flavours amalgamate for 2–3 minutes. Steam or microwave the asparagus tips. Spoon the risotto into warm bowls arrange the asparagus tips on top with a few shavings of Parmesan and trickle over a little olive oil.

VARIATIONS

If you have any leftover chicken you could add about 110g, finely chopped and fried in 1 tablespoon of oil and seasoned with a few drops of soy sauce. Alternatively you could add some peas, podded, skinned broad beans or some sliced mushrooms fried in butter. You can also, of course, make this with risotto rice.

THRIFTY TIP

It's worth buying less-than-perfect-looking spears as they're almost always cheaper. Always use the centre of the spear, preserving the tips for show off dishes and only discarding the woody ends which should easily snap off if the asparagus is fresh.

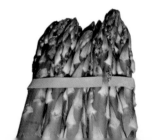

PEA AND BACON RISOTTO

A simple storecupboard recipe the Italians more impressively call *Risi e Bisi*. Adding extra puréed peas or pods at the end keeps the colour fresh.

SERVES 2–3

2 tbsp olive or sunflower oil
2 rashers of dry-cured streaky bacon, finely chopped
1 small onion finely chopped or $^1/_2$ bunch of spring onions, trimmed and finely sliced
150g risotto rice (such as Carnaroli or Arborio)
75ml white wine or 2 tbsp dry or sweet white vermouth
150g frozen peas
800ml chicken or vegetable stock made with 1 tbsp vegetable bouillon powder
1 sprig of mint
20g grated Parmesan or Grana Padano
2 tbsp finely chopped parsley
1 tbsp cream or crème fraîche (optional)
salt and freshly ground black pepper

Heat the olive or sunflower oil in a large saucepan, add the bacon and fry until starting to crisp. Stir in the onion or spring onions, turn the heat down and cook until starting to soften. Stir in the risotto rice and cook for 2–3 minutes then add the wine and bubble until it evaporates. Heat the stock until boiling add the mint and leave over a low heat.

Add half the peas to the rice, heat through for a minute or two then start to add ladlefuls of hot stock, stirring regularly until the stock is absorbed before adding the next batch of liquid. Continue until the stock is almost used up then take a ladleful, put it in a blender with the remaining peas and whizz until smooth. When the rice is cooked but still has some bite stir in the pea purée and heat through. Take the pan off the heat, stir in the grated Parmesan or Grana Padano, chopped parsley and a tablespoon of crème fraîche or double cream, cover the pan and rest for 2–3 minutes to let the flavours amalgamate. Spoon into warm bowls.

VARIATIONS

You could also add some asparagus stalks as in the previous recipe or some podded, skinned broad beans. Or add finely chopped tarragon instead of parsley.

THRIFTY TIP

In season you could use fresh peas (you'll need about 500g to give you 75–100g). Instead of making a purée with the peas boil up the pods with just enough stock to cover and pass them through a fine sieve. Use 50–75ml for the risotto and save the rest for a soup.

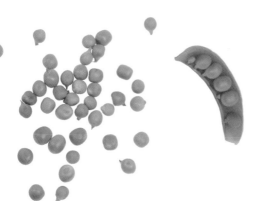

BIG
WEEKEND
COOK-UPS

WEEKENDS ARE WHEN THE FRUGAL COOK CAN GET SOME
REALLY THRIFTY RECIPES UNDER HIS OR HER BELT FOR THE
WEEK AHEAD. OR SIMPLY ENJOY THE PLEASURE OF FAMILY
MEALS COOKED THE OLD-FASHIONED WAY.

POACHED CHICKEN WITH PARSLEY AND LEMON DUMPLINGS

Assuming you have your favourite roast chicken recipe, as most families do, here's an alternative way to cook a chicken which keeps it beautifully succulent.

SERVES 4–6

a medium-sized free-range chicken (about 1.5kg)
1 medium-sized onion, peeled and cut into 8
2–3 carrots, peeled and sliced
1 small or $^1/_2$ larger bulb of fennel, quartered or two sticks of celery, cut into four
about 1 litre cold chicken stock or vegetable stock made with an organic stock cube or 1 tbsp vegetable bouillon powder
1 bayleaf
6–8 peppercorns

For the dumplings
200g self-raising flour
1 tsp baking powder
$^1/_2$ level tsp fine sea salt
$^1/_8$ tsp white pepper
finely grated rind of $^1/_2$ unwaxed lemon
75g suet
1 heaped tbsp finely snipped chives
1 heaped tbsp finely chopped parsley
125–150ml iced water

Put the chicken in a large pot with the onions, carrots and fennel, pour in the stock and enough water to cover and and bring to the boil over a moderate heat. (This will take about 20–25 minutes). Skim off any froth and add the bayleaf and peppercorns. Turn the heat down to a bare simmer and cook for 50–60 minutes or until the chicken is tender.

Make the dumplings about 10 minutes before the chicken is due to be ready. Sieve the flour, baking powder, salt and pepper into a bowl. Add the grated lemon rind. Tip in the suet and cut it in with a sharp knife. Mix in the chives and parsley then gradually add enough cold water to hold the mixture together, without handling the mixture too much. Form the dough into 8–10 small balls.

Once the chicken is cooked, set it aside on a warm plate to rest. Spoon out the vegetables and lay them alongside it. Bring the stock in the pan up to the boil again then drop in the dumplings, cover and simmer for 15 minutes. Remove the lid and cook for another 5 minutes to allow the dumplings to dry a little. Carve the chicken and serve in soup bowls with the vegetables and dumplings. You could also serve some extra freshly cooked veg such as carrots and fennel or leeks.

You can also get very successful results with this recipe in a slow cooker. Once you've brought the chicken and vegetables to the boil transfer them to a slow cooker and pour in just enough stock to cover, leaving about 2cm free at the top of the pot. Follow the cooking time recommended in the leaflet then carefully lift out the chicken and set it aside. You'll have to transfer the stock back to a saucepan again to cook the dumplings as they won't cook fast enough in a slow cooker.

VARIATIONS

You could serve the chicken with aioli rather than with dumplings and some boiled new potatoes tossed with butter and herbs.

LEFTOVERS

Don't make soup with the carcass as it will already have been boiled once, but any leftover chicken or stock will taste fabulous.

THRIFTY TIP

It's worth buying a couple of chickens if you find them at a good price and freezing one.

MEXICAN SALSA CHICKEN

There's a long, involved explanation as to how this recipe came about (check out the Frugal Cook blog, 26th May 2008) but suffice it to say it was originally designed to be made with tomatillos but works equally well with tomatoes.

SERVES 4–6

1kg chicken thighs or thighs and drumsticks
750g ripe tomatoes, skinned and chopped
1–2 mild onions (about 200g in total) peeled and roughly chopped
3–4 cloves of garlic, peeled and chopped
1–2 chillies, de-seeded and roughly chopped
rind and juice of 2 limes (preferably unwaxed)
a good bunch or large pack of coriander, well washed and trimmed
3–4 tbsp olive oil
1–1$\frac{1}{2}$ tsp salt
2 spring onions, trimmed and very finely shredded (optional)

You will need a large casserole or deep frying pan

Remove the skin from the chicken thighs and drumsticks. Skin the tomatoes by making a cut in the skin, pouring the boiling water over them, leaving them for a minute then plunging them into cold water. Put the peeled chopped tomatoes, onions, garlic, chillies and rind and juice of the limes in a blender. Cut the stalks off the coriander, chop roughly and add them to the blender goblet then whizz together until you have a liquid but still rough-textured sauce. Heat 2 tablespoons of oil in the casserole or frying pan and tip in the salsa. Add 1 teaspoon of salt and the skinned chicken, turning it in the sauce. Bring to the boil then turn the heat down low and simmer for about 45–50 minutes until the chicken is cooked and the salsa reduced and thick. Roughly chop half of the remaining coriander leaves and add them to the pan. Stir and cook for 3–4 minutes. Serve the chicken with warm tortillas or with brown rice, scattering over some more chopped fresh coriander and some finely shredded spring onions, if you have some.

VARIATIONS

You could add a bit of smoked chilli or pimenton to the salsa for a slightly smokier flavour.

LEFTOVERS

To die for. If there's any chicken, wrap it and the leftover sauce in a tortilla with some crumbly white cheese and extra spring onion and coriander as above. The sauce on its own would turn fried eggs into *huevos rancheros*.

THRIFTY TIP

This recipe will obviously be more economical and work much better in summer when tomatoes are ripe and in season.

SALT AND PEPPER WINGS

The main pleasure of eating chicken wings is the lovely sticky, finger-licking goo you get if you cook then sufficiently long, a texture and flavour that sometimes gets masked if you cover them with a marinade. If you can have salt and pepper squid I thought, why not salt and pepper wings? It cuts down on the other ingredients you need to use and makes them more child-friendly. A good dish to make when you have the oven on for something else.

SERVES 4–6

1kg free-range chicken wings, preferably organic
1–2 tbsp light cooking oil
freshly ground salt and freshly ground pepper

Pre-heat the oven to 180°C/350°F/Gas 4. Put the wings in a large roasting tin (or two smaller ones), pour over a little oil and turn the wings so they are lightly coated. Season generously with freshly ground salt and coarsely ground black pepper and roast for $1-1^{1}/_{4}$ hours, turning the wings two or three times. Remove the wings from the roasting tin, rolling them in the pan juices to pick up any sticky residues and leave until cool enough to handle (about 15–20 minutes). Eat warm or cold (but they're never as good once they've been refrigerated).

VARIATIONS

You could add a couple of crushed cloves of garlic to the pan half way through the cooking time to flavour the oil. If you do want a more flavoursome marinade brush on a Honey-Soy Marinade (see page 216).

LEFTOVERS

Save the fat from the pan which will have an excellent flavour.

THRIFTY TIP

You could remove the wing tips, if you prefer, and use them for stock.

ROAST BELLY PORK WITH BLACK PUDDING AND 'HEAVEN AND EARTH' MASH

Belly pork has become ultra-fashionable but it's still a good value buy for a weekend roast. It's worth buying from an independent butcher as they don't tend to vac-pack their meat which makes for drier skin and better crackling. The wackily-named mash is my version of a great German potato and apple recipe called *himmel und erde*. Perfect with pork.

SERVES 4–6

1 tsp coarse sea salt and 1 tsp black peppercorns
2 tsp coriander seeds
1 large clove of garlic, peeled and chopped
2 tbsp sunflower or light olive oil
1.35kg belly pork in a single piece on the bone
500ml chicken stock
salt and freshly ground black pepper
250g black pudding, skinned and sliced

For the 'Heaven and Earth' mash
600g boiling potatoes
500g Bramley apples or other sharp cooking apples

Preheat the oven to 230°C/450°F/Gas 9. Put the salt, peppercorns and coriander in a mortar and pound with a pestle until coarsely ground. Add the chopped garlic and pound again then add a tablespoon of oil to create a thick paste.

With a sharp knife cut into the pork flesh either side so you can push the spice mixture into the meat and rub it over the flesh and into the cuts you've made (but not over the skin). Put the joint on a wire rack over a roasting tin and add a splash of the stock to the pan to stop the spices from burning. Roast for 20 minutes. Turn the heat down to 180°C/350°F/Gas 4 and cook for another hour and forty minutes, pouring off the fat half way through and adding a little extra liquid to the tin if the juices threaten to burn (don't baste it though – you'll spoil the crackling!). Transfer the joint to another roasting tin, turn the heat back up to 230°C/450°F/Gas 9 and continue cooking until the crackling is good and crisp. Set aside and rest for 10 minutes (but don't cover or the steam will make the crackling soft). Carefully pour any accumulated fat off the first roasting tin, pour in half the remaining stock and work round the tin with a wooden spoon to incorporate all the caramelised meat juices. Add more stock if needed to get a thin but tasty gravy and season with salt and pepper.

Heat the remaining oil in another pan and fry the black pudding slices on both sides until crisp. Carve the meat into chunks and serve with the potato and apple purée (below) and some lightly cooked, buttered Brussel tops or cabbage.

To make the 'Heaven and Earth' mash, cut the potatoes into even-sized pieces, cover with cold water, bring to the boil and cook until tender (about 18–20 minutes). Peel, core and slice the apples and put in a saucepan with two tablespoons of water. Cover and cook on a low heat, stirring occasionally until the apples are soft and fluffy. Beat well with a wooden spoon. Drain and mash the potatoes then add the apple purée and beat well. Season to taste with salt and freshly ground black pepper.

VARIATIONS

You can replace half the chicken stock with cider.

LEFTOVERS

Crisp up any leftover pork and crackling in a pan and serve with stir-fried cabbage.

THRIFTY TIP

You can always stretch a roast by padding it out with forcemeat balls, dumplings or stuffing.

BREAST OF LAMB WITH LEMON, GARLIC, MINT AND HONEY

It's not only pork that can get the ribs treatment. Breast of lamb can be great too. Note the ribs can go into the oven while it's warming up.

SERVES 4–5

5 tbsp sunflower, groundnut or grapeseed oil
2 breasts of lamb (about 1.3kg), cut into individual ribs
3 tbsp clear honey
1 tsp chilli flakes or $^1/_4$ tsp cayenne pepper or chilli powder
3 cloves of garlic crushed with 1 rounded tsp salt
juice of 2 lemons (about 6–7 tbsp)
2 tbsp finely chopped mint
2 tbsp sesame seeds (optional)

Turn the oven on to 200°C/400°F/Gas 6. Put 2 tablespoons of oil in a large roasting tin, arrange the ribs in the tin in a single layer and turn in the oil. Put the tin in the oven and roast for 40 minutes until the fat on the ribs starts to sizzle.

Meanwhile, make the marinade. Mix the honey with 2 tablespoons of boiling water then add the chilli flakes, crushed garlic and salt, lemon juice, remaining sunflower oil and chopped mint. Remove the tin of ribs from the oven, pour off any accumulated fat and liquid and pour over the marinade. Turn down the oven to 160°C/325°F/Gas 3 and continue to cook for a further hour to an hour and a quarter until the ribs are well cooked, turning them and basting them every 15–20 minutes. If the marinade starts to catch pour in a little boiling water (but not too much – you want the ribs to get sticky). About 15 minutes before the cooking time is up you could sprinkle a tablespoon of sesame seeds over the ribs, then after about 6–7 minutes turn once more and sprinkle the other side. Serve with flat bread and a tomato, cucumber and onion salad (like a Greek salad without the Feta).

VARIATIONS

You could use rosemary instead of mint. Or start the ribs in the oven and finish them off on the barbecue.

THRIFTY TIP

To make sure you measure honey or golden syrup precisely, dip your tablespoon in boiling water before you put it into the jar.

HOT HONEY RIBS

Every meat eater loves ribs. These ones are especially finger-lickin' good.

SERVES 4–5

1.5 kg pork spare ribs
2 tbsp sunflower oil or vegetable oil
200g clear honey
100ml ketchup or creamed tomatoes
50ml light or dark soy sauce
2 tbsp Dijon mustard
2 tbsp sweet chilli sauce
1 tsp Worcestershire sauce
1–2 tsp grated fresh ginger
2 cloves garlic, peeled and crushed
salt and ground black pepper

Heat the oven to 200°C/400°F/Gas 6. Pour the oil in a large roasting tin (or two smaller ones) lay out the ribs in a single layer, turn them in the oil then roast them for 30 minutes. Meanwhile combine the honey, ketchup, soy sauce, mustard, sweet chilli sauce, Worcestershire sauce, ginger and garlic in a saucepan and warm through until the honey has melted. Check the seasoning adding salt and pepper to taste if needed.

After their initial cooking, take the ribs out of the oven, drain off any excess fat and pour over the marinade ensuring all the ribs are coated. Reduce the oven heat to 160°C/325°F/Gas 3 and cook the ribs for a further $1-1^{1}/_{4}$ hours, basting them regularly until the sauce has all but disappeared and the ribs are lovely and sticky (pour in a little boiling water if the marinade starts to catch on the bottom of the tin). Serve with sweet potato wedges (which you can cook at the same time as the ribs) and a slaw.

VARIATIONS

So long as you include something sweet, something hot and something tomato-based you can produce endless variations on this marinade depending what you have in your storecupboard.

THRIFTY TIP

Sweet chilli sauce is much cheaper in Chinese or Asian supermarkets.

LOVELY LAMB AND LEEK STEW

This is my version of a Welsh recipe called Cawl. I've renamed it because I think its primary ingredient, scrag-end of lamb, needs a bit of a sell. It's a fabulous comfort dish but like other dishes that involve inexpensive cuts you need to make it ahead, skim it and take the meat off the bone.

SERVES 4

2 large or 3 medium leeks
2 tbsp light olive oil or other cooking oil
1kg neck chops (sometimes described as scrag end of lamb), preferably organic
3 carrots, scrubbed (or peeled) and sliced
1 sprig of thyme and a bayleaf (or $^1/_2$ tsp dried thyme)
750ml light chicken or vegetable stock made with 2 tsp vegetable bouillon powder or half a stock cube
25g butter
3 medium sized potatoes, peeled and thickly sliced
salt and white (or black) pepper
a large handful of parsley
crusty bread, to serve

Cut off the upper (green) half of the leeks, discarding the coarse outer leaves but retaining the flavoursome inner leaves. Heat 1 tbsp of oil in a casserole and brown the chops on each side. Remove from the pan and set aside. Add the tops of the leeks you've just sliced and one of the carrots, roughly sliced, stir and fry for a couple of minutes. Return the meat to the pan tucking the chops together in a single layer, add the herbs and pour over enough stock to cover. Bring to the boil then turn the heat down and simmer very slowly for about 1 $^1/_2$–1$^3/_4$ hours until the meat is beginning to fall off the bone. Remove the chops from the pan, strain the stock into a bowl and cool it for at least an hour. Discard the herbs and flavouring veg. Trim, slice and wash the remaining leek and carrots. Heat the remaining oil in a pan, add the

butter, add the leeks, carrots and potatoes, cover and cook over a low heat for about 7–8 minutes until beginning to soften. Skim the fat off the cooking liquid and return it to the pan, bring to the boil and cook until the veg are just tender (another 15 minutes). Take the meat off the bone, removing any excess fat or connective tissue. Return the boned lamb to the pan and heat through. Season to taste with salt and (preferably white) pepper. Finely chop the parsley and add to the dish before serving. Serve in soup plates with plenty of crusty bread alongside.

VARIATIONS

You could vary the veg in this dish, using onions instead of leeks (in which case it will become more like an Irish stew) adding a stick of celery to the flavouring vegetables or some diced turnip or swede at the final stage.

THRIFTY TIP

Discarding the first batch of vegetables might seem wasteful but the stew will have a much better flavour if you finish it with fresh veg. Treat the flavouring vegetables like bones – they are there to add to the taste.

ITALIAN-STYLE VEAL STEW

My local organic butcher sells rosé veal – the only type worth buying both on flavour and welfare grounds – for a very reasonable price. This is a simple Italian-style stew, padded out with extra vegetables.

SERVES 4

500g stewing veal
4 tbsp olive oil
1 onion, peeled and roughly chopped
1 large leek, trimmed, washed and sliced
2 carrots, trimmed, scrubbed and sliced
1 dsp plain flour
1 glass of dry white wine
175ml of chicken stock, preferably homemade
2 tomatoes, skinned and finely chopped
150g button mushrooms, wiped and sliced
salt and freshly ground black pepper
2 tbsp finely chopped flat or curly parsley or
    tarragon

Remove any excess fat from the veal and cut into largeish chunks. Heat half the oil in a casserole or sauté pan and lightly brown the meat. Remove with a slotted spoon. Add the remaining oil and the onion, leek and carrot, stir, put a lid on the pan and cook over a low heat for 8–10 minutes. Sprinkle in the flour, stir, then add the white wine and stock and bring to the boil, stirring until slightly thickened. Return the meat to the pan, turn the heat right down and simmer for about an hour and a half, or until the meat is tender. About 20 minutes before the end of the cooking time stir in the chopped tomatoes and mushrooms. Check the seasoning, adding salt and pepper to taste. Stir in the parsley or tarragon and serve with new potatoes, plain boiled rice or tagliatelle.

VARIATIONS

You could turn this into a goulash by adding a tablespoon of sweet paprika and a teaspoon of hot paprika, or $\frac{1}{2}$ tsp cayenne pepper when you add the flour and stirring in some sour cream at the end. You could also make it with pork rather than veal. Or with chicken thighs which would cut the cooking time.

LEFTOVERS

Good reheated the next day. Could be frozen.

THRIFTY TIP

Extending a stew with vegetables like this brings the cost down significantly and also saves last minute work as you don't have to cook any additional veg.

RABBIT, BACON AND PERRY PIE

The cost of rabbit depends very much on where you live. In the country it's a snip. In the city it may be as cheap to use chicken, (though you won't get quite as good a texture). This is a slightly more frugal version of the recipe in *Meat and Two Veg* (Absolute Press) using perry (pear cider) instead of white wine.

4–5 tbsp light olive oil or sunflower oil
100g smoked bacon bits or smoked streaky bacon, rinded and roughly chopped
1 rabbit, jointed
500ml chicken or light vegetable stock
1 medium onion
1–2 carrots
1 tsp finely chopped fresh thyme
1 bayleaf
1 tbsp plain flour
250ml medium dry perry or cider or dry white wine
125g chestnut mushrooms
3 tbsp finely chopped parsley
1 level tbsp Dijon mustard
salt and freshly ground black pepper

For the pastry
300g plain flour
$1/4$ tsp sea salt
125g chilled butter, cut into small cubes
75g chilled Cookeen or other vegetable shortening, cut into small cubes
3 tbsp iced water
1 medium egg, lightly beaten for glazing the pie

You will need a lightly greased shallow round pie dish or deep flan dish 24–26cm in diameter

Heat 2 tablespoons of the oil and fry the bacon pieces for 2–3 minutes until lightly browned. Scoop out with a slotted spoon and transfer to a deep casserole. Brown the rabbit pieces lightly on all sides and transfer to the casserole. Pour half the stock into the pan and bubble up for a minute. Pour over the rabbit. Wipe the pan, replace over a medium heat and add the remaining oil. Fry the onion and carrot until beginning to soften (about 5–6 minutes). Add the thyme and stir in the flour then gradually add the remaining stock and perry. Bring to the boil and simmer for a couple of minutes, then pour over the rabbit and bacon. Add the bayleaf and cover the meat closely with greaseproof paper. Put a lid on the pan, turn the heat right down, and leave to simmer for 50–60 minutes or until tender.

While the rabbit is cooking make the pastry. Place the flour and salt in a large bowl and add the cubes of butter and Cookeen. Cut the fat into the flour then rub it in with your fingertips until it looks like coarse breadcrumbs. Sprinkle over the iced water and work it in with a flat bladed knife, pulling the mixture together as you go. Using your hand, pull it together into a ball, then shape the pastry into a flat disc. (You can obviously also make this in a food processor). Cover with clingfilm and refrigerate for 30 minutes.

Once the rabbit is cooked, remove the pieces from the pan and strip the meat off the bones, leaving it in largeish chunks. Reduce the sauce by about half until thickened then take off the heat and add the sliced mushrooms, parsley and mustard. Stir well, check the seasoning, adding salt and pepper to taste, and leave to cool.

When the filling is cold, heat the oven to 200°C/400°F/Gas 6. Spoon the filling into the pie dish. Roll out the pastry quite thickly to a circle slightly larger than the width of the dish. Carefully lower it over the filling. Using a pastry brush, moisten the rim of the dish under the pastry with beaten egg then press the edges down and trim off the excess pastry round the edges. Cut a slit in the middle of the pie. To decorate the pie, press the remaining scraps of pastry together then roll it out and cut rabbits' faces or any other shapes you like from it. Brush the pie with beaten egg then decorate it, glazing the decorations with more beaten egg. Bake the pie for 35–40 minutes until the pastry is well browned. Serve hot with buttered new potatoes and peas or cold with a simple green salad.

VARIATIONS

Use chicken instead of rabbit.

LEFTOVERS

Really excellent cold – almost better than hot.

THRIFTY TIP

Look out for rabbit in country butchers and farm shops.

BASIC BOLOGNESE

You don't have to add the vegetables if you're short of time but it does stretch the meat and make the recipe healthier!

MAKES 8–10 PORTIONS

1kg beef mince
4 tbsp olive oil
1 medium onion, peeled and very finely chopped
1 medium carrot, peeled and very finely chopped
1–2 sticks of celery peeled and very finely
  chopped
2 cloves of garlic, peeled, crushed or finely
  chopped
2 heaped tbsp concentrated tomato purée
1½ level tsp dried oregano, marjoram or Herbes
  de Provence
2 x 400g cans tomatoes
salt and pepper
finely chopped fresh parsley, to serve
grated Grana Padano or Parmesan, to serve

Heat a large frying pan over a moderately high heat. Add 2 tablespoons of the oil, swirl round the pan then add half the mince spreading it around the pan. Fry until beginning to brown then turn it over with a wooden spoon or spatula. Keep frying until all the mince is browned (about 1½–2 minutes). Then, tipping the pan away from you so the fat runs away, scoop out the mince onto a large plate and pour the fat that has accumulated in the pan into a cup or bowl to discard later. Replace the pan on the hob and repeat with the remaining mince, discarding the fat again at the end.

Heat the remaining oil, add the onion, carrot and celery and cook over a low heat for about 7–8 minutes until soft but not coloured. Stir in the crushed garlic and cook for a minute or two. Return the meat to the pan, stir in the tomato paste and cook for a couple of minutes. Add the herbs and tinned tomatoes, breaking them up with a wooden spoon. Season with salt and pepper, bring up to boiling point then turn the heat right down and leave to cook gently for 30–40 minutes. Roughly 15 minutes before the cooking time is up, start to cook any accompanying pasta (for half this batch of mince you'll need 500g of pasta which should serve up to six people). Spoon off half the sauce for one of the variations below.

Add 3–4 tablespoons of the pasta cooking water to the remaining mince. Tip the drained pasta into the sauce and toss together, adding a couple of tablespoons of finely chopped fresh parsley. Serve with grated Grana Padano or Parmesan.

THRIFTY TIP

Don't feel you have to use the extra lean mince that supermarkets promote so heavily as the initial browning of the meat gets rid of any excess fat.

AND WITH THE OTHER HALF OF THE SAUCE...

SPAGHETTI BOLOGNESE

If you're reheating a batch of the bolognese sauce above you could add half a glass of leftover red or white wine or some fried up, sliced mushrooms to stretch it a bit further.

COTTAGE PIE

To make the mince beefier and more savoury, add some leftover gravy, meat juices or braising liquid from a beef stew otherwise a teaspoon of Bovril or Marmite dissolved in 2 tablespoon boiling water should do the trick. Put the meat in a pie dish and top with mashed potato (about 800g potatoes, boiled and mashed with a little milk and butter) or a root vegetable mash such as carrot and swede or celeriac and potato. Bake for 30–35 minutes in a moderately hot oven (190°C/375°F/Gas 5).

MEAT PIE

As above but put the mince mixture into a pie dish and top with a puff pastry lid. If you had a few leftover carrots you could add those as well.

CHILLI CON CARNE

Add 2–3 teaspoons of mild chilli powder and $1/4$ teaspoon of ground cumin to half the basic recipe then add a drained, rinsed 400g can of red kidney beans and about 4 tablespoons of water. Bring up to boiling point then turn the heat down and simmer for 5 minutes until thoroughly heated through. Serve on its own or with boiled rice or a baked potato.

LASAGNE-STYLE PASTA BAKE

Cook 350g of penne or rigatoni pasta for a minute or two less than the time recommended on the packet. Make a quick cheese sauce (page 217). Heat up half the basic mince recipe above. Drain the pasta and tip into a lightly oiled shallow oven-proof dish. Mix in the mince and then the cheese sauce without totally combining the two. Sprinkle with grated cheese and put under the grill until the top is brown and bubbling.

NORWEGIAN MEATBALLS

I have to confess a fatal addiction to meatballs, especially Swedish ones. These, which come from a young Norwegian food writer Signe Johansen, should more strictly be dubbed Norwegian. Same difference.

SERVES 8

5–6 tbsp sunflower or other light cooking oil
1 onion, peeled and finely chopped
3 slices stale country bread, crusts removed, torn into small pieces (about 110g weight in total)
225ml milk mixed with a tablespoon of yoghurt
500g veal or beef mince
500g pork mince
2 level tsp allspice
1 level tsp nutmeg
$^1/_4$ level tsp ground ginger (optional)
1 level tsp salt
$^1/_4$ level tsp ground white or black pepper
1 large egg yolk
25g butter

Heat 2 tablespoons of the oil in a pan and cook the chopped onion over a low heat until soft (about 8–10 minutes). Set aside to cool. In a small bowl, combine the bread with the yoghurt infused milk. Make sure all the bread is moistened and leave until the liquid has been absorbed.

In a larger bowl, combine the mince, cooked onion, the spices and seasoning. Add the milk-soaked bread and mix together thoroughly (easiest with your hands). Rest the mixture for 10 minutes then take small spoonfuls of the mixture and lightly roll between your palms to form small walnut-sized meatballs. Complete rolling the meatballs before you start frying them.

Heat the oven to 110°C/225°F/Gas $^1/_2$ and place a baking dish in it. Heat a tablespoon of oil in a medium to large frying pan, add half the butter and fry a batch of meatballs, browning them well on all sides but taking care not to burn them. Transfer them to the warm baking dish and repeat with the remaining batches, adding extra oil and butter as necessary.

When the meatballs are cooked, serve warm with steamed new potatoes, a dollop of sour cream and a spoonful of lingonberry and cranberry sauce or with the cream gravy below.

For the cream gravy
After frying the meatballs, drain off the fat leaving 2 tablespoons in the pan, add 2 tablespoons of flour and cook over a low heat until golden. Gradually add 450ml beef stock, bring to the boil and reduce the liquid by a third. Take the pan off the heat and stir in 150ml double cream, sour cream or crème fraîche. Season with salt and pepper and a few drops of Worcestershire sauce. Add the meatballs back to the sauce and warm through.

VARIATIONS

You could reduce the amount of spice and add some chopped dill or parsley to the meatballs instead. Or use minced turkey and pork instead of beef or veal.

LEFTOVERS

Very tasty cold.

THRIFTY TIP

Adding a high proportion of bread to meatballs like this not only makes the meat go a lot further but makes the meatballs much easier to roll.

BUDGET MEATLOAF

Meatloaf is one of those comforting dishes that appeals to adults and children alike. This is a frugal version, stretched with pinhead (coarse) oatmeal.

SERVES 4 HOT, 6 COLD

400–450g good quality, simply flavoured sausages
  e.g. Cumberland
400–450g lean minced beef
100g finely chopped smoked bacon rashers,
  lardons or bacon bits
2 cloves of garlic, peeled and crushed
1 small onion, peeled and finely chopped
3 heaped tbsp chopped parsley
50g coarse oatmeal
1 large egg, lightly beaten
4 tbsp milk or oat milk
ground black pepper

You'll need a 900g loaf tin or ovenproof dish,
  lightly oiled

Preheat the oven to 180°C/350°F/Gas 4. Cut through the skin of each sausage and pull it off. Put the sausagemeat into a large bowl with the mince. Add the bacon, crushed garlic, chopped onion and parsley and mix well together (easiest with your hands, to be honest). Sprinkle over the oatmeal, add the egg and milk and mix together thoroughly (this time with a wooden spoon). Season generously with pepper and mix again. Pack the mixture into a lightly oiled large loaf tin or an ovenware dish. Place the dish in a roasting tin and pour boiling water around it up to the depth of about 1.5cm. Bake for about an hour or until the meatloaf has shrunk well away from the sides of the tin.

Carefully pour off any fat that has accumulated then tip the meatloaf onto a serving plate. Turn it back upright and slice it thickly. Serve hot with tomato sauce or onion gravy and mash or cold with potato salad and pickles.

VARIATIONS

You could make this with pork rather than beef mince or use a spicier sausage.

THRIFTY TIP

You'll get more out of the meatloaf if you serve it cold (simply because it's easier to cut thin slices).

PIZZA GIARDINIERA

Quickly stir-frying the veg before you put them on the pizza makes for a better (if, admittedly, less authentic) flavour.

MAKES 2 LARGE PIZZA BASES OR 8 SMALL PIZZA BASES

For the dough

250g strong white flour (or, better still if you have some, 100g '00' flour and 150g strong white flour)

$^1/_2$ level tsp fine sea salt

1 level tsp quick-acting yeast

2 tbsp olive oil

about 175ml hand-hot water

fine semolina for dusting the baking tin

For the topping

1 bunch spring onions, trimmed and sliced

2 small courgettes, finely sliced

100g broccoli florets

a few thin asparagus spears in season (optional)

a few shelled peas (optional)

about 400ml homemade or shop-bought passata (see opposite)

a handful of fresh, chopped herbs

200g Mozzarella

olive oil for drizzling

You will also need two large rectangular baking tins sprinkled with fine semolina

Sift the flour(s) into a bowl along with the salt and yeast. Mix together then form a hollow in the centre. Pour in the olive oil and half the warm water and stir to incorporate the flour. Gradually add as much of the remaining water as you need to pull the dough together. (It should take most of it – you need a wettish dough). Turn the dough onto a board and knead for 10 minutes until smooth and elastic, adding a little extra flour as you need it to prevent the dough sticking. Put the dough into a lightly oiled bowl, seal with clingfilm and leave in a warm place to double in size (about an hour).

Heat 3 tablespoons of olive oil in a wok or large frying pan. Add the sliced spring onions and stir-fry for a minute then add the sliced courgettes, broccoli, asparagus and peas if using. Stir-fry for a couple of minutes then remove from the heat, season and set aside.

Preheat the oven to its maximum setting. Knock the dough down and divide in half. Roll and shape each piece of dough into a large rectangle. Place one of the rectangles on top of a baking tray and spread with half the passata. Distribute half the vegetables over the pizza. Sprinkle with herbs and arrange half of the sliced Mozzarella over the top. Repeat with the other pizza. Trickle a little olive oil over the top of the two pizzas and bake for 8–10 minutes until the dough has puffed up and the cheese has melted.

FOR A GREAT HOMEMADE PASSATA

Heat 2 tablespoons of olive oil in a large frying pan or wok, add 1 clove of crushed garlic, fry for a few seconds then add 1 level tablespoon of tomato paste. Tip in 500g of chopped, skinned fresh tomatoes and stir well. Cover for 5 minutes to soften the tomatoes then break the tomatoes down with a fork or wooden spoon and simmer uncovered for a further 5 minutes until the mixture is thick and pulpy. Season with pepper and a little salt and then cool.

VARIATIONS

Well, almost any pizza topping you like. Pizzas are a great refuge for leftovers. You could make a summery, Spanish-style pizza for example based on chorizo, peppers, olives and sheep's cheese. A simple cheese and bacon one is great for kids. Mushroom pizzas are always good. Crisp streaky bacon, Italian grilled artichokes (the ones in jars) and Taleggio cheese is wonderful. If you cook the base without a topping (prick it well before it goes into the oven) you can then add an uncooked topping such as rocket, parma ham and shaved Parmesan or Pecorino drizzled with olive oil or, one I recently had in Paris, soft goat's cheese with wafer thin slices of raw beetroot and fennel.

LEFTOVERS

Shape and freeze any leftover dough to use straight out of the freezer.

THRIFTY TIP

As Mozzarella is a fashionable ingredient check the price carefully. Often it's cheaper in Italian delis but basic supermarket mozzarella can be quite a bargain.

RED ONION, ROSEMARY AND STILTON TART

One convenience product I really think is worth the money is ready-rolled pastry which makes it possible to put together an impressive looking tart with just a few minutes' preparation. Keep the cost of the recipe down with this delicious blue cheese and onion topping, based on the underrated Stilton.

SERVES 4–6

2 tbsp olive oil
50g butter
600g red onions, peeled and thickly sliced
1 tbsp finely chopped fresh rosemary leaves
1 tbsp brown sugar
2 tsp balsamic vinegar
1 x 375g pack fresh ready-rolled puff pastry
1 medium egg yolk
175g Stilton or other mellow blue cheese with the rind removed

You will also need a rectangular baking tray about 34 x 24cm

Heat a large frying pan or wok, add the oil and 25g of the butter and fry the onions and rosemary over a moderate heat for about 10 minutes or until soft and golden. Add the sugar and continue to fry, stirring, until deep brown (about another 8–10 minutes) then season with the balsamic vinegar, salt and pepper. Meanwhile heat the oven to 220°C/425°F/Gas 7. Lay the pastry on a lightly greased rectangular baking tray, trimming the pastry, if necessary, to fit. With a sharp knife score a line around the edge of the pastry about $1^{1}/_{4}$cm from the edge to create a rim. Brush the edge and the base of the tart with lightly beaten egg yolk taking care not to brush over the cut you've made. Spread the caramelised onions over the base then crumble the cheese over the top. Bake in the pre-heated oven for 10 minutes then reduce the heat to 200°C/400°F/Gas 6 and bake for a further 15–20 minutes until the tart is well puffed up and the top nice and brown.

VARIATIONS

You could use onions and peppers as the base and top the tart with goat's or sheep's cheese.

THRIFTY TIP

Red onions vary hugely in price depending on where you buy them. Sometimes they cost much the same as conventional onions, sometimes they're considerably more, so watch out!

CHEDDAR, HAM AND ONION QUICHE

The quality of the ingredients you use for this makes all the difference. A perfect way to use up a ham hock.

SERVES 4–6

1 tbsp olive oil
15g butter
1 medium onion (about 175g), peeled and roughly
   chopped
375g shop-bought or homemade shortcrust
   pastry (see page 214)
2 large or 3 medium eggs, lightly beaten
225ml single cream or cream and milk, mixed
100–110g ham, ideally off the bone, cut into small
   pieces
125g mature Cheddar, grated
salt and freshly ground black pepper

Preheat the oven to 200°C/400°F/Gas 5. Heat a frying pan over a moderate heat, add the oil and butter then, when it has melted, fry the chopped onion for about 5 minutes until soft. Set aside.

Unroll the pastry, if ready-rolled, or roll it out in a circle big enough to fit a 25cm/10-inch diameter flan tin. Carefully lower the pastry into the tin, pressing it into the sides, trim any overhanging edges and lightly prick the base with the prongs of a fork. Line the pastry case with a piece of greaseproof paper or foil weighed down with some baking beans and bake the pastry shell for about 10 minutes. Remove the paper and beans and return the pastry case to the oven for another 4 minutes. Brush a little of the beaten egg over the part-cooked pastry base and return to the oven for another minute or two (this stops it going soggy).

Reduce the heat to 190°C/375°F/Gas 5. Add the milk and cream to the remaining beaten eggs and season with salt and pepper. Scatter half the grated cheese over the base of the tart then sprinkle over the onions and ham and top with the remaining cheese. Carefully pour the egg and cream mixture over the top. Put the flan tin on a baking sheet and bake for about 30 minutes until the top is puffed up and lightly browned. Leave for 10–15 minutes before serving or cool completely and serve cold.

VARIATIONS

Use half a bunch of spring onions or a trimmed, washed, sliced leek instead of the onion. Replace the ham with lightly fried bacon or with flaked fish such as salmon or smoked mackerel. Or with vegetables such as mushrooms, spinach or broccoli (all lightly pre-cooked). You could also use other kinds of cheeses. Blue cheese makes a great quiche for example. You can make up the liquid with whatever you have available – double or single cream or crème fraîche so long as it ends up the consistency of single cream.

LEFTOVERS

Save a slice for a lunchbox.

THRIFTY TIP

Make two quiches at once and freeze one.

SALMON FISHCAKES WITH LEMON BUTTER

It's almost worth cooking salmon and potatoes just to make these fabulous fishcakes which I think were first invented by Charles Fontaine when he worked at the Ivy. A great way to use up leftover salmon.

SERVES 4

For the fishcakes
350g cooked salmon
350g freshly cooked mashed potato with no milk
   or butter added, cooled
1 tbsp tomato ketchup
1 tsp anchovy essence
1 tsp English or Dijon mustard
2 tbsp finely chopped fresh parsley
salt and freshly ground black pepper
plain flour, for dusting
1 tbsp olive oil
15g butter

For the lemon butter sauce
3 tbsp freshly squeezed lemon juice
40g unsalted butter
125ml double cream
2 tbsp finely chopped chives
salt and pepper

Carefully flake the salmon fillets, removing all skin and bones. Mix half of the salmon fillet with the mashed potato, tomato ketchup, anchovy sauce and mustard, mashing them together thoroughly. Season to taste with salt and pepper. Add the remaining salmon and parsley and mix in gently without breaking up the fish.

Divide the mixture into four, then lightly flour your hands and shape each piece into a deep fishcake. Place on a tray, cover with clingfilm and refrigerate for at least half an hour.

Preheat the oven to 200°C/400°F/Gas 6. Lightly flour the fishcakes. Heat a frying pan over a moderate heat, add the oil and then the butter. When the butter starts foaming add the fishcakes and fry for about 3 minutes each side until browned. Transfer to a baking dish and bake for 10–15 minutes until hot.

Meanwhile make the sauce by heating the butter in a saucepan. Add the cream and heat through without boiling. Add the lemon juice and chives and warm through thoroughly. Season with salt and pepper. These fishcakes are great with buttered spinach.

VARIATIONS

You can use other types of fish and other seasonings. White fish and mashed potato flavoured with finely chopped capers, gherkins and parsley is good for example.

THRIFTY TIP

It's worth buying a pack of salmon fillets when you see them on offer and keeping them in the freezer.

FRUGAL FISH PIE

Fish pie is always a favourite but here's a particularly economical version.

SERVES 4–5

500g frozen white fish (such as Sainsbury's 'Basics' range)
150g basic frozen peeled prawns (small ones are cheaper than big ones)
600ml semi-skimmed milk
40g butter
40g plain flour
2 tbsp chopped parsley if you have some
salt, ground black pepper and a good squeeze/squirt of lemon juice

For the potato topping
750g potatoes, cut into even-sized pieces
15g butter
50–60ml warm milk
salt and pepper

Cut the fillets into pieces that will fit into a medium to large saucepan (if frozen rock-hard, leave for 15 minutes or so before you attempt this). Lay them in the pan skin side up (if they still have a skin). Bring slowly to the boil then turn the heat right down and simmer for 3–5 minutes (depending on the thickness of the fillets). Remove the fish with a fish slice and strain the milk into a measuring jug.

Melt the butter in a non-stick saucepan, stir in the flour and cook for a few seconds. Take the pan off the heat and tip about two thirds of the hot strained milk into the flour, all in one go, whisking continually. Bring to the boil, turn the heat down and leave to simmer, adding a little more of the reserved milk if the sauce seems too thick. Season with pepper and a little salt.

Remove any skin from the fish and flake it into largeish chunks, carefully removing any bones. Tip the fish and prawns into the sauce and fold in the parsley. Check the seasoning, adding lemon juice, extra salt and pepper to taste and tip into a shallow pie dish or baking dish.

While you're assembling the pie, put the potatoes in a saucepan, cover with cold water and bring to the boil. Cook for about 20 minutes until you can stick the point of a knife in them easily. Drain the potatoes, return them to the pan and cut them up roughly with a knife. Mash them thoroughly with a potato masher or fork. Beat in the butter and warm milk. Season with salt and pepper. Spread the potato evenly over the top of the fish roughing up the surface with the prongs of a fork. Bake in a hot oven (200°C/400°F/Gas 6) for about 20–25 minutes until the base is bubbling and the top is nicely browned.

VARIATIONS

Substitute smoked haddock for half the white fish. You could also replace the prawns with quartered hard boiled eggs or skinned, seeded, diced tomato and/or top the potato with a layer of grated cheese.

THRIFTY TIP

Frozen fish is generally a good deal cheaper than fresh – and may well be fresher. It hasn't quite the same texture but is fine for a dish like this.

PORTUGUESE-STYLE SALT COD BAKE

Like lasagne, this is not a dish to be attempted if you're short of time. But it has the similar advantage of being able to be prepared ahead and feeding substantial numbers for a very modest outlay. All you need do on the night is toss up a green salad. Note you need to soak the salt cod 24 hours before using it.

SERVES 6–8

400g salt cod
4 tbsp olive oil
40g butter
500g onions, peeled and thinly sliced
2 large cloves of garlic
25g plain flour
600ml whole milk
1 bayleaf
1 heaped tbsp capers, finely chopped if large
2 tsp white or red vinegar
900g potatoes, well scrubbed and thinly sliced
3 hard boiled eggs, peeled and cut into 8 wedges
salt and freshly ground black pepper

Soak the salt cod in water 24 hours before you intend to use it, changing the water two or three times. Cover it with fresh cold water, and bring it slowly to the boil. If the water is still salty repeat this, then leave it to simmer over a very low heat for 7–8 minutes until tender. Reserve a little of the cooking water, drain off the rest and set the cod aside to cool.

Meanwhile heat 3 tablespoons of olive oil in a large frying pan, add half the butter and fry the onions over a low heat until soft and translucent. Add the garlic and cook a couple of minutes more. Stir in the flour then gradually add the milk and cook until thickened. Add the bayleaf and capers and leave to infuse over a low heat. Bring the sliced potatoes to the boil and drain. Flake the fish, removing any bones and add it and the vinegar to the onions, adding a little of the reserved cooking water to thin the sauce. Remove the bayleaf and season generously with pepper. If you've soaked the fish thoroughly it may also need some salt.

Generously oil a large rectangular ovenproof dish. Put a third of the potatoes in the base, cover with half the eggs and half the fish and onions, then repeat the layers finishing with a layer of potato. Brush the top of the potatoes with the remaining melted butter and bake in a moderately hot oven 190°C/375°F/Gas 5 for about 45–50 minutes until the filling is bubbling and the potatoes nicely browned. Serve with a sharply dressed green salad.

VARIATIONS

You could add some diced, seeded tomatoes.

THRIFTY TIP

Salt cod is a useful ingredient to have to hand because it keeps for weeks.

SMOKED MACKEREL AND POTATO GRATIN

Smoked mackerel is such good value; I'm always trying to find new ways to use it. Cue this great little recipe from gastropub chef Trish Hilferty's *Lobster and Chips* (Absolute Press). It takes a while to cook but the preparation is so easy it would also make a good mid-week supper.

SERVES 4

20g unsalted butter
250g smoked mackerel
1 small white onion, sliced as thinly as possible
500g waxy potatoes, peeled and cut into slices
    5mm ($^1/_4$ inch) thick
250ml milk
2 tsp Dijon mustard
250ml double cream
sea salt and freshly ground black pepper

You will also need a 20cm (8-inch) gratin dish

Preheat the oven to 180°C/350°F/Gas Mark 4. Grease the gratin dish with the butter. Skin the mackerel and flake the flesh into bite-sized chunks, discarding any bones. In a bowl, gently mix together the fish, onion and potatoes and then put them in the gratin dish. Mix a little of the milk into the mustard then mix in the remaining milk and cream, season with salt and pepper, and pour it over the potatoes. Cover the dish with foil and bake for 45 minutes. Remove the foil and continue to cook for 10–15 minutes, until the top of the gratin is golden brown, the cream is bubbling and the potatoes are tender. Serve with a dark green leafy salad.

VARIATIONS

If you're an IKEA fan you could replace the mackerel with a couple of tins of the Swedish 'anchovies' (actually sprats) they sell in their food section. Or add a couple of skinned, de-seeded chopped tomatoes to the bake.

THRIFTY TIP

Buy potatoes loose rather than pre-packed in bags.

HOMEMADE HUMMUS

This is my favourite hummus recipe. There are quicker ways of making it but none quite as tasty or which stretch quite as far. While you're cooking chickpeas from scratch you might as well set aside some to make a veggie stew or bake, such as the one opposite. You will need to soak the chickpeas overnight.

250g dried chickpeas
3–4 large cloves of garlic
I bayleaf
3 tbsp tahini paste, well stirred (20g per tbsp)
2 tbsp plain, unsweetened yoghurt
3–4 tbsp freshly squeezed lemon juice
$1/_2$ tsp ground cumin
$1/_2$ tsp salt

Put the chickpeas in a bowl, cover them generously with cold water and leave them to soak for at least 12 hours. The next day discard the water and rinse the chickpeas then put them in a saucepan of fresh cold water. Bring them to the boil, skim off any froth, add 3 cloves of garlic and the bayleaf (but no salt) and boil them for about $1^1/_2$–2 hours, topping up the water as necessary, until the skins begin to come away and they are soft enough to squish between your fingers. Turn off the heat and leave them to cool in the pan. Once they are cold, drain the chickpeas, reserving the cooking water. Save half for another dish and put the rest in a food processor or blender. Start to process them, adding enough of the cooking liquid to keep the mixture moving until you have a thick paste. Add the tahini paste, yoghurt, 3 tablespoons of lemon juice, cumin and salt and whizz together until smooth, (if you want to add a touch of garlic, crush a chopped clove with the salt). Check seasoning, adding more lemon juice if you think it needs it.

VARIATIONS

I like to keep this plain because it's more flexible but there are lots of variations. Add more lemon juice, a little grated lemon zest and some finely chopped coriander. Add some roasted peppers and extra garlic and a pinch of paprika or pimenton. Replace the yoghurt with soy yoghurt for those who are dairy intolerant.

LEFTOVERS

Store in a lidded plastic box to use with pitta bread, raw vegetables and grilled or roasted vegetables.

THRIFTY TIP

You can cut the cooking time for chickpeas considerably if you have a pressure cooker (see page 29).

SWEET POTATO, SPINACH AND CHICKPEA BAKE

A very easy and moreish vegetarian bake. Leftovers are particularly tasty – if there are any.

SERVES 4–6

3 medium onions
6 tbsp light olive or sunflower oil
450g sweet potatoes, peeled and cut into chunks
2 red peppers, quartered, de-seeded and cut into thick strips
2 large cloves of garlic
2–3 tsp Moroccan Spice Mix (page 27)
400g can whole or chopped tomatoes
250 ml (9 fl oz) stock made with 1 tsp Marigold vegetable bouillon powder
300–400g cooked chickpeas (see preceding recipe) or a 400g can of chickpeas, drained and rinsed
a good handful of fresh spinach leaves
1 small carton sour cream
salt, pepper and sugar, to taste

Peel two of the onions and cut each into eight wedges. Pour 4 tablespoons of the oil into a large roasting tin. Add the onion, cubed sweet potatoes and peppers and mix well with the oil. Turn the oven to 200°C/400°F/Gas 6, put the tin in the oven and roast the vegetables for about 35 minutes, turning them half way through. Meanwhile, peel and roughly chop the other onion. Heat the remaining 2 tablespoons of the oil in a large frying pan and fry the onion until beginning to soften. Add the garlic and spice mix and stir well. Add the tinned tomatoes and their juice, breaking them up if necessary with a wooden spoon and cook for about 5 minutes. Stir in the stock then check the seasoning adding salt and a little sugar to taste. Stir in the chickpeas. When the vegetables in the oven have been cooking for 35 minutes, pour over the spiced tomato and chickpeas and mix well. Turn the oven temperature down to 190°C/375°F/Gas 5 and cook for another 20–30 minutes until the vegetables are well cooked, turning them half way through. Just before the end of the cooking time wash the spinach, remove any tough stalks, slice the leaves finely and stir them into the bake. Return the tin to the oven for another 5 minutes. Serve with sour cream or a mild onion raita (page 118).

VARIATIONS

You could substitute butternut squash for the sweet potato or add courgettes or aubergines and add chopped fresh coriander rather than spinach.

LEFTOVERS

This is one of those veggie bakes that tastes good cold.

THRIFTY TIP

Whole tinned tomatoes are generally cheaper than ready-chopped ones.

PEACH AND BLUEBERRY COBBLER

This is a perfect dessert to make in high summer when both peaches and blueberries are in season but can be made with frozen fruit at other times of year.

SERVES 4

4 ripe, but not overripe peaches
150g fresh or frozen blueberries (if frozen, taken out of the freezer half an hour before baking
1–2 tsp lemon juice, depending how ripe the peaches are
15–20g caster sugar
$\frac{1}{2}$ tsp cinnamon

For the cobbler topping
110g chilled butter
110g plain flour
grated zest of half a lemon
45g caster sugar
$\frac{1}{2}$ tsp baking powder
$\frac{1}{8}$ tsp bicarbonate of soda
$\frac{1}{8}$ tsp salt
50–75g plain yoghurt (not low fat)

You will also need a pie dish 18–20cm in diameter

Pre-heat the oven to 200°C/400°F/Gas 6. Peel and quarter the peaches and place them in a bowl, (if you don't think they'll peel easily blanch them in boiling water for 10 seconds). Mix the sugar with the cinnamon, sprinkle over the peaches and mix lightly. Set aside while you prepare the topping.

Cut the cold butter into small cubes. If you have a food processor sift the flour, raising agents and sugar into the processor and whizz with the lemon zest. Add the cubed butter and whizz again until the mixture resembles breadcrumbs (about 20–30 seconds). Otherwise, sift the dry ingredients together and rub the butter in by hand. Add the blueberries and lemon juice to the macerating peaches, mix gently, then transfer to a lightly greased pie dish.

Transfer the cobbler mixture to a bowl and fold in just enough yoghurt to bring the topping together (too much will result in a tough consistency). Using your hands, roughly shape the mixture into five flatish rounds and place them on top of the peaches, leaving some of the fruit showing.

Bake for 25–30 minutes until the topping is golden and a skewer comes out clean when inserted. Serve the cobbler warm with Greek yoghurt or vanilla ice cream.

VARIATIONS

The filling could be made with nectarines, apricots or plums or with berry fruits and apples. Anything you can put in a crumble you can put in a cobbler.

THRIFTY TIP

Freeze blueberries when they're in season and cheap.

EMPRESS OF PUDDINGS

A slightly swankier version of Queen of Puddings, hence the name, including some fresh or frozen berries. But you can simply use jam if you prefer.

SERVES 4

400ml whole milk
finely grated rind of 1 small unwaxed lemon
15g butter
25g caster sugar
80g fresh breadcrumbs
2 large egg yolks
3 tbsp raspberry jam
125g fresh or frozen raspberries or mixed small berries

For the meringue
2 large egg whites
110g caster sugar

You will need a lightly greased small to medium-sized shallow oven-proof dish about 750ml in capacity

Pour the milk in a saucepan, add the lemon rind and stir then place over a low heat until the milk is hot but not boiling. Add the butter and caster sugar and leave a couple of minutes until melted then strain the milk over the breadcrumbs. Stir and leave for 20 minutes.

Meanwhile heat the oven to 160°C/325°F/Gas 3. Beat the soaked breadcrumbs, then beat in the egg yolks and tip the mixture into the greased pie dish. Place the dish in a roasting tin of water and bake for about 45 minutes until the top is lightly set. Take out of the oven. Put the jam in a small saucepan with the frozen fruit, warm through and spread gently over the pudding without breaking the surface. Whip the egg whites until stiff then whisk in half the sugar until the mixture is thick and shiny. Fold in the remaining sugar and spread evenly over the pudding. Put the pudding back in the oven, turn the heat down to 150°C/300°F/Gas 2, and cook for a further 15–20 minutes until the meringue is golden brown. Serve immediately, with cream if you're feeling indulgent.

VARIATIONS

You could make this with apricot rather than raspberry jam.

THRIFTY TIP

Look out for old fashioned Pyrex dishes in charity shops. They're perfect for cooking a dish like this.

WARNING

The meringue topping is only lightly cooked so may not be suitable for your pregnant friends or elderly relatives.

DANISH APPLE CHARLOTTE

A simple but delicious pudding which comes from a well thumbed copy of the *Hamlyn All Colour Cook Book* (Hamlyn), one of the books I used to teach myself to cook. For some unfathomable reason it's also referred to as Danish Peasant Girl with a Veil.

SERVES 4–6

75g butter
225g fresh white breadcrumbs
$^1/_2$ tsp cinnamon (optional)
50g Demerara sugar
700g Bramley or other cooking apples
juice of $^1/_2$ lemon
3 tbsp unrefined caster sugar
284ml whipping or double cream
plain dark chocolate for grating

You will need a large glass dessert bowl

Melt the butter in a large frying pan. Tip in the breadcrumbs and fry over a low heat, stirring regularly until crisp and golden. Stir in the cinnamon and Demerara sugar, then fry for another couple of minutes.

Quarter, peel and slice the apple and put in a pan with the lemon juice, caster sugar and 2 tablespoons of water. Cover the pan and bring to the boil then turn down the heat and cook until the apple is soft. Beat the apple to a purée with a wooden spoon. Check for sweetness, adding more sugar if needed and set aside to cool.

Spoon half the apple into a glass pudding bowl, cover with half the breadcrumbs then repeat the layers. Cover with clingfilm and chill. Whip the cream lightly and spread over the top of the pudding. Shave or grate over the chocolate.

VARIATIONS

You could replace the apple with a mixture of rhubarb and strawberries but don't let the mixture get too wet.

THRIFTY TIP

It's worth making a batch of breadcrumbs whenever you have some leftover bread. Keep them in a plastic bag in the freezer so they're ready whenever you need them.

LEMON DRIZZLE TRAYBAKE

This is one of those simple but infallible recipes that everyone loves – an easy all-in-one recipe from the doyenne of British baking, Mary Berry. It's worth making this amount because it freezes well but you can halve the quantities and make it in a smaller tin if you prefer.

MAKES 30 PIECES

For the cake
225g butter, softened
225g caster sugar
275g self-raising flour
2 tsp baking powder
4 eggs
4 tbsp milk
grated zest of 2 unwaxed lemons

For the crunchy topping
175g granulated sugar
juice of 2 lemons

You'll also need a large 30 x 23cm baking tin, lightly greased and lined with non-stick baking parchment

Preheat the oven to 160°C/325°F/Gas 3. Measure all the ingredients for the tray-bake into a large bowl and beat well for about 2 minutes, until well blended. Turn the mixture into the prepared tin, scraping the bowl with a plastic spatula to remove all of the mixture. Level the top gently with the back of the spatula. Bake in the middle of the oven for about 35–40 minutes, or until the cake springs back when lightly pressed and is beginning to shrink away from the sides of the tin. Leave the cake to cool in the tin for a few minutes then lift it out of the tin while still in its lining paper. Carefully remove the paper and put the tray bake onto a wire rack placed over a tray. To make the crunchy topping, mix the lemon juice and granulated sugar in a small bowl to give a runny consistency. Spoon this mixture evenly over the tray-bake whilst it is still warm. Cut into squares once cold and store in an airtight tin.

VARIATIONS

You could make this with orange rind and juice instead of lemon.

THRIFTY TIP

You could replace half the butter with a buttermilk spread which would cut the cost and make the cake mixture slightly easier to beat.

CAPPUCCINO CAKE

Before you say it, yes, I agree this recipe – which I've adapted from a splendid book called *Cakes and Biscuits: Best Kept Secrets of the Women's Institute* (Simon & Schuster) – is hardly thrifty (or healthy, let's face it), but even frugal cooks deserve a treat. And it does involve economies. Leftover coffee. Cocoa instead of chocolate (for the cake at least). Buttermilk spread instead of butter. And just think how much you'd pay for a cake like this in Starbucks!

MAKES 12–16 SQUARES OR BARS

1 tbsp cocoa powder
2 tbsp hot strong black coffee
200g unrefined caster sugar
225g hard buttermilk spread (e.g. Willow) at room temperature
4 medium eggs at room temperature
225g self-raising flour sifted with 1 tsp baking powder

For the icing
90g milk chocolate
40g butter or buttermilk spread
2 tbsp strong black coffee or milk
125g icing sugar

You'll also need a medium-sized shallow rectangular cake tin about 18 x 32cm lined with baking parchment (if not non-stick)

Set the oven to 180°C/350°F/Gas 4. Sift the cocoa into a large bowl, pour over the hot coffee and stir. Add the caster sugar, stir then tip in the spread, eggs and half the self-raising flour and beat thoroughly together with a wooden spoon or an electric hand whisk. Fold in the remaining flour. Spoon the mixture into the tin and level the surface. Bake for about 35–40 minutes until well risen and firm to the touch. Leave in the tin for 10 minutes then carefully tip out on a wire rack to cool. To make the icing, break up the chocolate and put it in a basin with the butter and coffee or milk. Place the bowl over a pan of hot water, taking care that it doesn't touch the water. Once the ingredients have melted, remove from the heat and beat in the sifted icing sugar. Spread over the surface of the cooled cake and leave to set for a couple of hours. Cut the cake into 16 squares or bars – or smaller pieces, if you prefer.

VARIATIONS

You could make a more economical chocolate frosting for this with cocoa powder using twice the quantity on page 211.

THRIFTY TIP

Buy your milk chocolate in the bakery section rather than from the confectionery shelves. It's cheaper there. Belgian chocolate is generally the best.

BANANA CHIFFON CAKE

More cakey than the normal banana tea bread. The
perfect way to use up leftover bananas.

75g broken walnuts (optional)
200g plain flour
1 tsp baking powder
$^1/_4$ tsp bicarbonate of soda
a pinch of salt
3 medium-sized ripe bananas
2 medium eggs
125g butter at room temperature
100g unrefined caster sugar plus 1 extra tsp
$^1/_2$ tsp vanilla extract
icing sugar for decoration (optional)

You will also need a lightly greased cake tin, 20cm
in diameter

Preheat the oven 180°C/350°F/Gas 4. If using the
walnuts tip them on a tray and crisp them for a few
minutes in the oven as it warms up. Sift the flour,
baking powder, bicarbonate of soda and salt and
set aside. Peel and mash the bananas.

Separate the egg whites from the yolks. Beat the
butter, sugar and vanilla until pale and fluffy, add
the egg yolks one at a time and beat until
incorporated. Mix in the banana. Whisk the egg
whites to a stiff peak. Add the remaining teaspoon
of sugar to the whites and beat again. Take a
heaped tablespoon of the egg whites and lightly
mix it into the cake mixture. Then fold in the
remainder of the egg whites. Fold in the sifted flour
and toasted walnuts, being careful not to knock the
air out of the mixture. Carefully pour the cake
mixture into the tin and bake on the middle shelf
of the oven for 30 minutes until the cake is golden
and feels springy to the touch.

VARIATIONS

You could add a butter icing similar to that on the
Carrot Muffins (page 165) if you wanted to make
the cake more luxurious. Or a simple orange
drizzle icing (icing sugar mixed with orange juice
and a little lemon juice).

THRIFTY TIP

The ideal point at which to use bananas for a recipe
like this is when they're still yellow and firm but
beginning to get black spots.

BARM BRACK

The beer, which I discovered when I was researching my beer and food book *An Appetite for Ale* (Camra), gives this traditional Irish recipe an extra dimension. This is a great recipe for using up leftovers. Good to make after Christmas if you've got a lot of dried fruit around. Note, this is a 3-day affair – you soak the fruit overnight then leave the bread overnight before slicing it.

175ml freshly brewed strong tea, cooled
(best to use a classic builders' tea for this rather than anything fancy)
150ml brown ale (e.g. Mann's)
150g dark muscovado or soft dark brown sugar
350g mixed dried fruit – or use up what's in the storecupboard
1 large egg, lightly beaten
275g self-raising flour or plain flour mixed with 2 tsp baking powder
$\frac{1}{2}$ tsp mixed spice

You will need a well-greased 900g loaf tin, lined with baking parchment

Pour the tea and ale into a large bowl, stir in the sugar then add the fruit and leave in the fridge overnight. When ready to cook preheat the oven to 180°C/350°F/Gas 4. Add the beaten egg to the soaked fruit, sift in the self-raising flour and mixed spice and mix thoroughly. Tip the mixture into a well greased, lined loaf tin and bake for $1\frac{1}{2}$ hours, turning the heat down to 170°C/325°F/Gas 3 half way through the cooking time. Leave in the tin for 10 minutes then turn out and cool on a wire rack. Wrap in foil and leave till the following day. Serve sliced with butter.

VARIATIONS

You could make this with a sweet stout like Mackeson's – or without beer at all in which case, increase the amount of tea. You can also vary the dried fruits you used – chopped up dates, prunes or unsulphured dried apricots would all be good.

LEFTOVERS

Will keep well for a week if stored in an airtight tin.

THRIFTY TIP

You can use the rest of the brown ale to make a particularly tasty Onion Gravy (page 219).

GRANNY SMITH SCONES

Scones are unbelievably easy once you get the hang of them. The trick is not to overwork the dough once you add the liquid and not to make them too thin.

MAKES 8 SCONES

1 tbsp lemon juice
1 medium Granny Smith or other tart eating apple
225g plain flour plus 3 level tsp baking powder or 225g self raising flour plus 1 1/2 level tsp baking powder
a pinch of salt
50g cool, firm butter (not straight from the fridge but cooler than room temperature)
40g unrefined or ordinary caster sugar
1 medium-large egg
milk

You will need a baking sheet

Preheat the oven to 220°C/425°F/Gas 7.
Put the lemon juice in a small bowl. Quarter, core and peel the apple and cut into small dice, adding each batch to the lemon juice to stop it discolouring. Sift the flour, baking powder and salt into a large bowl. Dice the butter and tip into the flour then carry on cutting it with a knife until you have very small pieces. Rub the butter lightly into the flour until it becomes coarse and grainy. Stir in the sugar and diced apple. Beat the egg in a measuring jug, add milk up to the 150ml mark and beat again. Make a hollow in the flour mixture and pour in most of the egg, leaving just over a tablespoon. Using a knife, mix it in lightly and quickly drawing the mixture together then gently pull the dough together. It should be soft but not sticky – add the extra liquid if it seems too dry. Transfer the dough to a floured board or work surface and shape into a rectangle about 2.5cm deep. Using a medium-sized cutter, cut the scones into rounds, re-rolling the offcuts, and transfer to a lightly greased baking tray. Brush the tops of the scones with the remaining egg and milk or, if you've incorporated that, with a little extra milk and bake for about 10–12 minutes until well risen and browned. Remove from the oven, cool for 5–10 minutes, then eat while still warm.

VARIATIONS

You could replace half the apple with chopped blueberries or blackberries and/or add 1/2 teaspoon of cinnamon to the dough. To make cheese scones, leave out the apple and sugar and add 25g of grated Parmesan or 40g of a mature hard cheese such as Cheddar or Gruyère.

LEFTOVERS

You could freeze the scones as soon as you cool them but they are better eaten straight away.

THRIFTY TIP

If you cut your scones into squares rather than rounds you don't need to buy a set of cutters.

CRUNCHY PEANUT COOKIES

I always thought the idea of peanut cookies was vaguely repellent until I tried these. Disastrously moreish.

MAKES 24–26

75g shelled peanuts
125g crunchy peanut butter (e.g. Whole Earth Original)
125g butter at room temperature
75g golden caster sugar plus 2 rounded tbsp
100g light soft brown sugar
$^1/_2$ tsp vanilla extract or essence
1 medium egg
175g plain flour
$^1/_4$ tsp bicarbonate of soda

You will need 2 large lightly greased baking sheets

Preheat the oven to 190°C/375°F/Gas 5.

Roast the peanuts for 10 minutes, cool then place them in a clean tea towel and rub off the skins. Chop roughly. Cream the butter and peanut butter together. Work in the two sugars (apart from the extra tablespoons) then add the vanilla extract and the egg. Mix in the chopped peanuts and the flour and bicarbonate of soda. Chill the dough for 20 minutes. Take heaped teaspoons of the mixture and form a ball the size of a large walnut. Roll each one in the remaining caster sugar. Space them out on the baking trays and flatten each one gently with the prongs of a fork. Bake for about 15 minutes until light brown. Cool on the baking sheet for 5 minutes, then remove to a wire rack until cold. Store in an airtight tin.

VARIATIONS

None really. The whole point is the peanuts.

THRIFTY TIP

Roast the peanuts while you have the oven on for something else.

CARROT, OAT AND CINNAMON MUFFINS

A batch of muffins can be rustled up at short notice from store-cupboard ingredients. This unusual recipe has the virtue of being slightly less sweet (and more sustaining) than many muffins which makes them a good lunchbox treat.

MAKES 9–12 MUFFINS

55g porridge oats plus a few more oats for
    decoration
55g butter
3 tbsp sunflower oil
4–5 level tbsp clear honey
200g carrots, trimmed and peeled
110g plain flour
55g plain wholemeal flour (not bread flour)
1 tsp baking powder plus $1/8$ tsp bicarbonate of
    soda
1 tsp cinnamon
a pinch of salt
2 medium eggs
1 tbsp plain yoghurt mixed with 75ml milk
$1/4$ tsp vanilla extract

You will also need a standard muffin tin lined with
    paper cups or brushed with a thin coating of oil
    (the mixture should make 9–10 muffins)

Preheat the oven to 180°C/350°F/Gas 4.

Toast the oats for 5–6 minutes in the oven while it warms up. Melt the butter in a small saucepan with the oil and honey and set aside to cool. Sift the two flours, raising agents, and cinnamon into a large bowl, add the salt and mix thoroughly. Grate the carrots on the medium side of a grater and tip into a sieve to drain. Lightly beat the eggs then beat in the yoghurt, milk and vanilla. Lightly mix the toasted oats with the flour mixture, make a hollow in the middle then pour in the milk and eggs and melted butter and honey. Fold the mixture together swiftly with a large metal spoon without over-mixing it then carefully fold in the grated carrots. Spoon the mixture into the paper cases, taking it almost up to the brim if you want them to rise gratifyingly high. Sprinkle with extra porridge oats and bake for 20–25 minutes in the top half of the oven, until golden brown, firm and springy to the touch.

VARIATIONS

You could use grated apple instead of carrot, or ginger instead of cinnamon. You could also ice the muffins with a Philadelphia cheese icing. Take 75g of soft butter and cream with 40–60g of icing sugar (depending on how sweet you like your icing). Add a few drops of vanilla extract, then work in 150g of Philadelphia Cream Cheese (not the low-fat version!).

THRIFTY TIP

Mixing yoghurt and milk is cheaper than using the frequently recommended buttermilk.

LEMON AND GINGER FLAPJACKS

A flapjack with a difference based on crunchy oatmeal with a zesty lemon and ginger kick.

MAKES 12–16 SQUARES OR BARS

150g coarse (pinhead) oatmeal
50g plain flour
$^1/_2$ tsp baking powder
$^3/_4$ tsp salt
150g muesli, preferably unsweetened
150g butter
100g Demerara sugar
50g golden syrup
a 2.5 cm cube of peeled fresh ginger, grated or a
    tsp of ground ginger
grated zest of 1 small unwaxed lemon

You will need a 20cm square or 27cm by 17cm
    rectangular baking tin, lightly greased

Pre-heat oven to 180°C/350°F/Gas 4. Put the oatmeal in a baking tin and toast in the oven for about 10 minutes while preparing the other ingredients. Sift the flour, baking powder and salt together, mix together then add the muesli. Place the butter, sugar, golden syrup, ginger, lemon zest and juice in a medium-sized saucepan, warm gently to melt the butter and syrup, then bring up to boiling point and take off the heat.

Tip the flour and muesli mixture into the saucepan together with the toasted oatmeal and stir swiftly with a wooden spoon. Spoon into the baking tin, level the surface and bake for 20–25 minutes until golden and springy to the touch. Cool for 10–15 minutes then mark out into squares or bars with a sharp knife. Leave to cool until hardened then remove from the tin.

VARIATIONS

You can play around with all sorts of flapjack flavours. Dried berries such as cranberries and cherries and raisins are good or snipped up dried banana.

THRIFTY TIP

You could substitute porridge oats for the oatmeal or muesli.

WHOLEMEAL PORRIDGE BREAD

I adapted this recipe from one by food writer Signe Johansen who has a bit of a thing about oats. Great fresh but makes really delicious toast.

MAKES 1 LARGE LOAF

30g butter or 2 tbsp sunflower oil
1 level tbsp dark soft brown or other brown sugar
150g jumbo oats or porridge oats plus an extra
 tbsp for the topping
250g strong wholemeal flour
200g strong white flour
2 tsp salt
1 level tsp quick-acting yeast (e.g. Dove's)
beaten egg or egg white for glazing

You'll also need a lightly greased 900g loaf tin, preferably non-stick

Heat 250ml water until hot but not boiling, add the butter and sugar and stir until melted. Add the oats, stir and leave to cool whilst assembling the rest of the ingredients. Tip the wholemeal flour in a large bowl, sift in the white flour, salt and yeast, and mix thoroughly so the salt and yeast are evenly distributed. Have 125ml of warm water to hand. Make a hollow in the flour, add the soaked porridge oats and half the water and stir with a wooden spoon. When the mixture begins to come together, scrape the dough off the spoon and bring the mixture together with your hands, adding as much extra water as you need to form a dough (the texture should be slightly sticky, but not wet). Turn the dough onto a board and knead for 10 minutes until it springs back when you press it lightly with your thumb.

Transfer the dough back to the mixing bowl, cover lightly with clingfilm and leave to rise somewhere warm for an hour.

Once the dough has risen, knock it back and knead gently then shape the loaf so that it will fit into the tin leaving the join underneath. Re-cover it with the oiled clingfilm and leave it until it has doubled in size (about another 30–40 minutes). Turn the oven on to 220°C/425°F/Gas 7 about 15 minutes before the dough is due to be ready.

Brush the top of the loaf with the beaten egg then sprinkle over the remaining oats. Place the loaf in the oven and bake for 20 minutes then turn the heat down to 190°C/375°F/Gas 5 and bake for a further 25 to 30 minutes or until you can insert a skewer or sharp-pointed knife in the bread and it comes out clean. Leave in the tin for 10 minutes then turn out to cool on a wire rack. This bread is particularly good with cheese or toasted with honey.

VARIATIONS

You could make it entirely with wholemeal flour but it will come out slightly heavier.

LEFTOVERS

Freeze in slices.

THRIFTY TIP

Since you have to have the oven on at such a high temperature it would be worth baking some more bread or a pizza at the same time.

SHEEP'S CHEESE, OLIVE AND OREGANO BREAD

Flavoured breads always command a premium in smart delis and bakers but can actually be a great way of using up leftovers. This is a simple soda bread that doesn't need kneading.

200ml sheep's yoghurt or low-fat bio yoghurt
I level dsp clear honey
225g self-raising flour
225g plain wholemeal flour (not bread flour) plus extra for dusting
$^1/_2$ level tsp cream of tartar
I level tsp bicarbonate of soda
$^1/_2$ tsp fine sea salt
50g strong sheep's cheese (e.g. Berkswell), rinded and finely sliced
60g marinated olives with herbs, stoned and finely chopped
I tsp finely chopped fresh or dried oregano

Measure the yoghurt into a measuring jug and add enough water to bring it up to the 275ml mark. Tip into a pan with the honey and warm very gently until the honey dissolves. Stir well then take the pan off the heat and cool until you can comfortably hold a finger in the milk.

Combine the two flours, cream of tartar, bicarbonate of soda and salt in a large mixing bowl. Pour over the milk and honey mixture and mix with a wooden spoon until it comes together. Tip the cheese, olives and oregano into the dough then work the mixture with your hands into a ball, adding a little extra water if necessary. The dough should be soft but not sticky.

Shape the dough into a ball about 16cm wide and place on a floured baking tray. Cut a deep cross in the centre of the loaf, dust with a little more flour and bake for about 35–40 minutes until the bread is well browned and the bottom of the loaf sounds hollow when you tap it. Transfer to a wire rack and cool for about 20 minutes. Serve while still warm.

VARIATIONS

You could play around with all sorts of different cheeses and complementary ingredients. Mature Cheddar, chopped sun-dried tomatoes and basil for example or Stilton, thyme and crisp fried onions.

THRIFTY TIP

It's generally cheaper to buy olives with their stones still in although pitted olives are obviously quicker to chop up. Whatever you have in the fridge or storecupboard really.

THE FRUGAL HOST

GOOD HOUSEKEEPING DOESN'T HAVE TO FLY OUT OF THE WINDOW JUST BECAUSE YOU'RE HAVING FRIENDS ROUND. MAKE YOUR GUESTS FEEL PAMPERED BY THE WARMTH OF YOUR WELCOME AND THE FACT THAT YOU'VE TAKEN THE TROUBLE TO COOK THEM SOMETHING FROM SCRATCH, RATHER THAN THE EXPENSE OF THE INGREDIENTS YOU'VE LAVISHED ON THEM.

It seems like the antithesis of hospitality to skimp on what you offer your guests, but inviting friends round can totally blow your month's food budget. So how do you cut back what you spend without seeming ungenerous? Here are a few ideas....

ENTERTAINING ON A BUDGET

CUT DOWN ON THE AMOUNT OF TIME YOU HAVE PEOPLE ROUND

Instead of inviting people for dinner (or rather, supper – see below) just have them round for a drink and a few nibbles. Or coffee and cake. It not only cuts down the amount of food you have to buy but the amount of time you need to spend preparing it. (See more on drinks parties on pages 194–197.)

BE IMAGINATIVE

Make up for your lack of cash by inviting friends to a meal that sounds fun. You could tie it to an event such as the Mexican national holiday *Cinco de Mayo* (maybe the occasion for a tortilla party), or Bastille Day on July 14th (a French picnic), or an *Oktoberfest 'bier and wurst'* evening. Or focus it on a type of food like a cup cake tea, a jelly and ice cream party or a soup supper.

SHARE THE COST

Band together with friends or neighbours to put a meal together. That obviously cuts down on the workload too.

GET ALL YOUR ENTERTAINING OVER WITH IN ONE WEEKEND

There's a lot to be said, if you can face the washing up, for having the same or a similar meal two consecutive nights for two different groups of friends. Less work for the cook and no leftovers problem. Restaurants do it all the time....

FORGET THE THIRD COURSE (AND THE CHEESEBOARD)

You don't actually need to cook three courses. Just have something light to nibble with a pre-dinner drink and go straight to the main course or have a starter, skip the main course and go on to the cheese or pud (note: pud *singular*, you don't need to show off and make three!). Think supper rather than dinner party. And you can still offer your friends cheese; just don't feel obliged to offer them five or six different kinds, most of which you'll struggle to use up (see page 199).

GET AHEAD

This doesn't just apply to budget entertaining of course, but there are huge benefits in knowing what you're going to feed people, especially if they're staying for a few days (see How to Survive Christmas, pages 198–201). Have at least a couple of dishes ready-prepared so you don't have a last minute panic splurge.

PLAY TO YOUR STRENGTHS

What's frugal, as I've mentioned (pages 16–19) depends on where you live. In the country, game such as pheasant and rabbit can be dirt cheap and is also a treat for visiting townies. Whereas in a big city you're much more likely to be able to lay your hands on reasonably priced herbs and spices to make ethnic meals that country friends will really enjoy.

If you're a great baker put the emphasis on homemade bread, biscuits and desserts. If you make a mean green Thai curry from scratch, do that. It's all about giving people food they don't cook for themselves.

CARAMELISED CAULIFLOWER SOUP

You simply wouldn't believe cauliflower could taste so sumptuous – or that there's no cream in this luxurious soup, which was inspired by the brilliant Heston Blumenthal.

SERVES 4–6

1 medium to large cauliflower
75g unsalted butter
$\frac{1}{4}$ tsp curry powder plus a little extra for decoration
150ml semi-skimmed milk
600ml light vegetable stock made with 2 rounded tsp Marigold vegetable bouillon powder or an organic vegetable stock cube
salt, black pepper and lemon juice to taste

Trim the base and the leaves off the cauliflower, break into florets then chop them finely. Cut the butter into cubes, put them in a large saucepan and place on a medium to high heat. Add the cauliflower and cook, stirring occasionally until golden brown (about 12–15 minutes). Stir in the curry powder and cook for another 2–3 minutes then add the milk, and bring to the boil, stirring. Reduce the heat, cover the pan and simmer for 5 minutes. Add 300ml of the stock, bring to the boil again then cook gently until the cauliflower is soft (about another 5 minutes). Remove the pan from the heat, leave to stand for 5 minutes then tip the contents into a liquidiser and purée until smooth. Scoop the purée out of the blender and return to the pan. Whizz up the remaining stock in the blender to pick up the last bits of the purée and add to the cauliflower. Stir well and re-heat gently. Season to taste with lemon juice, salt and black pepper then add as much salt as you think the soup needs. Serve in small bowls with some snipped chives and a light dusting of curry powder.

VARIATIONS

You could add some cream but it's already quite rich.

THRIFTY TIP

It's always worth holding back some stock or other liquid to get the last bits of purée out of the blender.

POT ROAST PHEASANT WITH PORT

Game is one of those ingredients that's frugal (or not) depending on where you live. If you live in a city, it's dear. If you live in the country it can be cheaper than chicken and makes a great show-off meal to give townie guests who come to stay.

SERVES 4–6

3 tbsp olive oil
2 pheasants (hen pheasants for preference)
1 large or 2 smaller onions, peeled and roughly chopped
2 carrots, peeled and sliced
2 turnips and/or 2 sticks of celery, peeled or trimmed and sliced
2 cloves of garlic, peeled and finely chopped
1 1/2 tsp sweet pimenton
3/4 tsp cinnamon
100ml inexpensive vintage character or late bottled vintage port
100ml white or red wine
400ml chicken, pheasant or vegetable stock

Preheat the oven to 150°C/300°F/Gas 2. Heat the olive oil and brown the pheasants on all sides. Remove from the casserole and add the vegetables, turning them in the oil. Fry for a couple of minutes then add the garlic and stir. Add the pimenton and cinnamon, stir again and pour in the port. Wait for it to evaporate then add a similar sized glass of white or red wine. Stir, then place the pheasant back over the vegetables. Add half the stock, cover the pan and roast for an hour, turning the pheasant half way through. Take the lid off, increase the heat to 160°C/325°F/Gas 3, and cook for another 30–40 minutes until the pheasant is well browned and the liquid reduced, (again, turn it half way through this stage of the cooking time). Remove the pheasant, set aside and rest. Leave the pan juices and vegetables to settle for 10 minutes then carefully skim off the fat. Carve the pheasants and serve with the cooking vegetables and a parsnip mash or other root vegetable purée.

VARIATIONS

An alternative way to serve this for four is just to serve the pheasant breasts (if you serve enough vegetables it doesn't look ungenerous) and save the legs and carcass for other recipes.

LEFTOVERS

Cut the remaining meat off the legs and carcass, wrap in foil and refrigerate. Put the bones in a saucepan with a small onion, half a carrot, a stick of celery, a bayleaf and a few peppercorns, bring to the boil and simmer for an hour and a half. Cool, strain and skim then use as the base of a pilaf or soup or freeze for another occasion.

THRIFTY TIP

Leftover port makes a great addition to stews and mulled wine.

BRAISED BEEF SHORT-RIBS
WITH RED WINE AND POLENTA

Short-rib is a classic American and French cut which you seldom find here but my organic butcher has started selling it. They're thick chunky wedges of beef on the bone and need long slow cooking. Start the recipe a day ahead so you can skim off the fat.

SERVES 4–6

2 tbsp oil
1.2kg beef short ribs
2 medium onions, peeled and roughly chopped
2 medium carrots, peeled and sliced
2 cloves of garlic, peeled and crushed
2 tbsp tomato purée
1 rounded tbsp plain flour
600–700ml full-bodied red wine or wine and stock combined plus an extra half glassful
2 sprigs of thyme
salt and freshly ground black pepper

Heat the oil in a large ovenproof pan or casserole and brown the ribs on all sides. Set aside. Turn the heat down and fry the chopped onions and carrots in the oil until beginning to soften (about 7–8 minutes). Stir in the garlic and tomato purée and cook for a minute over a low heat then stir in the flour. Gradually add 500ml red wine then heat, stirring, until the sauce has thickened. Season with salt and pepper. Return the ribs to the pan, adding enough extra wine, stock or water to ensure they're covered with sauce and bring to the boil. Turn the heat right down and simmer on the lowest possible heat or transfer the casserole to a low oven (140°C/275°F/Gas 1) for 3 1/2–4 hours until the meat is falling off the bone. Check the casserole every hour or so to make sure it isn't cooking too fast. The surface should barely tremble. Remove from the heat and cool then refrigerate overnight. Skim the fat off the surface of the casserole and remove the ribs. Cut off the meat and cut into chunks and return to the liquid in the casserole. Add another half glassful of red wine then reheat the stew slowly. Serve with polenta (see page 221) or mash. A dark leafy vegetable like cavolo nero or kale makes a good accompaniment.

VARIATIONS

If you prefer you can substitute beef stock for half the wine but it will make the sauce taste more like a gravy (see thrifty tip below). You could also add some mushrooms to the recipe.

LEFTOVERS

If left with enough stew to make another helping, transfer it into a single-portion ovenproof dish, top with mashed potato and bake like a cottage pie.

THRIFTY TIP

This is a good dish to make after a party when you have various open bottles of wine of possibly dubious provenance lying around. It's never a bad idea to make more cooking liquid than you strictly need for a stew. Any leftovers can be frozen and used as the basis for a quick sauce or a gravy.

SLOW-ROAST SHOULDER OF LAMB WITH AROMATIC HERBS

I was given a bag of dried herbs from Cyprus which were more pungent and aromatic than any I'd ever tasted. They seemed to me the ideal accompaniment for a slow roast shoulder of lamb which is a frugal buy but can be quite fatty. If you can't lay your hands on Cypriot ones you can often find Greek dried herbs by the sprig in delis. Or, if you have a herb garden, grow and dry your own.

SERVES 4–6

some dried sprigs of Mediterranean herbs, ideally
    including rosemary, thyme and oregano
1 tsp coarse sea salt
1 tsp cumin seeds
1 tsp peppercorns
2kg lamb shoulder
2 large cloves of garlic, peeled and finely sliced
olive oil
175ml red or white wine
175ml light stock

Pre-heat the oven to 180°C/350°F/Gas 4. Take about six assorted sprigs of herbs, pull off the leaves and put them in a mortar. Add the sea salt, peppercorns and cumin seeds and grind together with a pestle until you have roughly ground powder. Trim off any extra thick patches of fat off the lamb shoulder with a sharp knife (but not all of it – you need to leave a thin layer over the joint). Make some small incisions all over the meat and stuff the garlic into the slits. Put the lamb in a roasting pan and rub all over with olive oil. Sprinkle half the herbs over the lamb and rub in well too. Put the lamb in the oven and roast for 20 minutes then turn the heat down to 140°/275°F/Gas 1 and cook for another 4–4½ hours. Ovens vary so you'll have to keep an eye on it. If it seems to be cooking too fast – unlikely, but ovens are odd – turn the heat down. Basically the fat and juices should be gently bubbling away and you should be able to smell the meat cooking.

Baste the meat occasionally and pour off (and keep) any surplus fat that accumulates but don't open the oven door too often as it reduces the heat. Once you appear to have got rid of most of the fat (after 2½–3 hours or once it stops accumulating in the pan) baste the meat again, sprinkle a little more herbs over the meat and add the wine to the pan. Keep checking to ensure the pan juices are not burning which will spoil your sauce, (add more wine or a little water if they look like getting dry). When the meat is cooked and falling away from the bone put it on a carving plate and leave it in a warm place. Add about 150ml stock and work off the stuck-on juices. Skim or spoon off the lamb fat you have set aside and you should find some jellied meat juices. Add those too. Check the seasoning, adding a little salt and pepper to taste, then strain the gravy into a small saucepan. If you have time, leave it to cool a little then you can skim the sauce again. Cut the meat into large chunks and serve on a large platter. Reheat the meat juices and serve in a warm jug.

VARIATIONS

You could roast a large joint of pork like this too.

LEFTOVERS

See idea for cottage pie adaptation in the previous recipe. If you just have meat leftover, shred it, fry lightly with a few spices and serve warm with a couscous or quinoa salad.

THRIFTY TIP

Because this dish cooks for such a long time it's best made with older lamb or mutton rather than expensive new season's lamb.

CHOUX PUFFS WITH CREAM AND WARM COCOA SAUCE (AKA PROFITEROLES)

How unfashionable profiteroles are now, but how much everyone loves them and how cheap and easy they are to make... I'm being upfront about the cocoa because it's a great substitute for – and often better than – chocolate.

SERVES 4–6

50g butter (preferably unsalted) cut into cubes
1 1/2–2 tbsp caster sugar
75g strong white flour sifted with a pinch of fine sea salt
2 large fresh free range eggs, lightly beaten
284ml double cream
a few drops of vanilla extract

For the cocoa sauce
175g caster sugar
50g cocoa powder

You will also need two lightly greased baking trays

Turn the oven to 220°C/425°F/Gas 7. To make the choux puffs, put the butter and 2 teaspoons of the caster sugar in a saucepan with 150ml water. Place the pan over a low heat until the butter and sugar have melted, then bring to the boil. Take off the heat, add the flour all at once and beat energetically with a wooden spoon until the dough comes away from the sides of the pan. Leave to cool for 5 minutes then beat in the eggs bit by bit until you have a stiff, glossy mixture. This process is much easier in a food processor.

Rinse the two baking trays with cold water, shaking off any excess so they are slightly damp (this helps the pastry rise). Using two teaspoons, spoon blobs of the mixture onto the baking trays then place in the oven and cook for about 18–20 minutes until well risen and brown. Remove the profiteroles from the oven and cut a small slit in the base of each one so they don't collapse. Cool on a wire rack.

When they're cold whip the cream lightly until just holding its shape and sweeten to taste with sugar and a few drops of vanilla extract. Cut the profiteroles in half, fill them with the sweetened cream and pile them up on a plate (you can refrigerate them for an hour or two at this point but not for any longer as the pastry will go soggy).

To make the sauce, sift the cocoa powder into a bowl. Put sugar in a pan with 150ml water and warm over a low heat until dissolved. Bring to the boil, cook for a minute then pour over the cocoa powder and stir well until smooth. Return the sauce to the pan, cook for a minute then set aside for 15 minutes before drizzling over the profiteroles.

VARIATIONS

Instead of sweetening the profiteroles add 50g of finely grated Gruyère or mature Cheddar cheese and serve them as a nibble with a glass of wine (i.e. gougères).

LEFTOVERS

The basic choux puffs can be frozen and reheated in a moderate oven.

THRIFTY TIP

Cocoa is a great alternative to chocolate for baking and desserts such as this.

HAZELNUT MERINGUE CAKE

Another delicious relic of the '70s updated from a very battered copy of *Cordon Bleu Desserts and Puddings* by Rosemary Hume and Muriel Downes (Penguin). Nowadays you don't even have to rub the hazelnut skins off (although it tastes fractionally better if you do).

125g skinned hazelnuts
4 egg whites at room temperature
250g caster sugar
a few drops of vanilla extract
$^{1}/_{2}$ tsp vinegar
150ml double cream
450g fresh or frozen raspberries
icing sugar to taste

You will also need two lightly oiled non-stick 20cm cake tins with the bases lined with baking parchment.

Put the nuts on a baking tray. Set the oven to 190°C/375°F/Gas 5 and roast the nuts until lightly browned (and smelling deliciously nutty) – about 10 minutes. Remove from the oven, leave to cool then pulse in a food processor until finely chopped but not powdery. Whisk the egg whites until just holding their shape then gradually beat in the caster sugar, a heaped tablespoon at a time, adding the vanilla extract and vinegar with the last addition. Fold in the finely chopped nuts and spoon the mixture into the prepared tins. Bake for 30–40 minutes until the meringue cakes are well risen and firm. Cool, then carefully remove the baking parchment.

Whizz half the raspberries in a food processor or blender and sieve into a bowl. Beat in sifted icing sugar to taste – about 4–5 tablespoons – and pour into a small glass jug. Whip the cream lightly and spread over the upturned base of one of the meringue cakes. Scatter over half the raspberries and carefully place the other half of the meringue 'cake' on top. Sift over a little icing sugar and serve with the raspberry sauce.

VARIATIONS

You could use toasted walnuts or pecans instead of hazelnuts or fill the cake with fresh peaches or nectarines.

THRIFTY TIP

Look up page 213 to see what you can do with the leftover egg yolks.

SUMMER PUDDING

This is adapted from one of my oldest cookbooks, the Penguin Freezer Cookbook. A perfect pudding to make in high summer when berries are at their best. You can vary the fruit depending on what you have available (see below) but you will need some dark fruits such as blackcurrants and blackberries for colour.

150g–175g stale white bread with the crusts removed
125g de-stalked blackcurrants
125g redcurrants or pitted cherries
125g blackberries
250g strawberries, hulled and halved or quartered
200g raspberries
200–225g unrefined granulated or caster sugar
thick pouring cream to serve

You will need a medium-sized pudding basin which will hold about 850ml (1½ pints) of liquid and a plate that fits into the top (see method).

Cut the bread into thin slices. Arrange round the base and sides of the basin leaving two or three slices for the lid. Put the sugar in a medium to large saucepan with 150ml water and place over a low heat until the sugar has dissolved. Bring to the boil without stirring, cook for a couple of minutes, then tip in the fruit, stir and cook for about 5 minutes or so until beginning to soften. Sweeten with an extra spoonful or two of sugar if you think it needs it.

Tip the hot fruit into the bread-lined basin and cover with the remaining bread slices. Put a plate over the top and weigh down with a weight or heavy tin. Cool, transfer to the fridge and leave overnight. To serve, carefully run a flat-bladed knife round the edge of the pudding, place a plate over the bowl and invert the pudding onto the plate. Serve with thick pouring cream.

VARIATIONS

You could include gooseberries in the fruit mix. You could also freeze the pudding (in which case you might want to make it in a foil basin but it will be slightly harder to line).

THRIFTY TIP

You could base this on a frozen summer fruits mix which can be cheaper than fresh fruit, even in season.

APPLE, BLACKBERRY AND NUT CRUMBLE

Freshly picked blackberries are free food at its best – a real seasonal treat.

SERVES 6

800g Bramley or other cooking apples
200g fresh or frozen blackberries, preferably wild
3–4 tbsp unrefined caster sugar

For the crumble topping
50g walnut pieces
125g plain flour
100g butter at fridge temperature
50g Demerara or unrefined caster sugar

Peel and core the apples and slice thickly into a large saucepan. Add the blackberries, 3 tablespoons of the sugar and 3 tablespoons of water, mix in lightly, cover and bring to the boil. Cook until the apple is tender but still holding its shape. Check for sweetness, adding more sugar if you think it needs it then set aside to cool for at least 30 minutes or until you are ready to cook the crumble. Meanwhile, break up the walnut pieces in a food processor, add the flour and the chilled butter cut into cubes and pulse until the mixture resembles large breadcrumbs. Add the sugar and process briefly, (if you do this by hand, chop the walnuts as finely as you can, rub the butter into the flour, then stir in the chopped walnuts and sugar). Transfer the cooked fruit to a medium to large, lightly greased pie dish or similar ovenproof dish and spoon the crumble mixture evenly over the top. Bake in a hot (200°C/400°F/Gas 6) oven for 30 minutes until the crumble is brown and the juices are beginning to bubble through. Serve with cream or custard.

VARIATIONS

You could reduce the cost still further by making this with windfall apples though you may need to adjust the quantity of sugar and water. If you haven't got any blackberries, increase the amount of apple, add a handful of raisins and mix a little cinnamon with the sugar. Other fruits such as rhubarb, plums and gooseberries are also great in a crumble. Or change the nuts in the topping. Almonds are good, for example.

LEFTOVERS

It's worth making extra fruit filling to save for a breakfast compôte (pages 47 and 55).

THRIFTY TIP

Broken walnut pieces are cheaper than buying walnut halves.

SUMMER FRUIT PAVLOVA

Pavlova might seem like a well-worn cliché but it's easy, frugal and delicious. What more do you want?

3 large egg whites
175g caster sugar plus 2–3 extra tsp for sweetening the cream
$^1/_2$–1 tsp vanilla extract or essence plus a few extra drops for the cream
$^3/_4$ tsp malt or wine vinegar
1 tsp cornflour
500g mixed berries such as strawberries, raspberries and blueberries
284ml carton of double cream
Grenadine (optional)

You will need some non-stick baking parchment

Pre-heat the oven to 150°C/300°F/Gas 2. Roll out the baking parchment. Take a large plate, turn it upside down on the paper and draw round it with a pencil or pen then cut round the circle you've made. Place it on a baking sheet. Whisk the egg whites in a deep bowl until just holding a peak. Gradually whisk in one third of the sugar then keep whisking until the mixture is very stiff and shiny. Fold in the remaining sugar, then finally fold in the vanilla essence, vinegar and cornflour (sieved over the top of the mixture to avoid lumps). Spoon the meringue onto the circle of paper hollowing out the centre slightly so the edges are higher than the middle. Bake for about 1 hour until the top is pale golden brown. When cool enough to handle (about 10 minutes) carefully peel off the baking parchment then leave to get completely cold.

Prepare the fruit, hulling and slicing the strawberries. Whip the cream lightly until holding its shape. Add $^1/_4$ tsp vanilla extract and 2 teaspoons of caster sugar and fold carefully into the cream. Spread half the cream over the pavlova, top with half the berries then spoon over the remaining cream and scatter the remaining berries over the top. Drizzle with a little grenadine if you have some.

VARIATIONS

You could top with other fruits such as peaches and passionfruit.

THRIFTY TIP

If you're using thawed frozen berries add them at the last minute before you take them to the table otherwise their juice will run all over the cream.

POACHED SALMON

Whole salmon is generally much cheaper than salmon fillets and makes an impressive centrepiece to a summer meal. If you're lucky you'll also get some leftovers for fishcakes or other recipes too. The ideal way to cook this is in a fish kettle but if you don't have or can't borrow one you could either halve the fish or bake it in foil. The advantage of this method though, which I first got from food writer Katie Stewart, is that it's so easy and keeps the fish beautifully moist. The salmon is fantastic served with the Cucumber and Herb Salad, opposite and the Mayonnaise Verte over the page.

SERVES 8–10

3–4 kg whole salmon, gutted and cleaned
2 tsp salt
a tablespoon of wine vinegar

Put the fish in the pan and cover with cold water. Remove the fish and bring the water to the boil. Add the salt and vinegar, return the salmon to the pan, bring back to the boil and boil hard for two minutes. Turn the heat off, cover the pan and leave the salmon until cold (this could take up to 12 hours so you could leave it overnight). Peel off the skin and carefully transfer the fish to a large platter. You could decorate it with fine cucumber slices rather than making an accompanying cucumber salad but I don't mind leaving it as it is. Serve with the green (or ordinary homemade) mayonnaise (over the page) and buttered new potatoes.

VARIATIONS

To bake the fish, turn the oven to 190°C/375°F/ Gas 5. Line a large roasting tin (one of the oven's own tins is most likely to fit best) with a double layer of foil and oil lightly with a neutral flavoured oil (e.g. sunflower oil). Place the salmon on top and stuff the cavity with a couple of slices of lemon and a handful of parsley. Splash over a half a small wine glass of dry white wine and loosely wrap the foil around the fish, pulling the edges of the foil together to create an airtight parcel. Bake for 40–50 minutes depending on the size of the fish then leave the fish to cool in the foil. Remove the skin and serve with Cucumber and Herb Salad (page 187) and Mayonnaise Verte (page 188).

THRIFTY TIP

Whole salmon are often on promotion in the early summer.

LEFTOVERS

Cooked salmon makes great fishcakes (see page 147) or you could combine it with pasta in a salad, with rice in a kedgeree or mix it with a little white sauce and some mushrooms or peas and asparagus and top it with a pastry lid for a salmon pot pie.

CUCUMBER AND HERB SALAD

A delicate and fresh-tasting salad that contrasts well with the richness of the salmon and with any accompanying mayonnaise.

SERVES 6

1 cucumber, peeled and finely sliced
2 tbsp white wine vinegar or Japanese seasoned
    rice vinegar
2 level tbsp scissor-snipped chives, chervil, dill or
    tarragon – or a mixture of these
caster sugar to taste (optional)
fine sea salt and freshly ground black pepper

Place the cucumber on a large flat dinner plate and sprinkle with a teaspoon of sea salt. Place another plate on top of the cucumber and weight it with a heavy tin or other weight. After about 30 minutes, drain off any liquid that has formed, rinse the cucumber and pat dry with kitchen towel. Place in a shallow dish, dress with the vinegar and sugar if using (you may not need it with the Japanese rice vinegar), and mix well. Season with freshly ground black pepper and extra salt and sugar to taste.

VARIATIONS

If you're not making mayonnaise you could add a little cream or Greek yoghurt to this salad.

THRIFTY TIP

Watch out for cucumber prices. It's one of the staples on which supermarkets often over-charge.

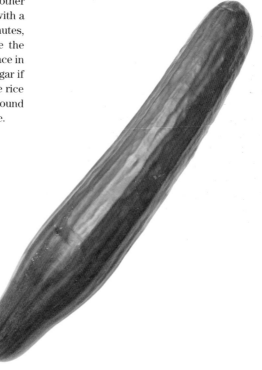

MAYONNAISE VERTE

This is the classic French way of making a green mayonnaise by hand. You can save time by making it in a food processor, adding the oil slowly to begin with and speeding up as it thickens or doctor shop-bought mayonnaise as suggested below.

40g watercress or watercress and spinach leaves
5g chopped chervil or parsley leaves
2g tarragon leaves
4 medium or 3 large egg yolks at room temperature
1 tsp Dijon mustard
1 tbsp white wine vinegar or tarragon vinegar
575ml oil at room temperature (I usually use $^1/_3$ olive oil to $^2/_3$ of a neutral oil such as sunflower or grapeseed oil)
salt, freshly ground black pepper and lemon juice to taste

Wash the watercress and spinach leaves if using and put in a pan with the water that is still clinging to the leaves. Cover the pan and put on a very low heat until the leaves collapse. Add the chervil or parsley and tarragon, stir and leave off the heat for a minute. Strain the leaves and leave to cool.

Put the egg yolks in a bowl with the mustard, salt, pepper and a teaspoon of vinegar. Whisk well. Start to add the oil, drop by drop, whisking all the time then once the mixture begins to thicken, increase the speed at which you add the oil to a thin stream. You can speed up as the mixture becomes thicker. Add a few drops of vinegar from time to time along with the oil – you may not need the whole amount.

Squeeze the blanched leaves and chop them as finely as you can (or pass through a sieve) then fold the purée into the mayonnaise. Adjust the seasoning with salt, pepper and lemon juice.

VARIATIONS

You can create a much simpler herb mayonnaise by finely chopping a mixture of fresh herbs such as dill, parsley and tarragon and adding them to some shop-bought French-style mayonnaise.

LEFTOVERS

Make a pavlova with the whites. Save the watercress and herb stalks for soup (see page 78).

THRIFTY TIP

Creating your own oil mix from a decent quality olive oil and an inexpensive neutral oil is much better value than buying a basic olive oil.

BEER-CAN CHICKEN

I'm not including this just because it's frugal but because it's the best way I know of roasting chicken. And the most fun.

SERVES 4–6

1 small to medium-sized chicken – about 1.3–1.5kg (3lb–3lb 5 oz)
about 1 tbsp jerk seasoning or other spicy rub
a little oil
1 330ml can of lager

You will need a barbecue with a high-domed lid

Rinse the chicken inside and out and dry thoroughly with kitchen towel. Remove any surplus fat from the carcass and sprinkle the inside of the chicken with about 1 teaspoon of the rub, rubbing it in well. Rub a little of the oil into the chicken skin, sprinkle the remaining rub over the rest of the chicken and rub it in. Fire up the barbecue. Pour half the contents of the beer can into a glass. Lightly oil the can and lower the chicken onto the can so that it stands upright propped up by its legs (yes, it does look ludicrous...). Lay the can and chicken carefully on the barbecue rack then cover and cook over an indirect heat for about 50 minutes to an hour until the juices run clear when you pierce the leg with a skewer. Holding the can with a pair of tongs very carefully remove chicken from the can and transfer to a carving tray. Rest for 5–10 minutes then carve and serve with a barbecue sauce or a salsa.

VARIATIONS

You could use other types of dry rub – or none at all and simply season your bird with salt and pepper. It'll still taste good.

THRIFTY TIP

The beer you use doesn't make a massive difference to this. The small cans of own brand German or Belgian lager are good value.

MOROCCAN-STYLE LAMB WITH DATES, PRUNES AND APRICOTS

A gorgeously rich, sweet tagine that makes a brilliant centrepiece for a supper party. Make it a day ahead – in a slow cooker if you have one – for minimum last-minute hassle.

SERVES 8–10

5–6 lamb knuckles (about 2kg meat in total)
pinch of saffron (optional – good if you have some)
600ml hot chicken or vegetable stock
2 tbsp light olive or sunflower oil
2 medium onions, peeled and roughly chopped
2 carrots, peeled and sliced
1 clove of garlic
1 tbsp Moroccan Spice Mix (see page 27) or
   1 rounded tsp each of ground cumin and ground coriander, $^1/_2$ rounded tsp turmeric and $^1/_4$ tsp hot paprika or chilli power
1 cinnamon stick or 1 tsp ground cinnamon
2 tbsp passata or juice from a tin of tomatoes
250g mixed dried fruit including prunes, apricots and dates, larger pieces cut into half
2 sprigs of fresh thyme or 1 tsp dried thyme, marjoram or oregano
1 small to medium (125–150ml) glass of red wine or stock
2 heaped tbsp chopped parsley or coriander
salt and freshly ground black pepper

With a sharp knife trim any obvious excess fat off the lamb knuckles, (don't worry too much, you're skimming the stew later on). Infuse the saffron, if using, in the hot stock. Heat the oil in a deep frying pan or sauté pan and fry the onions and carrots over a low heat until starting to soften. Add the garlic and spices, stir, then stir in the passata and stock. Add the lamb knuckles, mixed fruit and thyme and bring slowly to the boil then turn the heat right down and simmer for about $2^1/_2$ hours or until the meat is tender. The liquid probably won't cover the meat at this stage so you may need to turn the lamb knuckles every half hour or so. Cool the stew, removing the meat and bigger chunks of vegetable before it's completely cold. Chill the liquid then skim off the fat. Cut the meat off the bones, removing any remaining skin or connective tissue, cut into large chunks, and return to the pan along with the skimmed liquid and a glass of red wine or stock. Reheat gently. Season with salt and pepper and an extra pinch of cinnamon if you think it needs it. Serve with roast carrots and parsnips seasoned with crushed coriander seeds and Crunchy Almond Couscous (make up couscous in the normal way then fork through almonds fried in butter – about 50g of almonds to 250g of couscous).

VARIATIONS

Although quite un-Moroccan this would also be good made with pork shoulder which would cut the meat cooking time by about half an hour. You could also add extra root veg such as carrots turnips and parsnips to extend the meat. Part-cook them and add them to the stew when you reheat it

LEFTOVERS

Heats up well the next day. And freezes for up to a month. Use any leftover dried fruits for a compôte (see page 55).

THRIFTY TIP

Knuckles, if you can find them, are cheaper than lamb shanks, particularly if you buy them direct from the producer.

PERSIAN CHICKEN

This terrific one-pot dish was inspired by one of my favourite cookery books, *Persia in Peckham* by Sally Butcher (Prospect Books). The original contained lamb and beans but when I realised I was cooking almost nothing but lamb for this book I decided to adapt it to chicken. And made a few other changes, as you do. What you can't do without are the dried limes (available from middle-eastern grocers or by mail order from Sally's shop Persepolis) and ridiculously large amounts of herbs (so no use buying them in a supermarket). This makes a great meal for sophisticates who have been everywhere and eaten everything. The tangy lemon and herb flavours are really quite unique. And incredibly addictive.

SERVES 6–8

8 chicken thighs, ideally still on the bone
1 large onion, peeled and roughly chopped
3 large cloves of garlic, peeled and roughly chopped
4–6 dried limes (depending on size) washed and pierced in several places with a skewer or sharp knife
about 1 litre cold chicken stock, either homemade or made with an organic stock cube
1–1 1/2 tsp ground turmeric
8 waxy small to medium-sized potatoes (about 500–600g) quartered or cut into eight
2 tbsp oil
a large bunch of chives or spring onion tops (the green bits), finely sliced
a bunch of spinach
a good-sized bunch each of parsley and coriander
yoghurt, finely sliced onion and hot pepper sauce, to serve

Remove the skin from the chicken thighs and put them in a large casserole or sauté pan. Add the onion, garlic and dried limes, cover with stock and sprinkle over a good teaspoon of turmeric. Bring slowly to the boil then turn the heat down and simmer for 20 minutes. Add the potatoes and continue to cook until tender. Meanwhile, wash the herbs and spinach thoroughly, removing the tougher stalks and chop roughly. Heat the oil in a frying pan, add the onion and herbs and spinach and fry them quickly until they wilt. Tip them into the stew, stir, put the lid back on and cook for another 10–15 minutes. Season to taste with salt and pepper. Traditionally, this type of dish would be served with boiled basmati rice but you could serve it with couscous. Good accompaniments are plain yoghurt, very finely sliced onion and hot chilli sauce.

VARIATIONS

You could add some cauliflower florets or runner beans to the stew instead of – or as well as – the potatoes or add a drained can of chickpeas.

LEFTOVERS

Remove the meat from any remaining chicken pieces, chop up and return to the pan. Serve as a soup, adding a little more stock and some more fresh herbs.

THRIFTY TIP

Go to a middle-eastern or Asian grocer to buy your herbs and greens. Far cheaper than your local supermarket.

CHARGRILLED CHICKEN, PEPPER AND HERB COUSCOUS SALAD

What to do with any leftover chicken. In fact it's almost worth grilling more than you need just so that you can make it.

SERVES 4–6

5 tbsp olive oil
2 tbsp pinenuts (optional)
1 onion, peeled and finely chopped
1 clove of garlic, peeled and crushed
250g instant couscous
400ml vegetable stock (or whatever quantity the couscous pack recommends)
1–1 $\frac{1}{2}$ tbsp wine vinegar or lemon juice
1 chargrilled chicken breast or a couple of barbecued legs, cut into strips
leftover grilled peppers, courgettes, tomatoes and aubergines, diced
3 heaped tbsp chopped fresh herbs such as fresh basil, tarragon, chervil parsley or coriander
salt and pepper

Heat 2 tablespoons of the oil in a small frying pan, add the pinenuts and fry for 30 seconds or so until lightly browned. Remove from the pan with a slotted spoon and set aside. Add the onion, stir, turn the heat up a little and fry until the edges of the onion start turning brown (about 5–6 minutes). Meanwhile make up the couscous, following the instructions on the pack but don't add any oil. When the onions are brown, take them off the heat and stir in the garlic, then tip them and the pinenuts into the couscous, fork through and leave to cool. Make the dressing by whisking the vinegar or lemon juice with the remaining oil and season to taste with salt and pepper. When the couscous has cooled down add the chopped up chicken and vegetables, the dressing and herbs and toss together. Serve straightaway.

VARIATIONS

You could also add some roasted corn kernels to the recipe.

LEFTOVERS

If you've already made a couscous salad to go with your barbecue you could simply mix in the chopped leftover chicken and vegetables, a splash of dressing and a few herbs.

THRIFTY TIP

If you have some leftover green pesto you could add that to the dressing.

I remember when I was a child my parents were always asking people 'round for a drink'. And they meant literally that (with a few nuts and cheesy biscuits thrown in). There was no expectation that people would stay for the rest of the evening or need to be given supper.

Nowadays, having people 'round for a drink' seems to involve the kind of elaborate canapés that you would at one time only have been able to provide if you had caterers but can now buy straight from the chill cabinets at Marks and Spencer and Waitrose. And I don't need to tell you that they don't come cheap.

The fact is however that people are perfectly happy with much simpler fare. Who can resist honey-glazed sausages on sticks? Or crumbly homemade cheese straws? What's wrong with handing round a few crostini or crackers topped with a thrifty but delicious spread like the mushroom caviar or smoked mackerel pâté overleaf? Even the much-maligned chips and dips deserve to be resurrected, if updated a tad for today's healthier lifestyle. I don't know anyone who doesn't enjoy eating tortilla chips dunked in a zesty fresh tomato salsa (page 83). Or warm pitta bread strips with homemade hummus (152) come to that.

If you genuinely want to cut down the amount you spend on entertaining you need to set some parameters. Like 'come round for a quick drink' or 'drop in for a coffee' rather than an open-ended invitation to eat you out of house and home.

For a bigger party give your guests an idea just when you expect them to drop by – say from 6pm–8pm and underline what's on offer whether it's beer and sausages (a good idea for a cheap party) or sherry and tapas (which needn't amount to much more than olives, nuts and a few chunks of chorizo and cheese). Just limit the invitation in some way.

HOMEMADE CHEDDAR STRAWS

I got the recipe for these cheese straws from chef Paul Hayes who was the chef at my son's pub The Marquess Tavern. They look so wonderfully rustic that no-one would mistake them for the shop-bought version. A great way to use up leftover Cheddar.

SERVES 6-8

150g plain flour
$^1/_4$ tsp cayenne pepper
$^1/_4$ tsp English mustard powder
a pinch of sea salt
100g chilled, unsalted butter, cut into cubes
150g strong, mature farmhouse Cheddar, coarsely grated
1 egg yolk
2 tbsp water

Sift the flour with the cayenne pepper, mustard and salt and tip into a bowl. Cut in the butter and rub through the flour with your finger tips as if you were making pastry. Add the cheese and cut and rub in thoroughly. Beat the egg yolk with the water and add just enough to the mix to enable you to pull it together and shape into a flat disc. Wrap in clingfilm and refrigerate for 30 minutes then take out and allow to come back to room temperature. Preheat the oven to 190°C/375°F/Gas 5. Roll out the dough thinly then cut into long strips about 2–3cm (1 inch) wide and 30cm (12 inches) in length. Using a palate knife, lay the strips carefully on a couple of lightly oiled baking sheets and bake for about 12–15 minutes until golden brown. Leave on the trays for 10 minutes then transfer them to a wire rack to finish cooling.

VARIATIONS

You could make these with other regional British hard cheeses such as Lancashire or Red Leicester or a mixture of cheeses.

LEFTOVERS

Can be stored in an airtight tin and refreshed in a moderate oven before serving.

THRIFTY TIP

Tail-end pieces of hard cheese can be grated and frozen until you have enough to make this recipe.

MUSHROOM CAVIAR

A deceptively simple recipe with a sophisticated taste from my favourite local restaurant Culinaria. Perfect to pass around with pre-dinner drinks – then skip the starter.

ENOUGH FOR 6–8

2 shallots or I small onion, peeled and roughly chopped
I clove of garlic, peeled and chopped
350g button mushrooms, wiped clean and quartered
3 tbsp sunflower oil
200g tub of crème fraîche
2 tbsp finely chopped tarragon leaves
salt and pepper and a good squeeze of lemon juice

Put the onion and garlic in the bowl of your food processor and pulse until finely chopped. Heat the oil over a low heat in a medium to large heavy bottomed saucepan or frying pan and cook the onion and garlic gently until starting to soften (about 4–5 minutes). Chop the mushrooms very finely in the food processor and tip into the pan with the onions. Stir and cook over a very low heat, stirring occasionally, for about 30 minutes until the mushrooms have the consistency of a thick paste. Take off the heat, stir in the crème fraîche and return to the pan until the mixture has thickened again (about another 15 minutes).

Stir in the chopped tarragon and season to taste with salt, pepper and a good squeeze of lemon juice. Tip into a bowl, trickle over a tablespoon or so of good olive oil to stop the surface from discolouring, and refrigerate. Bring to cool room temperature before spreading on crostini (below).

FOR THE CROSTINI

While I reckon ciabatta is normally a bit pricey, it's perfect for crostini bases.

MAKES ABOUT 30–32 SLICES

2 ready-to-bake ciabatta loaves
olive oil spray or 4–6 tbsp light olive oil
2 baking trays

Preheat the oven to 180°C/350°F/Gas 4. Cut the ciabatta on the slant into fairly thin slices. Spray both sides with olive oil or pour the olive oil on the baking trays and dip the slices of ciabatta in it. Bake for 15 minutes, turning the slices half way through. Repeat with any remaining ciabatta slices. Cool then store the toasts in an airtight tin.

VARIATIONS

You could add dill rather than tarragon.

THRIFTY TIP

Buy mushrooms loose rather than pre-packed.

SMOKED MACKEREL PÂTÉ

An inexpensive but really delicious dip based on smoked mackerel and the light, healthy German cheese Quark.

SERVES 8

250g smoked mackerel
250g Quark or sieved cottage cheese
4 tbsp mayonnaise
3–4 tbsp lemon juice
4 tbsp roughly chopped fresh parsley
a few drops of Tabasco or a pinch of cayenne
    pepper
freshly ground black pepper

With a knife and fork slip the mackerel off its skin and flake it roughly. Put in a food processor with the Quark or sieved cottage cheese, mayonnaise, lemon juice and pulse until the ingredients are amalgamated. Add the parsley and whizz briefly again. Check the seasoning adding more lemon juice if you think it needs it, a little black pepper and some Tabasco or cayenne pepper if you want to spice it up a bit. Tip into a bowl and refrigerate until ready to use. Serve on wholewheat or spelt crackers.

VARIATIONS

You could try substituting cooked kipper fillets but nothing works quite as well as smoked mackerel.

THRIFTY TIP

Quark is a really good value soft cheese which also makes a good basis for cheesecakes.

What on earth is it about Christmas that makes us panic-buy? You'd think the shops were closing for a month rather than for a couple of days.

Maybe it's some primitive instinct to provide for our families. More probably, we haven't the faintest idea what we need and get caught up in the collective hysteria. Whatever – you can probably cut your shopping bill in half.

HOW TO SURVIVE CHRISTMAS
WITHOUT BLOWING THE BUDGET

Even if you don't normally write a menu plan I'd urge you to do so for Christmas. Working out what you actually need not what you might need if the entire neighbourhood camped out on your doorstep for the next fortnight. Look up what size turkey and Christmas pudding you need unless you still want to be eating it in January. In fact, pass on the Christmas pudding if nobody actually likes it and make something like a French chocolate 'buche' (yule log) instead. Do this in time so that you don't end up having to rush round the supermarket on Christmas Eve manically scooping up anything edible. Try and put a couple of dishes like a casserole, lasagne or a fish pie in the freezer so that you've got something available if unexpected guests drop by. Ask yourself if you really need a whole, or even half, a Stilton or endless packets of nuts and dried fruits. Not to mention enough booze to sink a cross-channel ferry... Make a list, take it with you to the shops or supermarket and stick to it!

You'll find suggestions for many Christmas ingredients within the A–Z of Ingredients and Leftovers (pages 203–225), but over these next few pages I've included some leftover ideas to get you started: ones that might particularly appeal to a jaded palate.

TURKEY

You'll find many of the suggestions for using up leftover chicken work for turkey, but here's a star recipe from my friend and cookery writer Andrea Leeman. Posh enough to serve for a post-Christmas dinner party.

TURKEY AND TARRAGON TERRINE

SERVES 6

500g chunks of cooked turkey or turkey and ham
1 tbsp chopped tarragon
1 tbsp shelled pistachio nuts, roughly chopped
4 tbsp dry or medium dry sherry or montilla
6 sheets of gelatine (or whatever amount is
    recommended to set 584ml/1 pint of liquid)
425ml strained turkey or chicken stock
6 tbsp mayonnaise
6 tsp grain mustard

Can be moulded in a 900g loaf tin, 6 ramekins or a 2 pint china pudding bowl.

Remove the skin and any gristly bits from the turkey (and ham, if using), and cut into largeish chunks about 2cm square. Put the sherry into a shallow dish, add the gelatine and rest for about 10 minutes until the gelatine softens. Heat the turkey stock, remove from the stove and stir in the gelatine until dissolved. Leave to cool for 30 minutes. Pour half the stock into the loaf tin or ramekins, add half the turkey, tarragon and pistachio nuts and refrigerate until it just begins to set. Add the remaining half of the ingredients and refrigerate for a further few hours. Mix the mayonnaise with grain mustard to taste. To turn out the terrine, dip the container(s) briefly into hot water and invert on a plate(s). Good with wholemeal toast or jacket potatoes and salad.

HAM

Can also be used in the terrine above or try the ham and parsley pâté and other suggestions on page 215.

VEG SUCH AS CARROTS, CELERY AND PARSNIPS

Large batches of homemade soup will use up most of these but take care what you combine with what or you may end up with an unappealing sludge. You can also roast a big tin of cut up root veg. Or make an invigorating slaw.

SPROUTS

Can't beat Bubble and Squeak!

BUBBLE AND SQUEAK

SERVES 4–6

About 500g each of cold boiled potatoes and
  cooked sprouts or cabbage
1 tbsp olive oil
20g butter
salt and freshly ground black pepper

Roughly chop up the potato and sprouts, mix together and season generously with salt and pepper. Heat a large frying pan over a moderate heat, add the oil, heat for a minute then add the butter. Tip in the potato and cabbage mix and flatten into a cake with a fork or a spatula. Let it cook for about 3–4 minutes then start to turn it over. Keep turning it every few minutes until the crispy bits on the bottom of the pan get well mixed in to the hash – about 8–10 minutes in all.

SMOKED SALMON

Unlikely to be a problem getting rid of this but offcuts and scraps can be whizzed into a tasty spread with cream cheese and flavoured with a little lemon rind or juice and chopped chives or dill.

CRANBERRIES

Use to make a crumble or the compôte below.

CRANBERRY, RASPBERRY AND APPLE COMPOTE

SERVES 4

500g pack of cranberries
250g pack of frozen raspberries
3–4 medium eating apples, quartered, peeled and
  cut into chunks
4–5 tbsp unrefined caster sugar
2–3 tbsp sloe gin or late bottled vintage port
  (optional)

Wash and pick over the cranberries, removing any that are bruised or damaged. Put them in a pan with the frozen raspberries, apple and 4 tablespoons of sugar. Add 4–5 tablespoons of water and slowly bring to the boil. Simmer until the fruits are soft. Add sloe gin to taste and more sugar if you think it needs it. Leave to cool then pour into a glass dish. Serve with cream.

CHRISTMAS PUDDING

Microwaves really well. Restores its texture.

CHRISTMAS CAKE

Cut off the icing and marzipan (nibble instead of sweets) and serve fingers of cake with a strong Cheddar.

MINCE PIES

Can be smashed up and folded into softened vanilla ice cream then refrozen as a mince pie crumble ice cream (obviously this whole process needs to take place quickly so you don't run any health risks).

MINCEMEAT

Add a little water, fruit juice or brandy and use as an ice cream sauce. Mix with chopped apples or oranges and make a mincemeat tart or pie.

CHESTNUTS

Leftover chestnuts can be stir-fried with bacon and sprouts or combined with lentils as in the luxurious soup below. Sweetened chestnut purée can be mixed with cream and melted chocolate and used to sandwich meringues.

CHESTNUT AND LENTIL SOUP

A great way to use up your turkey stock so that it doesn't taste like turkey stock. You don't have to peel your own chestnuts but they do taste better.

SERVES 6–8
450g whole chestnuts or 350g ready-prepared
  chestnuts
4 tbsp light olive oil
I large leek, washed, trimmed and finely sliced or
  2 medium onions, peeled and chopped
I large carrot (about 110g), peeled and finely diced
I stick of celery, trimmed and finely sliced
  (optional)
I clove of garlic, peeled and crushed
I level tsp sweet pimenton or sweet paprika
1.5–1.75 litres turkey, duck, ham, chicken or game
  stock
175g whole brown or green lentils
2 tbsp montilla, Madeira, dry marsala or
  amontillado sherry (optional)
1/2–I tsp Worcestershire sauce or dark soy sauce
10g butter
100ml whipping cream
salt and freshly ground black pepper

Wash the chestnuts and make a cut with a sharp knife in the curved side of each one. Put in a saucepan of boiling water, bring back to the boil and boil for 3 minutes. Turn the heat off and remove the chestnuts two at a time, letting them cool a few seconds then peeling off both the hard outer shell and inner brown papery skin. If they become harder to peel, bring the water back to the boil again. Chop the chestnuts roughly, saving a few to decorate the soup.

Heat the oil in a large saucepan, add the leek, carrot and celery, stir well and cook over a moderate heat until the vegetables start to soften (about 5–6 minutes). Stir in the crushed garlic and pimenton or paprika and cook for a minute then add the chopped chestnuts and 1 litre of the stock and bring to the boil. Rinse the lentils and add them to the vegetables then cook for about 35–40 minutes until the vegetables are soft. Cool for 10 minutes then pass the soup in batches through a blender or food processor, using some of the remaining stock to blitz up the last remaining bits of soup in the blender. Return all the soup and the remaining stock to the pan, add the montilla, Madeira or sherry and reheat gently. Add more stock if necessary and season with salt, freshly ground black pepper and a dash of Worcestershire sauce or soy sauce if you feel it needs it. To serve, roughly chop the remaining chestnuts and fry in a little butter. Season the cream with salt and pepper and whip lightly. Serve the soup with a spoonful of whipped cream and a few fried chestnut pieces sprinkled over.

STILTON

Make potted Stilton by mashing 3 parts Stilton with 1 part softened butter, adding a little mustard and a splash of port (preferably tawny as Late Bottled Vintage will turn it a sickly pink) and seasoning it with freshly ground black pepper. Good with toast and crackers. See also Linguine with Stilton and Onion (page 110), and Blue Cheese Butter (page 210).

PORT

Use up in mulled wine. (Unless it's vintage port, obviously).

SATSUMAS AND CLEMENTINES

Peel, removing as much of the pith as possible, then slice horizontally into thin slices and cover with sugar syrup (made by dissolving sugar in an equal quantity of water, bringing to the boil and boiling for 2–3 minutes and cooling). A few drops of orange flower water will make it taste even better.

A–Z OF INGREDIENTS AND LEFTOVERS

SOMETIMES I THINK I PREFER TO COOK FROM LEFTOVERS THAN FRESH INGREDIENTS. IT REQUIRES MORE CREATIVITY YET LESS IS EXPECTED OF YOU. IF YOU MANAGE TO CONJURE UP A MEAL FROM NEXT TO NOTHING EVERYONE IS WILDLY IMPRESSED. AND YOU HAVE A SMUG FEELING OF SATISFACTION AT ALL THE MONEY YOU'VE SAVED.

ANCHOVIES

Can be used to top pizzas, added to a salade Niçoise with tuna, eggs and green beans or added to a pasta sauce such as the punchy puttanesca (garlic, olives, capers, anchovies and parsley). Dissolved in a pan with a little oil they also add a mysterious smoky flavour to a creamy pasta sauce. Save any leftover oil for drizzling over pizza.

APPLES

Although cooking apples like Bramleys are the best for making apple pies, crumbles or tart apple sauces (*see* opposite), you can cook with many eating apples too. Try adding chopped or grated apple to scones (page 162), make an apple cake or simply pan-fry some sliced apple in butter and sugar or honey and top with yoghurt or crème fraîche for a quick, tasty dessert.

Eating apples work well in savoury salads especially with celery, ham, cheese and nuts. Grate a little apple into a shop-bought coleslaw to zip it up. Add some to your breakfast muesli.

If you have a glut, make chutney or juice with carrots for an invigorating start to the day. Or make a batch of apple compôte or apple sauce which you can freeze.

APPLE AND CINNAMON COMPÔTE FOR 4–5

Quarter, peel and core 3 large Bramley or other cooking apples (about 700g) and slice thickly into a large saucepan. Sprinkle with 2–3 tablespoons of unrefined caster sugar and $^1/_4$ teaspoon cinnamon and add 3 tablespoons of water. Put a lid on the pan, put over a moderate heat and cook for about 10–15 minutes until the apples have broken down. Stir with a wooden spoon and cool. You could replace some of the apple with other fruit such as blackberries, raspberries or frozen mixed berries, in which case you may want to leave out the cinnamon.

APPLE AND ONION SAUCE

Similar ingredients to the above without the sugar or cinnamon. Soften a chopped onion (and a couple of chopped sage leaves if you have them) in melted butter then add the sliced apple and water and cook as above. Season with salt and pepper. Good with pork or sausages.

APPLE LEMONADE

Don't discard the apple peel when you make a pie or crumble. Put it in a saucepan along with a couple of leftover lemon shells, cover with water, bring to the boil and simmer for 20 minutes. Add sugar to taste then leave it to cool. Strain and refrigerate.

ASPARAGUS

The main thing is not to waste half the spears. Although the bottom quarter can be woody the middle section is fine for salads, soups, pasta and risotto dishes and stir-fries. If it's nearing the end of the season you may need to peel them first with a vegetable peeler. Asparagus has an affinity with all kinds of seafood especially crab, prawns and salmon and with eggs and goat's cheese.

AUBERGINES

Slice and spray lightly with olive oil, and roast in a hot oven or cook in a ridged grill pan or on a barbecue. Can be used for salads or sandwich fillings. Can also be roasted whole and combined with olive oil and spices for a smoky middle-eastern spread (*baba ganoush*). Aubergines go well with cooked tomatoes, Mozzarella, cumin and coriander.

AVOCADOS

Great added to salsas (*see* page 83) and salads, especially with seafood such as prawns and crab. Ripe avocados that are about to go over can be whizzed up into a cold soup or guacamole (though remove any blackened sections which will affect the colour of the finished dish).

MEXICAN-STYLE GUACAMOLE

Peel 3 medium-sized avocados and scoop their flesh into a large bowl, removing any black bits. Mash with a fork until you have a chunky paste. Pour over 2 tablespoons of lime juice then mix in 3 heaped tablespoons of finely chopped onion, a small green chilli, de-seeded and finely chopped, a large clove of garlic crushed with $\frac{1}{4}$ teaspoon salt and 1 tablespoons of olive oil. Season with black pepper and extra salt if you think it needs it. Stir in 2–3 tablespoons of finely chopped fresh coriander and a couple of chopped, skinned, de-seeded tomatoes if you have some. Cover closely with clingfilm to exclude any air and refrigerate until ready to serve, but don't make it more than a couple of hours in advance. Serve with tortilla chips.

BACON

Everyone knows what to do with a decent amount of bacon, it's the odd rasher that might pose problems. Another reason (apart from the cost) to favour streaky over lean – it can be fried crisp and added to sandwiches, salads, scones and muffins. An odd rasher or offcuts can also be chopped and fried to give flavour to stews, pulses and pasta sauces such as the classic carbonara. Adding a spoonful of sweet or hot paprika to bacon is a good substitute for chorizo.

BANANAS

Just-ripe bananas can be fried up with a little butter, brown sugar and rum or bourbon for an indulgent dessert or baked on the barbecue. Once they're very ripe they're best used for smoothies or baking as banana bread, cake or muffins (*see* Banana Chiffon Cake, page 160). Or, even simpler, mash them with a little brown sugar or honey and drizzle over a little cream. You can freeze them if you think they're about to go over but they will go quite soft as they thaw. Bananas go particularly well with chocolate, nuts, orange, strawberries, blueberries, yoghurt, cream and vanilla.

BASIL

Doesn't keep well so best made into pesto if you can't use it within a couple of days. **Goes well with** tomatoes, Mozzarella, olive oil, Parmesan and Cheddar. Add a few leaves to a pizza topping or salad.

FRESH PESTO
Cut up 50g of mature Parmesan or Grana Padano and put it in a food processor. Add 50g of pinenuts and a finely chopped small clove of garlic and pulse/process in short bursts until the mixture is the consistency of large breadcrumbs. Add two large handfuls of fresh basil leaves and process briefly then gradually add olive oil until you have a thick paste. Tip into a bowl and season with freshly ground black pepper, a small squeeze of lemon and a little salt and some more olive oil if you think it needs it.

BEANS

Fresh green beans can be added to stir-fries and chunky vegetable soups such as minestrone. Lightly blanched, they can be added to salads such as salade Niçoise or to a mixed bean or tomato salad.

Cooked skinned broad beans are a decorative and tasty addition to salads, pasta dishes and risottos. You could also cook them, unskinned, with garlic and bacon, ham or chorizo as a tasty tapas. Canned beans such as cannelini beans or flageolets can also be added to soups or stews or whizzed up with some crushed garlic and a little stock for a tasty, hummus-style spread.

BEEF

It's hard to beat cold roast beef served rare, but more well-cooked leftovers can be incorporated in a cottage pie (preferably with some added fresh mince – *see* page 137) or spicy beef hash. Beef **goes well with** onions, carrots, tomatoes, mushrooms, red wine, beer, garlic, soy, Worcestershire sauce, chilli and blue cheese.

BEER

In the unlikely event you have some leftover, a good robust beer makes a great addition to a gravy (page 219) or stew, or can be used as a marinade for dried fruit (*see* Barm Brack, page 161). Unlike wine it won't keep for more than 24 hours once opened though.

BEETROOT

Scrub clean, oil lightly and wrap loosely in foil and roast in a moderate oven for about an hour until tender. Peel and slice or cut into wedges to add to a salad such as the one on page 59. Raw beetroot can be used raw in a borscht (Russian beetroot soup), mixed with carrot in a slaw or roasted along with other root vegetables.

Don't throw away the leaves which can be cooked in the same way as spinach or chard. **Goes well with** goat's cheese, yoghurt, hummus chives, fennel, walnuts and walnut oil, carrots and orange.

BLUEBERRIES

Can be used along with other berries in a fresh fruit compôte or cheesecake or tart topping. Good for baking in muffins, crumbles, cobblers (page 154), etc., as they hold their shape well (frozen blueberries are often cheaper than fresh). Blueberries go well with other berries such as raspberries, strawberries and cherries, with peaches and nectarines and creamy desserts.

BREAD

Undoubtedly one of the most useful leftover ingredients so long as you buy a loaf with some substance, texture and keeping quality. Sliced two or three day old bread makes a good base for simple snacks (*see* toast toppings pages 60, 61 and 63), great toasted sandwiches such as Croque Monsieur (*see* below) and quick breakfast or teatime treats such as cinnamon toast and French toast (*see* page 53). It's also a classic base for inexpensive desserts such as bread pudding, bread and butter pudding and Summer Pudding (page 82).You can also use roughly torn bread to stretch meatballs (*see* page 138) or to make a rustic Tuscan-style panzanella salad.

CINNAMON TOAST

A great winter tea-time snack. Pop a couple of slices of white bread under the grill. Turn and lightly grill the other side. Spread with soft butter and sprinkle with cinnamon sugar. Put back under the grill until bubbling.

CROQUE MONSIEUR

A French-style ham and cheese toastie dipped in beaten egg mixed with a splash of milk or cream then pan-fried in butter.

CIABATTA AND BAGUETTES

CROSTINI BASES

Although this is a good way to use up leftover ciabatta or baguette it's almost worth starting from scratch just to make these incredibly useful bases for pre-dinner nibbles. Pre-heat the oven to 180°C/350°F/Gas 4. Cut the ciabatta or baguette into thin slices, about 1 cm thick. Spray both sides with an olive oil spray or pour some olive oil on a baking tray and dip the slices of bread in it. Bake for 15 minutes, turning the slices half way through. Repeat with any remaining bread slices. Cool, then store the crostini in an airtight tin for up to a week.

CROÛTONS

Similar to crostini but need to be baked longer (and possibly cut smaller) if you're making them for soup, like the classic French onion soup. Follow the method above but cook at a slightly lower temperature (160°C/325°F/Gas 3) and for about 10–15 minutes longer. You can make nice crunchy croûtons for a salad by spraying cut up bread crusts (or pitta breads) with oil and dry-frying them in a frying pan until crisp.

GARLIC BREAD (ENOUGH FOR 6–8)

Heat the oven to 200°C/400°F/Gas 6. Cut 1 large or 2 medium day-old baguettes or French sticks in thick diagonal slices without cutting right through the loaf (i.e. leave it attached at the base). Mash 125g soft butter with a wooden spoon until creamy then add 4 cloves of crushed garlic, 4 tablespoons of parsley and season with salt and pepper. Spread the butter generously on either side of the cuts you've made. Wrap the bread in foil and bake for 10 minutes. Loosen the foil and replace in the oven for another 5 minutes to brown and crisp the top.

BREADCRUMBS

TO MAKE FRESH BREADCRUMBS
Use two- to three-day-old bread that has dried slightly. Cut away the crusts (which you can use for croûtons if not too hard – *see* above) and cut the remaining bread into cubes. Whizz them in batches in a liquidiser or food processor until fine then use as follows or transfer to plastic bags and freeze (invaluable for gratin toppings, stuffings, dumplings, meatballs, classic English puddings such as Queen of Puddings (page 156) and treacle tart. *See also* Danish Apple Charlotte (page 157) and Spaghetti with Breadcrumbs (page 111).

BREAD SAUCE
A Christmas classic but great with roast chicken at any time of year. Peel and halve a medium onion. Stick two cloves in each half, place them in a small saucepan with a bayleaf, pour over 300ml ($\frac{1}{2}$ pint) of milk and heat until just below boiling point. Turn the heat down to a bare simmer and cook for 15 minutes then set the milk aside for another 15 minutes so that the flavours can continue infusing. Put 75g of breadcrumbs in a bowl, strain over the warm milk then tip the sauce back into the saucepan and heat gently over a low heat for about 10 minutes until thick. Season with salt, pepper and a little freshly-grated nutmeg. Just before serving stir in a knob of butter.

HOW TO MAKE DRIED BREADCRUMBS
Slice stale bread thinly and bake as described under croûtons above but without spraying them with oil first. Cool then whizz in a food processor or blender, taking care not to reduce them to powder. (You can also buy them dried and readymade from Italian delis). You can use them for coating chicken, veal or turkey escalopes (page 88) or Scotch eggs or as an alternative to fresh breadcrumbs in a gratin topping.

BROCCOLI

Small amounts of broccoli can be broken into florets and stir-fried on its own (good as a warm salad with spring onions, garlic and chilli) or with other veg. It can also be incorporated into frittatas (page 48) and quiches (broccoli works well with eggs and cheese). The stalks can also be added to a stir-fry or soup (peeled first if they're tough). A small amount of broccoli works well in a pea soup.

BUTTERNUT SQUASH

Add to a selection of roast vegetables or a mixed vegetable bake such as the one on page 218 or add to a risotto. Roast butternut squash, along with red peppers, makes a colourful addition to a couscous salad or the flesh can be scooped out for a soup. Butternut squash **goes well with** dark leafy greens and strong-washed rind cheeses.

CABBAGE/GREENS

Rather than boiling, try shredding and stir-frying cabbage and spring greens with oil and garlic (remove the tough central leaf first) or slow-braise with spices such as juniper or caraway. Finely shredded leaves can also be added to soups as a replacement for parsley. Crisper varieties can be turned into a good coleslaw with finely chopped onion, grated carrot and sliced green pepper and apple (soak the shredded leaves in iced water first). Cooked cabbage can be turned into Bubble and Squeak (page 200). You can braise red cabbage with onion, apples, cloves and red wine or again, turn it into a slaw.

CARROTS

One of the most versatile vegetables, raw carrots can be used for salads and slaws, to dunk in dips such as hummus (page 152) or to make soup. Small amounts can be added to all sorts of stews and braises. They can also be roasted along with other roast veg or turned into purées (they mix well with swede) and soups. You can also use them to make carrot cake and muffins (page 165) and to make healthy juices if you have a juicer. Carrots go well with beef, cabbage, swede, onions and other root veg, Jerusalem artichokes, apples, hummus, olives and spices such as cumin and coriander, peanuts and fresh parsley.

MOROCCAN-STYLE SPICED CARROT SALAD

To make a quick salad for two, cut the tops and tips off two carrots and grate them coarsely. Mix with the juice of half an orange, a tablespoon of sunflower oil and season to taste with Moroccan Spice Mix (page 27) or curry powder, salt and a little sugar. Sprinkle with finely chopped coriander or parsley (you could also add a few black olives or some sesame, sunflower or pumpkin seeds).

CAULIFLOWER

Much more versatile than you'd think from cauliflower cheese. Best lightly blanched before using in salads (see page 68), dry curries or pakoras. Good in a vegetable curry or couscous. Also makes fabulous soup (page 174). Cauliflower goes well with cheese sauces, potato, spices such as coriander and turmeric and fresh coriander.

CELERY

A useful addition to add bulk to soups, stews and pasta sauces without affecting the taste. A crunchy addition to salads. Good as a braised vegetable with a little stock too. Celery goes well with most cheeses especially blue cheese such as Stilton, carrots and apples and cashew nuts. Can be substituted for fennel.

CHEESE

Most uses for leftover cheese are pretty obvious – sandwiches, cheese on toast, salads, quiches, pizza toppings and pasta bakes – but sometimes the cheese you have isn't suitable for any of those uses. Mature-washed rind cheeses for example are very hard to use in recipes. The only answer is buying less to ensure you don't have leftovers (page 24).

Small amounts of cheese can be turned into a spread with or without the aid of butter (see below). You can also experiment with the cheeses you use for familiar recipes. Taleggio, for example, makes a great pizza topping, sliced Brie can be used for a melt with a few fried mushrooms on toast. Other regional cheeses such as Lancashire and Red Leicester can be used for cheese sauces and for scones and muffins, crumbly white cheeses such as Caerphilly and Wensleydale can replace Feta in salads and blue cheeses can be used in a pasta sauce like the Stilton Sauce on page 110. Oh, and a useful tip – save any rind from a hard cheese like Gruyère or Parmesan to add to a vegetable or bean soup.

FROMAGE FORT

Fish out all your bits and pieces of cheese, cut off any rind or mould and cut into cubes. Put one or two roughly chopped cloves of garlic in a food processor, whizz until finely chopped then add the cheese and enough white wine to make a smooth spread and whizz again. Season with ground black pepper and cayenne pepper or a little chilli powder (it should be quite spicy).

BLUE CHEESE BUTTER

You can make this with any mellow blue cheese such as Gorgonzola, Fourme d'Ambert or Cashel Blue (but not Roquefort as it is too salty unless you combine it with another milder cheese). Cut 100g unsalted butter and 100g blue cheese into chunks, having first removed any rind. Place in a bowl and beat together (easiest with an electric hand-held mixer but you can use a wooden spoon). Crush a teaspoon of peppercorns and mix them in together with a tablespoon of finely snipped chives. Spoon the flavoured butter into a rough rectangle onto a piece of foil, and then roll it into a sausage shape. Twist the ends of the foil at either end like a Christmas cracker and refrigerate until firm. Remove from the fridge about 20 minutes before serving. Great on burgers or steaks.

CHICKEN AND TURKEY

A whole chicken is possibly the thriftiest meal going. A medium to large bird can easily be stretched to serve 10–12.

I find it helps to divide the leftovers into three categories – white meat, brown meat and the carcass.

White meat's not the problem. Everybody loves it – it eats well cold: in sandwiches or in salads.

Brown meat (the kind you get on legs and thighs and on the underside of the carcass) I find needs to be cooked up into something else – a pasta bake or a pilau or saved for a soup or soupy stew. Which is where your third component comes in – the carcass – which you should, if you're feeling truly frugal, use to make a stock (or freeze until you have several cooked carcasses then make a big batch).

The key thing to remember is to cover the bones with cold rather than hot water which will make the stock cloudy, to skim it once you've brought it to the boil (again to keep it clear) and to cook it slowly so that you don't extract the more bitter compounds from the bones. Then cool it, refrigerate it and skim it. That may sound like quite a palaver but it's a routine that becomes familiar and it's worth it for a really great tasting base for soups, stews and risottos.

RECIPES THAT USE LEFTOVER CHICKEN OR TURKEY, OR STOCK:
Chicken and Celery Sandwich Filling (page 65)
Sweet Potato and Chicken Hash (page 74)
Chicken and Mushroom Pasta Bake (page 112)
Spiced Game Pilaf (can be made with chicken or turkey, page 117)
The two risottos on pages 120–121
A Soothing Chicken Curry (page 107)
Asian-Style Chicken Broth with Coriander and Noodles (page 109)
Chargrilled Chicken, Pepper and Herb Couscous Salad (page 192)

CHICKPEAS

Small amounts of chickpeas can be added to a leftovers fry-up. They combine especially well with Spanish-style ingredients such as onion, chorizo and peppers (*see* page 115) and with North African and Indian spices with added fresh coriander (*see* Sweet Potato, Spinach and Chickpea Bake on page 153). *See* also Homemade Hummus on page 152.

CHOCOLATE

Leftover chocolate? You're joking....

CIDER

A good addition to casseroles and pies, especially with pork or chicken. An economical alternative to white wine (like beer, cider doesn't keep well once open. Use within 24 hours). You can also mull cider.

COCOA

A cheap alternative to chocolate for cakes and icing. To make a chocolate frosting for a small cake, sift 75g of icing sugar and 1 tablespoon of cocoa powder into a bowl. Put 25g sugar and 15g butter into a saucepan with 2 tablespoons of water. Heat until the sugar has dissolved then bring to the boil. Pour into the icing sugar and beat well till smooth. Use straight away or wait for it to harden for a fluffier frosting.

COD

See fish.

COFFEE

Leftover black coffee can be used for coffee cakes and also makes a great addition to chocolate cakes and icings (*see* Cappuccino Cake, page 159). Or mix it with iced milk, sugar and vanilla ice cream for an indulgent iced coffee.

CORIANDER (FRESH)

You might buy coriander for Thai and other Asian dishes but the leftovers can be used in curries, Middle-Eastern and Mexican dishes such as tomato salsa (page 83). Washed roots and stalks can be added to curries and stews for extra flavour. Chopped coriander leaves are good added to scrambled eggs if you want to make them a bit more exotic. Note that coriander is best kept in the fridge door in a jar or glass of water with a plastic bag secured over the top with a rubber band. Change the water every couple of days and it'll keep for up to a week. You can also freeze the leaves but crumble them into a dish while still frozen.

FRESH CORIANDER CHUTNEY
Wash half a large bunch of coriander thoroughly, shake it dry then chop off the thicker stalks and freeze or save for another recipe. Chop the leaves as finely as possible. Wash 2–3 sprigs of mint, strip the leaves from the stalks and chop finely. Tip 300ml plain yoghurt into a bowl and mix in the coriander and mint, a crushed clove of garlic and a de-seeded, finely chopped chilli. Season to taste with salt, lemon juice and a pinch of ground cumin. Cover the bowl and leave in the fridge for half an hour to let the flavours infuse but eat within 2 hours.

COURGETTES

Not great reheated but the odd courgette can be incorporated into a pasta sauce (page 111), frittata (page 48), quiche, soup, couscous or Mediterranean vegetable bake or cooked *a la grècque* (*see* page 218). Sautéed courgettes are good cold as a salad. Courgettes go well with Feta and other white cheeses, lemon, mint, dill, olive oil, tomatoes, prawns, pasta and couscous.

STIR-FRIED COURGETTES WITH DILL OR MINT

For a quick vegetable meal for one, top and tail one or two courgettes and grate them coarsely. Heat a tablespoon of oil in a pan then, once it's hot, add a similar amount of butter. Tip in the grated courgettes and stir-fry for a minute. Stir in a tablespoon of chopped dill or mint and serve.

COUSCOUS

Leftover couscous can be reheated in a microwave or steamer or dressed lightly with olive oil and vinegar and added to chopped grilled or roasted vegetables such as onions, peppers and courgettes (*see* Chargrilled Chicken, Pepper and Herb Couscous Salad on page 192) or Red Peppers, White Cheese and Butternut Squash.

CRAB

You're unlikely to be left with surplus white crab meat (if so, season with a little chilli, coriander and lime and serve on small lettuce leaves), but brown is less immediately appealing. The taste is fabulous though. Combine with pedestrian white fish to give a luxurious taste to fish soups, quiches, fish pies and fish cakes. Brown crab meat **goes well with** cream, saffron, tomato and brandy.

CREAM/CRÈME FRAÎCHE

A luxurious last-minute addition to all kinds of dishes from soups to quiches, to sautés and casseroles. Probably only our anxiety about weight gain holds us back. Buy double cream and full-fat crème fraîche then at least they freeze (though may be a bit grainy and won't whip when thawed).

CUCUMBER

Curiously unfashionable these days but a brilliant base for such quintessentially English dishes as cucumber sandwiches, cucumber and herb salads (page 187) cucumber and cream cheese mousse and chilled cucumber soup. Can also be served stir-fried as a veg, (peel, cut in half lengthways, run the tip of a teaspoon down the centre to scoop out the seeds then slice into half-moon shapes). **Goes well with** salmon, white crab meat, dill, tarragon and mint, cream cheese.

DUCK

Not much on a duck but maybe enough leftover to make an elegant little starter salad combined with some of the ingredients below or to make a pilaf with the scraps (*see* Spiced Game Pilaf page 117). Duck **goes well with** honey, orange, mango, raspberries, blackberries and plums, pomegranate seeds, soy and hoisin sauce.

EGGS

Whole eggs are never really a leftover though they are the invaluable basis for many a scratch meal such as frittatas (page 48), pancakes, spaghetti carbonara and such old-fashioned favourites as egg mayonnaise, stuffed eggs and egg Florentine (with cheese sauce and spinach). And, of course, all kinds of baking. It's leftover yolks and whites that pose the problem.

EGG YOLKS

Perfect for a plain or herb-flavoured homemade mayonnaise (page 188) or aioli, for desserts such as crème brulée and crème caramel, or simply add an extra yolk (and a little extra milk, cream or water) to scrambled eggs or an omelette or quiche. You can also use a leftover yolk to glaze a pie.

EGG WHITES

Save for meringues and pavlovas (page 185) – they can be frozen.

MERINGUES

Preheat your oven to 150°C/300°F/Gas 2. Put 2 large fresh egg whites in a large, scrupulously clean bowl and whisk them with a hand held electric whisk or rotary whisk until they hold a peak when you draw the whisk up through them. Add 110g unrefined caster sugar a heaped tablespoon at a time, beating the whites well between each addition. Lay a sheet of baking parchment over a baking tray. Using two dessertspoons, scoop out spoonfuls of the mixture onto the tray – you should get 8–10 meringues. Put the tray in the oven and turn down the heat to 140°C/275°F/Gas 1. Cook for an hour then turn off the oven and leave the meringues to cool in the residual heat until completely cold. You can serve them as they are or sandwich the halves together with whipped cream.

FAT AND DRIPPING

It's well worth saving leftover fat from a roasting tin or frying pan (in the case of bacon) as the flavourful base for another dish. Goose and duck fat is great for roasting potatoes, beef dripping is gorgeous slathered on toast (with a little coarse salt sprinkled on the top) and bacon, chicken and pork fat all good for frying other meats. Only lamb fat is rarely appealing. When you pour off the fat and have refrigerated it, retrieve the jellied meat juices underneath which make a fantastic addition to a pasta sauce, risotto, pie or stew.

FENNEL

A mainstay of Italian cooking. Finely sliced it makes a great raw salad (*see* page 100). You can also braise it with a little onion and serve it at room temperature as an antipasto salad or blitz it into a purée with cream (great with grilled fish). Makes a good risotto base too. Fennel **goes well with** prawns and other seafood, poached chicken, cream, Parmesan and dill.

FISH

The ideal use for leftover fish is fishcakes (*see* page 147). Small amounts of cooked white fish can also be lightly dressed with olive oil and lemon juice and served with a few chopped capers, some finely chopped gherkin and parsley. Or there may be enough, with a few frozen prawns and a hard boiled egg, to knock up a mini fish pie. *See also* Salmon and Smoked Fish (both page 223).

FLOUR

Not so much a leftover as a storecupboard staple but so useful it's worth listing here, not least for the opportunity to include this lovely shortcrust pastry recipe.

OLD-FASHIONED SHORTCRUST PASTRY

Sift 250g of plain flour and $\frac{1}{4}$ teaspoon of salt into a large bowl and add 110g of chilled butter and shortening cut into small cubes. Cut 50g of chilled vegetable fat (such as Cookeen) into the flour then rub it in with your fingers until the mixture is the consistency of coarse breadcrumbs. Add 4 tablespoons of chilled water and quickly mix into the pastry with a round-bladed knife, pulling the mixture together until it begins to form a ball. If it seems a bit dry add a little more water. When you have a rough ball of pastry put it on a lightly floured work surface or chopping board and press it lightly into a flat disc. Wrap it in clingfilm and chill for half an hour (or make considerably more quickly in a food processor). This is a very short, crisp, crumbly pastry, helped by the Cookeen. It makes enough for a 25cm quiche tin or to top a similarly sized pie.

* You could make a wholewheat pastry by replacing half the pastry with stoneground flour.

FRUIT

The tail ends of fruit bowls or leftover berries can get wasted unless you salvage them in a smoothie, compôte (pages 55) or simple fruit salad (if you don't have that much left over, mix them with some frozen or tinned fruit as in the Strawberry and Apricot Fruit Salad on page 52). You can grill, barbecue or roast fruit such as pineapple, peaches and nectarines.

See also suggestions for Apples, Bananas, Lemons and Limes and Oranges. Berries such as Blueberries (page 207), Raspberries (page 222) and Strawberries (page 224) are good for baking too and if still fresh can be frozen.

AN EXOTIC SYRUP FOR FRUIT SALADS

Put 125g of caster or granulated sugar in a saucepan with 125ml of water and heat over a low heat, stirring occasionally until the sugar has completely dissolved, brushing any remaining grains down the side of the pan into the syrup. Add 6–8 lightly crushed cardamom pods, bring to the boil and boil without stirring for two minutes then take off the heat and cool. Remove the cardamom pods, pour the syrup into a clean jar or plastic container, refrigerate then use as needed (good for cocktails too!). Will keep for 2–3 weeks.

DRIED FRUITS

There are often half-used packs of dried fruits leftover from a cake or pudding recipe (particularly after Christmas). Make a cake or teabread (page 160) just to use them up. Dried fruits such as apricots, prunes and dates can be used in tagines (page 190), pilafs or turned into a dried fruit compôte (page 55). Dried fruits work particularly well in lamb and pork dishes (see Pork and Prunes page 89).

GAME

Leftover feathered game can be treated much as any other bird such as chicken, guineafowl, turkey and duck. Use prime breast meat for sandwiches and salads, tougher leg meat for pilaus and pilafs (see Spiced Game Pilaf, page 117), and the carcass for a particularly flavourful stock. Game **goes well with** redcurrant, orange, apricots and other dried fruits, bacon, chestnuts, cabbage, celeriac, mushrooms, pastry and port (see Pot Roast Pheasant page 176). Leftover venison can be treated much as beef.

GOOSE

There isn't much flesh on a goose so you're unlikely to have much prime quality meat left over but what there is will make a great pilaf (see Spiced Game Pilaf, page 117). The prize leftover though is the accumulated fat which is fantastic for roasting potatoes (see Fat and Dripping, page 213). Goose **goes well with** potatoes, apples, oranges and red cabbage.

GRAVY

Always worth making extra to add to a shepherd's or cottage pie or to freeze so that you have an instant gravy when you need it. Add some leftover stock, beer, cider or wine if you have some. *See* Onion Gravy (page 219).

GREENS

See Cabbage, page 208.

GUINEAFOWL

See suggestions for chicken and game.

HAM

Apart from the obvious (cold cuts and sandwiches), a bit of ham makes a good addition to all kinds of dishes such as omelettes, scrambled egg, frittata, quiche (*see* page 146) spaghetti carbonara (instead of bacon), macaroni cheese, rice dishes such as jambalaya or a pie (with cold chicken or turkey). A ham bone makes a great basis for a soup (*see* page 79). Or try the tasty spread below.

POTTED HAM
Cut about 140g of lean ham up roughly and process in a food processor until finely chopped. Dice 150g unsalted butter, add it to the ham and process until smooth. Add 1½–2 teaspoons of English or Dijon mustard and enough water to make a spreadable consistency. Transfer the pâté to a bowl and stir in about 3 tablespoons of finely chopped parsley and a few finely snipped chives. Season with white pepper and a little salt if you feel it needs it (it may well not if the ham is salty). Refrigerate for an hour or two to allow the flavours to develop then allow to come back to room temperature before serving with crusty fresh bread or toast.

HERBS

You use very little of some herbs such as bay leaves, sage, rosemary and thyme which is why it's worth growing your own rather than buying them by the pack. Other herbs such as chervil, chives, coriander (page 215) dill, parsley and tarragon can be used lavishly. Woody herbs such as rosemary and thyme are the kind to use in long slow cooking or for roasting. Sage is best fried or used (in small quantities) in a stuffing. Parsley is the most versatile herb and can be used both to flavour or garnish dishes or as a basis for a soup or sauce (*see* page 219).

WHAT GOES WITH WHAT
Basil: tomatoes, Mozzarella
Chervil: eggs, mayonnaise
Chives: eggs, soft cheese, can replace spring onions
Coriander: Asian and Middle-Eastern dishes
Dill: cucumber, goat's cheese, pickled fish such as herring, smoked salmon
Mint: lamb, Feta, new potatoes, cucumber
Marjoram/oregano: cooked tomatoes and other Mediterranean veg
Rosemary: lamb, olives, tomatoes, potatoes and other root vegetables
Sage: onions, butternut squash, butter, pork, bread (as part of a stuffing), good deep-fried with pasta
Tarragon: cucumber, soft cheese, very good stuffed into a roast chicken or with a creamy sauce to serve with chicken
Thyme: good with chicken and pork

HONEY

Keeps well but not always used as widely as it might be for sweetening fruit or as a substitute for sugar in baking. Can also be used as a glaze for grilled meats such as chicken wings as in the simple marinade below from Jill Dupleix.

HONEY-SOY MARINADE

Mix a crushed garlic clove with a teaspoon of grated fresh ginger or ginger paste and a few drops of chilli sauce or a pinch of chilli powder or cayenne pepper. Add 2 tablespoons of soy sauce, 1 tablespoon of clear honey, 1 tablespoon of lime or lemon juice, 1 tablespoon of vegetable oil or olive oil and 1 tablespoon of boiling water. Mix well and use to brush over chicken wings or drumsticks (*see* page 126).

LAMB

Reheated lamb takes spices well. Add to a rogan josh sauce (cheaper made with a curry paste) for a quick lamb curry or give it the pilaf treatment (*see* page 117). Cold lamb also works well with spicy chutneys. You can also use it to make shepherd's pie, but I think it's made better with fresh mince (*see* Meat, page 217). Lamb **goes well with** onion, leeks, tomatoes, courgettes, aubergines, rice, haricot beans and flageolets, garlic and a wide range of spices and herbs, especially mint and coriander.

LEEKS

Great in their own right but can be substituted for onions or spring onions in all sorts of dishes from soups to stir-fries to stews (page 132). Particularly good with eggs, cheese (especially goat's cheese) and cream – *see* the Spring Vegetable Frittata on page 48. Leeks also go particularly well with chicken and salmon.

LEMONS AND LIMES

Invaluable fridge ingredients, with a wide range of uses in sweet and savoury dishes. A squeeze of lemon or lime will often finish a dish off while lemon and lime-based desserts provide a refreshing and inexpensive way to finish off a meal. Unwaxed fruit is better for zesting but keeps less well so you need to step in and freeze it before it deteriorates. You can freeze the zest, juice or slices which can be dropped direct from frozen into drinks.

Lemons go well with practically all fish and shellfish, chicken, veal, lamb, courgettes, herbs such as parsley mint and dill, garlic and parsley and desserts that contain cream, almonds and eggs (*see* Empress of Puddings, page 156) and cakes such as the Lemon Drizzle Traybake on page 158.

Limes go particularly well with other Asian ingredients such as garlic, chilli and coriander, with avocados and fresh tomatoes (*see* Mexican Salsa Chicken page 125), and with tropical fruits, especially mango.

LEMON PARSLEY BUTTER

Work the rind and juice of half a lemon into 100g softened butter than mix in 2 tablespoons of finely chopped parsley. Use to top grilled fish or chicken.

LENTILS

Cooked whole green or brown lentils can be heated through and used as an accompaniment for grilled or fried sausages or turned into a salad with goat's cheese, beetroot, Jerusalem artichokes or artichoke hearts and plenty of parsley or other fresh herbs. Red lentils can be added to a vegetable soup to make it more substantial or, if already cooked as a dhal, just add a little stock to turn it into a soup. Lentils also go well with spinach and coriander.

LETTUCE AND SALAD GREENS

Outside leaves often get thrown away but if still in reasonably good condition can be added to a pea soup or a French-style dish of peas cooked with onion and bacon. Hold onto the stalks of leafy salad greens such as watercress and spinach and add them to a vegetable soup such as the Stalky Spinach, Pea and Mint Soup (page 78).

LIMES

See lemons and limes.

MANGOES

Once very ripe, mangoes are best whizzed up with yoghurt and a little lime juice for a refreshing mango lassi (thin with a little water to get the right consistency), or combined with a banana in a smoothie.

MEAT

The more meat is cooked the harder it is to transform it into another cooked dish. I'm absolutely not a fan of rissoles or shepherd's pie made with leftovers from the roast. If you want to make a shepherd's pie your best bet is to chop any meat up small and mix it with some freshly cooked mince and vegetables (good gravy also helps a lot). Or fry the last bits and pieces of meat (preferably in some of the tasty fat you've saved – see Fat and Dripping, page 213) and add them to a pilaf (page 17) or hash (page 74). Less well cooked meat can be cut into slices or chunks and reheated in gravy or turned into a curry or stew but don't cook it too long otherwise it will go unappealingly squelchy. See also Beef, Lamb, Chicken and Pork.

MELONS

Useful for savoury dishes as well as sweet ones. Try mixing ripe Charentais melon cubes with strawberries and/or raspberries or make a salad with cubes of honeydew melon, cucumber and seeded tomatoes, toss with a light salad dressing, leave for a couple of hours to extract the juices then scatter over some finely chopped herbs such as mint, parsley and chives. Melon goes particularly well with air-dried ham.

MILK

Like eggs, more a fridge staple than a leftover – an invaluable base for sauces, pancakes, Yorkshire pudding, toad-in-the-hole, milk puddings such as rice pudding and Empress of Puddings (page 156) and other British nursery treats. (Many of these can be made with soy milk if you're dairy-intolerant.)

QUICK CHEESE SAUCE
Put 20g of butter in a small saucepan with 20g of flour and 284ml ($^1/_2$ pint) of whole or semi-skimmed milk, bring gradually to the boil, whisking energetically with a wire whisk until thickened. Turn the heat down low and simmer for 5 minutes. Take the pan off the heat and add 40g of mature or extra mature Cheddar or other hard cheese and season with salt and white pepper to taste. To lighten the sauce, add a tablespoon or two of water you've used for cooking any accompanying vegetables or pasta. To make it richer, add a couple of tablespoons of double cream or a dollop of crème fraîche.

CARDAMOM RICE PUDDING
Another use for those cardamom pods I suggested for the Exotic Syrup on page 214. Put 55g of pudding rice in a saucepan with 500ml of milk, 50g of caster sugar and 5 or 6 lightly crushed cardamom pods. Bring to the boil and leave over a very low heat, stirring occasionally for about an hour until the rice has absorbed the milk and is rich and creamy. You could add a little cream at the end

– or a couple of tablespoons of sifted cocoa powder if you wanted a chocolate rice pud.

MINT

Apart from its use in recipes mint also makes a great fresh-tasting caffeine-free infusion. Simply pour boiling water over some sprigs and leave for 3–4 minutes or make it in a pot, Moroccan style. Put a green tea bag and 1–2 teaspoons of sugar in a pot with a handful of fresh mint, fill up to the brim of the pot with boiling water, stir and leave to infuse as before. Mint **goes well with** lamb, Feta and other crumbly white cheeses, couscous, new potatoes, tomatoes, cucumber and melon.

MUSHROOMS

Hugely versatile cheap ingredient that makes a fantastic spread (*see* Mushroom Caviar, page 196) or can be added to omelettes, quiches, pasta sauces, risotto and other rice dishes, casseroles and sautés or simply cooked up with a little butter, garlic and cream and served on toast (page 60) or as a filling for pancakes or pastry cases. Raw mushrooms are very good in a salad with Parmesan and watercress or rocket or can be cooked in white wine and olive oil (overleaf) for a simple starter salad. Mushrooms go particularly well with butter, cream, cheese, eggs, beef, chicken, pork, bacon, kidneys (page 97), white wine, onions and garlic. Their savoury flavour can be boosted by soy sauce, Worcestershire sauce, mushroom ketchup or a splash of Madeira, dry marsala or sherry.

MUSHROOMS A LA GRÈCQUE
Put 150ml of crisp dry white wine in a saucepan with a finely chopped clove of garlic and a bay leaf, bring up to the boil and simmer until the wine has reduced by half. Grind together $1\frac{1}{2}$ teaspoons of coriander seeds, $\frac{1}{2}$ teaspoon of sea salt, $\frac{1}{4}$ teaspoon of peppercorns and $\frac{1}{4}$ teaspoon of crushed chillies with a pestle and mortar. Tip into the reduced wine, add 3 tablespoons of olive oil and a tablespoon of lemon juice, stir and simmer

over a very low heat for 4–5 minutes. Wipe and thickly slice 350g of mushrooms. Put them in a large bowl, pour over the hot dressing and sprinkle with a tablespoon of chopped mint. Toss the mushrooms in the dressing then leave them to macerate for about an hour, turning them occasionally. Check the seasoning, adding more salt, pepper and lemon juice if you think it needs it. Add a little parsley, toss the salad again and serve with crusty bread or warm pitta bread.

NOODLES

Small amounts of rice noodles or egg noodles can be added to an Asian-style broth like the one on page 109, added to a stir-fry or cooked and rinsed with cold water and added to a salad (you can substitute ordinary spaghetti for noodles in many recipes).

NUTS

Nuts don't keep that well so you need to find ways to use them up. As well as adding them to cakes, cookies (page 163), flapjacks and puddings (*see* the Apple, Blackberry and Nut Crumble on page 184 and the Hazelnut Meringue Cake on page 181) you can add them to stuffings, gratin toppings, pilafs and couscous, salads or even pasta dishes such as Linguine with Stilton (page 110) for a bit of texture and crunch. And also, of course, serve them with cheese. If the pack has been open for a while refresh them in the oven before using.

WHAT GOES WITH WHAT
Almonds: apples, pears, apricots, lemon, raspberries
Brazil nuts: chocolate
Cashew nuts: Chinese style stir-fried vegetables, mushrooms and rice.
Hazelnuts: raspberries, peaches and nectarines and in coffee and chocolate- flavoured desserts
Peanuts: chilli, lime, carrot and cucumber in Asian-style salads (peanut butter is also good in a spicy dressing).

Pistachios: cream, rosewater, couscous
Walnuts: bananas, cream cheese, blue cheese, raisins and dates, orange, apples and celery

OATS/OATMEAL

As well as making porridge and muesli, oats can be added to flapjacks (page 166), muffins (page 165), wholemeal bread (page 167), and used to stretch a meatloaf (page 140). Refresh them in the oven as you warm it up to intensify their flavour.

OLIVES

Can be added to salads and pasta sauces and French-style daubes (beef or lamb stews), or North African tagines to give them a bit of a kick. You can also add them to breads like the Sheep's Cheese and Olive Bread on page 143. Olives go well with cooked tomato, Mozzarella and sheep's cheeses, basil, rosemary, oregano and thyme, chilli, lemon, orange and anchovies.

ONIONS

Rarely redundant but can be a useful base for a flavourful white sauce or gravy, a quiche, an onion marmalade or a cooling raita (see page 118). Or indulge yourself with some deep-fried onion rings. Spring onions can be used in stir-fries, salads, frittatas or quiches. Onions go well with milk, cream, yoghurt, thyme, sage, Parmesan, sausages, beef and tomatoes.

ONION GRAVY
Peel and slice 3 medium onions. Heat a heavy saucepan or casserole over a moderate heat, add a tablespoon of oil then, when that melts, a good slice (about 20g) of butter. Tip in the onions, stir well and cook over a medium heat for about 10 minutes until soft and beginning to brown. Stir in a tablespoon of flour then gradually add 350ml of beef stock – you can replace half the stock with beer or red wine – (or stock made with a teaspoon of Bovril or Marmite), stirring continually. Bring to the boil then turn the heat right down and simmer for 5 minutes or until ready to use. Season with pepper and a dash of Worcestershire sauce.

ORANGES, SATSUMAS AND MANDARINS

More versatile than generally assumed from their usual use as juice. Can replace lemon in many dishes such as salad dressings and cakes. An orange fruit salad is very refreshing. Skin the oranges by scoring them into quarters then put them in a bowl and pour boiling water over them. Leave for a minute then drain off the hot water and pour over cold water. The skin should peel away cleanly taking most of the pith. Slice the oranges horizontally and pour over the Cardamom Syrup on page 182 or plain sugar syrup and chill well. Oranges go well with duck, pork, mackerel, chicory, watercress, walnuts, almonds, olives, parsley and dill.

PARSLEY

Well worth buying in large bunches so it's likely you may have some left over which could be added in generous quantities to garlic or lemon butter (*see* page 184) a pea soup, a white sauce (great with boiled bacon) or used as the base for a pesto instead of basil (*see* page 173). Deep-fried parsley also makes a good accompaniment for fish. And don't forget the stalks which can be chopped and added to sauces, soups, stews and frittatas for extra flavour. Like other fresh herbs, it also freezes.

PARSNIPS

The odd parsnip can be added to a tray of roast veg or very finely sliced and deep-fried for delicious chips. If you have a few more you can make a purée, while part-cooked parsnips can be brushed with honey and finished under the grill. Leftover roast parsnips make great soup (*see* page 67). Parsnips go well with cream, Parmesan, nutmeg, curry powder, venison sausages, pheasant, carrots and other root veg.

PASTA

Leftover pasta can be used for pasta salads so long as you dress it soon after you've cooked it (*see* page 63). Alternatively, rinse it with cold water so it doesn't stick together, refrigerate it, then add it to a pasta sauce or stir-fry it with oil, garlic and chilli for a crisper effect.

PEACHES AND NECTARINES

For a quick dessert, fry a skinned, stoned, sliced peach in a little butter. Add some sugar (and a dash of bourbon, dark rum or marsala if you have some) and a few drops of vanilla extract or flavouring and serve with cream or vanilla ice-cream. You can also use peaches as the base of a crumble or cobbler (*see* page 131) or skin and poach in a red or sweet wine syrup. Also good in chutneys and relishes.

Peaches go well with chicken, ham, berries such as blueberries and raspberries and vanilla.

PEARS

Crucial to catch them in the narrow window between being completely hard and unripe and soft and woolly. If you have a glut of unripe pears poach them in leftover red wine or cider and sugar. Ripe pears can be added to fruit salads, smoothies and juices and also make very good tarts. Pears go well with blue cheese, walnuts and watercress, almonds, chocolate and vanilla ice cream.

PEAS

Everybody's favourite standby veg – can be used direct from the freezer so rarely wasted. A few leftover peas can be added to a salad, frittata, pasta sauce or pilaf. Peas go well with chicken, bacon, ham, salmon, prawns, rice, pasta, Parmesan, spring onions, carrots – virtually anything.

PEPPERS

Red peppers in particular are a useful standby veg to add to salsa salads (page 60) and stir-fries but can also be stir-fried on their own (*see* page 81). If you have a lot to use up, slow-roast them with oil and garlic and use for chunky Italian-style sandwiches or antipasti. Peppers go well with onion, butter beans, chorizo and eggs, tomatoes, courgettes and aubergines.

PHEASANT

See game.

PINEAPPLE

Marinate small cubes of pineapple for half an hour with lime juice, chilli and mint for a refreshing salsa (also quite good at the end of a spicy meal). Pineapple **goes well with** lime, chilli, coconut and rum and with ham.

PLUMS

Use for crumbles and cobblers. Stir-fry sliced plums in a little butter for a couple of minutes, sprinkle with sugar and a pinch of cinnamon and serve on toasted malt bread. Make chutney. Plums go well with apples, cinnamon, pork and duck.

POLENTA

It's worth cooking extra polenta so that you have some leftover for grilling – a great accompaniment to grilled or barbecued meat and vegetables. 'Wet', sloppier polenta **goes well with** dark winey stews.

To cook polenta, bring one litre of light vegetable stock (made with an organic stock cube or 1 tablespoon of vegetable bouillon powder) to the boil in a big (preferably non-stick) saucepan then reduce to a simmer. Tip 175g of polenta into a jug

then gradually pour it into the simmering stock, whisking all the time. Continue stirring until it begins to thicken then turn the heat right down and cook for about 15–20 minutes until thick, stirring it every couple of minutes. If you're going to grill it gradually beat in 50g of butter and 25g of freshly grated Parmesan, season with salt and pepper then pour onto a baking tray to a depth of about $1\frac{1}{2}$cm, evening the surface with a spatula. When cold you can cut up the polenta, brush it lightly with oil and cook it on a ridged grill. If you want a sloppier polenta to go with a stew, stop the cooking slightly earlier and add 25g more butter and another 15–20g of cheese and season as above.

PORK

Unless eaten as a cold cut, cold pork needs jazzing up with a bit of hot spice to boost the flavour. Good dishes to try are Jambalaya and the Indonesian dish Nasi Goreng. You could also turn it into a Cape Malay-style curry with apricots or brush thick slices of cold pork with a spicy marinade or barbecue sauce and heat them under the grill. Pork goes well with potatoes, onions, fennel, apricots, cheese, cream, mustard, curry paste, chilli and smoky barbecue sauces. See also Meat, page 217.

POTATOES

Possibly the world's most desirable leftover, perfect for sautéeing, turning into a hash (page 74) or Bubble and Squeak (page 200) a potato salad (*see* below) or, in the case of leftover mash, potato scones or fishcakes (page 147). Even a leftover baked potato can make a great topping for some leftover stew if you mash the flesh while it's still warm. Well-scrubbed organic potato peelings make great fried potato skins for dunking.

GERMAN-STYLE POTATO SALAD
Cut up leftover potatoes while still warm and dress lightly with a tablespoon or two of vinaigrette. Add 1 heaped tablespoon of finely chopped onion, a finely chopped sweet and sour cucumber, a

chopped hard-boiled egg and a heaped tablespoon of mayonnaise. Add a splash of liquid from the pickle jar, season with salt and pepper and sprinkle with chopped fresh parsley.

POTATO CAKES

The best way to make these is to set aside some mashed potato before you add any butter or milk – you want the potato to be quite firm and still warm. Add 20g of sieved flour for every 100g of potato, add an egg yolk (unless you've got a particularly small amount of potato) season the mixture generously with salt and pepper, divide up and shape into shallow patties. Cool and refrigerate until needed. Dust with flour and fry in a mixture of olive oil and butter. (You could also add some fried finely chopped bacon and chopped onion and/or a little crumbled blue cheese.)

PRAWNS

Prawns don't keep or reheat well, so leftovers are best used as soon as possible in a sandwich or salad. You can, however, make an excellent prawn-flavoured butter from the shells of whole prawns or shrimps. Put the shells in a saucepan with a generous amount of butter (about 125g for the shells of about 500g of prawns) and $\frac{1}{8}$ teaspoon of cayenne or chilli powder and heat slowly until the butter has melted. Bring to the boil then take off the heat and leave to cool for 15 minutes. Pulse the shells and butter briefly in a food processor then strain through a fine sieve. Cool and refrigerate then use in pasta sauces, risottos and fish pies. Prawns go well with hard boiled eggs, mayonnaise, lemon, lime, chilli, ginger, garlic, coriander, dill, tomatoes, cucumber, courgettes, pasta, rice and couscous.

RASPBERRIES

Can be used along with other berries in a fresh fruit compôte or cheesecake topping. Add to an apple crumble. Purée, sieve, sweeten with sieved icing sugar and serve as a sauce or turn into a sorbet or ice-cream. Heat frozen raspberries through with sugar for a fresh-tasting winter compôte (page 47) or soft-set fridge jam. Add fresh or frozen raspberries to a Queen of Puddings (page 156) or Bakewell tart. Raspberries go well with white and dark chocolate, cream and creamy desserts such as pannacotta, hazelnuts (page 181), toasted oatmeal, other berries such as blueberries strawberries and cherries, and peaches and nectarines.

RHUBARB

Makes a great breakfast compôte or pie or crumble base (delicious mixed with strawberries). Rhubarb goes with pastry, crumble toppings especially with almonds, ginger and orange, cream, sour cream cream cheese and yoghurt.

RICE

Can be reheated (best microwaved) but better cooled and refrigerated first. Egg-fried rice needs to be made with fridge-cold rice. If you're making a rice salad, dress the rice while it is still warm so that it absorbs the dressing and bring it to room temperature before serving. Leftover risotto can be made into tasty *arancini* (deep-fried risotto balls).

EGG-FRIED RICE

To make egg-fried rice for one, break 1 large or 2 medium eggs into a bowl and beat them lightly. Heat a wok or large frying pan over a moderate heat and pour in 2 tablespoons of oil. Tip in 2–3 finely sliced spring onions and stir-fry for a minute or two until beginning to soften. Add the beaten eggs and stir until almost all the liquid egg has disappeared (a few seconds). Add a portion of cooked, chilled basmati rice and a handful of thawed frozen peas and stir-fry for a couple of minutes until hot through. Sprinkle over about 1 tablespoon of soy sauce and mix in well.

SALAD LEAVES

See Lettuce.

SALMON

The best use for cooked salmon is in fishcakes (page 125) but you can also add it to a creamy sauce for a pancake filling or a fish pie, or add it to a risotto or kedgeree (taking care not to break it up too much). Other good uses include quiche or a pasta or cold noodle salads (it works well with a limey Thai-style dressing). Or make a quick salmon pâté by whizzing it up with some melted butter or cream cheese and seasoning it with a squeeze of lemon, a little mace or nutmeg if you have some and a pinch of cayenne or chilli pepper. You could also add a few finely chopped chives. Salmon **goes well with** butter, cream, asparagus, broccoli, peas, red peppers, cucumber (fresh and pickled) ginger, orange, lime, soy, coriander and dill.

SMOKED FISH

You're unlikely to struggle to think of what to do with a bit of leftover smoked salmon or trout but, in addition to most of the ingredients mentioned above in the Salmon entry, it goes particularly well with eggs. So odd scraps can be added to scrambled eggs, quiche or a spaghetti carbonara (instead of bacon). It also makes a great classic bagel filling with cream cheese and pickled cucumbers and also **goes well with** beetroot. Raw smoked fish such as smoked cod and haddock can be cooked up in a creamy sauce and frozen in portions to fill omelettes or pancakes or as a topping for toast.

SMOKED HADDOCK IN CREAM SAUCE

Take two big fillets of undyed smoked haddock or cod, cut it into pieces that will fit in a saucepan, add a medium onion, peeled and halved and a bay leaf and cover with milk. Bring slowly to the boil, then turn the heat off, put a lid of the pan and leave for 7–8 minutes. Carefully remove the fish from the pan and transfer to a serving plate. Strain the milk into a jug. Melt 40g of butter in a heavy bottomed saucepan and stir in 25g of flour. Cook for a minute then add about 400ml of the strained milk, and stir until thick. Bring back to the boil and simmer over a very low heat while you flake the fish off the skin, carefully removing any bones. Season the white sauce with pepper and a little salt and tip in the flaked fish. Add a little more strained milk if the sauce is too thick.

SPINACH

Uncooked spinach leaves can be shredded and added to a soup or curry instead of fresh herbs. Reheat cooked spinach in butter, add a little cream and nutmeg and use as an omelette or pancake filling or whizz up in a pea soup. Spinach **goes well with** eggs, cheese (especially Parmesan, Ricotta and – when raw – blue cheese) cream, ham, bacon, mushrooms, curry spices, potatoes and pulses like chickpeas and lentils.

SPROUTS

More versatile than you'd think. Very good stir-fried or shredded into winter salads. Cooked sprouts are perfect for Bubble and Squeak (page 200) or can be turned into a gratin. Sprouts go well with onion, bacon, potatoes, chestnuts, cream, parmesan, ginger and soy sauce.

STRAWBERRIES

Macerate with leftover red wine and a little sugar. Mix with less expensive fruit such as tinned apricots (page 55). Whizz up into a smoothie or ice-cream. Strawberries go well with cream, vanilla ice-cream, yoghurt, fromage frais, cream cheese, Mascarpone, other berries such as raspberries and blueberries, bananas, orange juice and vanilla.

SWEETCORN

Corn on the cob should be eaten as soon as possible after purchase. The kernels can be stripped off the cob and used for fritters or creamed corn, or almost dry-fried in a hot pan rubbed with a little oil to make a spicy salsa. Frozen sweetcorn can be used in a similar way or added to a chowder or a stir-fry. Sweetcorn **goes well with** butter, cream, chicken, ham, bacon, salad vegetables, spring onions, chilli, coriander.

TOMATOES

Easy to use up in salads, pasta sauces, soups and stews but don't forget Tomatoes on Toast (page 63) or fresh tomato salsa (page 83). Tomatoes go well with chicken, prawns, pasta, Mozzarella, Feta, basil, coriander, olives, capers, aubergines, courgettes and onions.

A SIMPLE FRESH TOMATO SAUCE

Heat 2–3 tablespoons of olive oil in a pan, add a crushed clove of garlic, a dessertspoon of tomato paste and 4–6 medium sized, skinned chopped tomatoes. Cook over a low heat for about 10 minutes until the tomatoes have broken down then season with salt and pepper and add a few torn basil leaves if you have some. Leftover tinned tomatoes can be used in a similar way though don't forget to transfer them into another container otherwise the juice can corrode the lining of the tin.

SLOW-ROAST TOMATOES

Another good use for a batch of small or medium-sized tomatoes. Cut them in half and lay them on a baking tray. Season with salt and pepper and drizzle over some olive oil and back in a slow oven (160°C/325°F/Gas 3) for about an hour and a quarter to an hour and a half until sweet and caramelised. Serve with mozzarella and basil as an antipasto or add to a pasta sauce or pasta salad.

TURKEY

See Chicken.

TUNA

Best used cold, added to salads or used to fill sandwiches (try a tuna version of the Chicken and Celery Sandwich Filling on page 65). Tinned tuna goes with hard boiled eggs, lettuce, cucumber, tomatoes, green beans, mayo, anchovies, olives, capers, and lemon. Fresh tuna **goes well with** Asian flavours such as soy sauce, ginger, chilli, lime and fresh coriander.

WALNUTS

See Nuts.

WATERCRESS

More robust than other salad leaves so can be successfully used in a quiche or a frittata or turned into a soup. (Note, the leaves discolour and lose their flavour quite quickly so use within 24 hours of purchase, ideally). Watercress goes with eggs, roasted or grilled meat, pâtés and terrines, oily fish such as mackerel and salmon, bacon and Cheddar and Feta cheese.

EASY WATERCRESS SOUP

You'll need one large or two smaller bunches of watercress. Wash thoroughly, chop off the stalks and roughly chop the leaves. Set both stalks and leaves to one side. Heat a saucepan or casserole and add 2 tablespoons of olive oil and 15g of butter. Add a medium to large chopped onion (or half a bunch of spring onions, trimmed and sliced) and cook for 3–4 minutes then add a finely sliced medium-sized potato, stir, cover the pan and cook on a low heat for another five minutes or so. Add the watercress stalks and 600ml of chicken or vegetable stock, bring to the boil and cook until the potatoes are almost tender (about 10 minutes). Add the chopped watercress leaves, bring back to the boil, cook for a couple of minutes then take off the heat and cool slightly. Pass the soup in batches through a liquidiser until smooth then return to the pan and reheat gently without boiling. You can add a little milk or cream at this stage if you want a creamier texture. Season to taste with salt, pepper and a squeeze of lemon juice.

VEGETABLES

Often vegetables are too far gone to do anything with them. By and large the longer they're cooked the less useful they are. Well cooked buttered veg or crispy roast potatoes rarely reheat well. A well-seasoned hash such as Bubble and Squeak (page 00) is about the only rescue remedy.

Lightly stir-fried or steamed veg on the other hand such as broccoli, cauliflower or peas are a useful addition to pasta sauces, curries, pilaus or frittatas.

And even rather scruffy raw vegetables from the bottom of the fridge or the tail end of a veg box can be salvaged if you get to them in time.

For more specific suggestions check individual entries – Tomatoes, Broccoli, Cauliflower, Cucumber, etc. – but if you've a mixture of veg to use up try either making a tray of roast veg, preferably of a similar type (in winter I base it potatoes, carrots, onions and parsnips, in summer on onions, courgettes, peppers and aubergines) or making a mixed vegetable soup, curry or couscous.

WINE

Great to have around the kitchen for marinades or to chuck into sauces, gravies and stews but don't use wine from bottles that have been open for weeks (or ones that are corked) otherwise it will taste like vinegar. If bottles are less than half full (the most likely scenario...) transfer the wine into a smaller bottle or container and refrigerate it or even, if you can't use it over the next few days, simmer it in a saucepan until reduced by about half in volume, cool and freeze it in an ice cube tray to take out as you need it. If you're slow cooking a stew or casserole with wine add a dash at the end of the cooking time to revive the flavour.

YOGHURT

Apparently yoghurt is one of the most frequently chucked out foods from the average household. Maybe it's all the flavoured ones no-one likes. If you buy plain yoghurt it's hard not to find a use for it. Mix it with puréed fruit for a smoothie or your own fruit-flavoured yoghurt. Stir it into a cooked fruit compôte. Serve dollops on spicy food such as curries. Make a raita or a tandoori marinade for chicken. Add to salad dressings or cold soups (great with cucumber). Use for yoghurt-based ice-creams. Yoghurt goes particularly well with bananas, berries, mango, cucumber, mint and lamb.

INDEX

a

almonds
Dried fruit compôte with redbush tea, cinnamon and honey 55

anchovies (204)
Smoked mackerel and potato gratin 151
Warm cauliflower, egg and anchovy salad 68

apples (204)
Apple and cinnamon compôte 204
Apple and cinnamon porridge 45
Apple and onion sauce for serving with pork or sausages 204
Apple, blackberry and nut crumble 184
Apple lemonade 204
Carrot, oat and cinnamon muffins 165
Cranberry, raspberry and apple compôte 200
Danish apple charlotte 157
French toast with Polish cherries 53
Granny Smith scones 162
Roast belly pork with black pudding and 'heaven and earth' mash 128

apple juice
Fresh fruit muesli with yoghurt 46

apricots
French toast with Polish cherries 53
Fresh fruit muesli with yoghurt 46
Moroccan-style lamb with dates, prunes and apricots 190

Strawberry and apricot fruit salad with orange and mint 52

asparagus (204)
Asparagus and barley risotto 120
Goat's cheese, beetroot and asparagus salad 66
Spiced game pilaf 177
Spring vegetable frittata 48

aubergines (205)
Chargrilled chicken, pepper and herb couscous salad 192

avocados (205)
Avocado salsa salad to go with tuna or mackerel 69
Mexican-style guacamole 205

b

bacon (205)
Budget meatloaf 140
Cheddar, ham and onion quiche 146
Chickpeas and chorizo 115
Pea and bacon risotto 121
Pollack, bacon and sweetcorn chowder 104
Rabbit, bacon and perry pie 134
Spring vegetable frittata 48
Two vegetable minestrone 77

bakes
Lemon drizzle traybake 158
Portuguese-style salt cod bake 149
Sweet potato, spinach and chickpea bake 153

bananas 205
Banana chiffon cake 160
Lemon and ginger flapjacks 166

barley
Asparagus and barley risotto 120

basil (206)
Fresh pesto 206

batter
Granny Smith scones 162
Ina Pinkney's buttermilk pancakes 56

beans (206)
Two vegetable minestrone 77
Summer sausages with peppers and butterbean mash 93

berries
Apple, blackberry and nut crumble 184
Cranberry, raspberry and apple compôte 200
Empress of puddings 156
French toast with Polish cherries 53
Granny Smith scones 162
Lemon and ginger flapjacks 166
Peach and blueberry cobbler 154
Strawberry and apricot fruit salad with orange and mint 52
Summer fruit pavlova 185
Summer pudding 182
Winter raspberry compôte with yoghurt and toasted oatmeal 47

beef (206)
Basic bolognese 136
Bavette aux echalotes 90
Braised beef short-ribs with red wine and polenta 177
Budget meatloaf 140
Norwegian meatballs 138
Thai beef salad 86
beer (206)
Barm brack 161
Beer-can chicken 189

beetroot (206)
Goat's cheese, beetroot and asparagus salad 66

blueberries (207)
Peach and blueberry cobbler 154

bread (207)
Bread sauce 208
Cinnamon toast 207
Croque monsieur 207
Crostini bases 207
Croûtons 207
French toast with Polish cherries 53
Garlic bread 207
Grilled tomatoes on toast 63
Grilled mushrooms on toast 60
Kidneys with mustard 96
Ciabatta and baguettes 207
Norwegian meatballs 138
Prawn and egg open sandwich 64
Sardine 'rillettes' with lemon and parsley 61
Sheep's cheese, olive and oregano bread 168
Spiced parsnip soup with garlic raita 81
Summer pudding 182
Wholemeal porridge bread 167

breadcrumbs
Chicken and mushroom pasta bake 112
Danish apple charlotte 157
Dried breadcrumbs 208
Empress of puddings 156
Schnitzel 88
Spaghetti with zucchini and garlic and lemon breadcrumbs 111

broad beans
Goat's cheese, beetroot and asparagus salad 66
Ham, broad bean and herb pasta salad 73
Spiced game pilaf 177
Spring vegetable frittata 48

broccoli (208)
Pizza giardiniera 141

Spiced game pilaf 177
Spring vegetable frittata 48

butterbeans
Summer sausages with peppers and butterbean mash 93

buttermilk
Cappuccino cake 159
Ina Pinkney's buttermilk pancakes 56

butternut squash (208)
Sweet potato, spinach and chickpea bake 153

C

cabbage (208)
Bubble and squeak 200

cakes
Cappuccino cake 159
Hazelnut meringue cake 181

carrots (209)
Braised beef short-ribs with red wine and polenta 177
Carrot, oat and cinnamon muffins 165
Chestnut and lentil soup 201
Italian-style veal stew 133
Lovely lamb and leek stew 132
Moroccan-style lamb with dates, prunes and apricots 190
Moroccan-style spiced carrot salad 209
Pea and ham soup 79
Poached chicken with parsley and lemon dumplings 124
Winter sausages with stoemp 91

capers
Portuguese-style salt cod bake 149
Roast pollack with tomatoes, olives and capers 101

Sardine 'rillettes' with lemon and parsley 61
Warm cauliflower, egg and anchovy salad 68

cauliflower (209)
Caramelised cauliflower soup 174
Persian chicken 191
Warm cauliflower, egg and anchovy salad 68

celery (209)
Basic bolognese 136
Chestnut and lentil soup 201
Chicken and celery sandwich filling 65
Pea and ham soup 79
Pot roast pheasant with port 176
Spiced parsnip soup with garlic raita 81
Two vegetable minestrone 77

cheese (209)
Asparagus and barley risotto 120
Blue cheese butter 210
Cheddar, ham and onion quiche 146
Chicken and mushroom pasta bake 112
Croque monsieur 207
Fresh pesto 206
Fromage fort 210
Goat's cheese, beetroot and asparagus salad 66
Homemade Cheddar straws 195
Just-like-tuna pâté 82
Linguine with Stilton and onion 110
Pea and bacon risotto 121
Pizza giardiniera 141
Quick cheese sauce 217
Red onion, rosemary and Stilton tart 144
Sheep's cheese, olive and oregano bread 168
Smoked haddock, Parmesan and chive omelette 50

Smoked mackerel pâté 197
Spinach and Ricotta pasta bake
113

cherries
French toast with Polish cherries
53

chestnuts
Chestnut and lentil soup 201

chicken (210)
A soothing chicken curry 107
Asian-style chicken broth with
coriander and noodles 109
Asparagus and barley risotto 120
Chargrilled chicken, pepper and
herb couscous salad 192
Chicken and celery sandwich
filling 65
Chicken and mushroom pasta
bake 112
Italian-style veal stew 133
Mexican salsa chicken 125
Persian chicken 191
Poached chicken with parsley and
lemon dumplings 124
Rabbit, bacon and perry pie 134
Salt and pepper wings 126
Schnitzel 88
Sweet potato and chicken hash 74

chickpeas (211)
Chickpeas and chorizo 115
Homemade hummus 152
Persian chicken 191
Sweet potato, spinach and
chickpea bake 153

chicory
Mackerel, olive and orange salad
71

chillies
Asian-style chicken broth with
coriander and noodles 109
Avocado salsa salad to go with

tuna or mackerel 69
Honey-soy marinade 216
Mexican salsa chicken 125
Mexican-style guacamole 205
Seared tuna with fennel, mint and
chilli salad 100
Spicy cashew and mushroom rice
118
Sweet potato and chicken hash 74
Thai beef salad 86
Tortilla chips and salsa 83

chocolate (211)
Cappuccino cake 159
Choux puffs with cream and
warm cocoa sauce 180
Danish apple charlotte 157

chorizo
Chickpeas and chorizo 115

cider (211)
Rabbit, bacon and perry pie 134
Roast belly pork with black
pudding and 'heaven and earth'
mash 128

cocoa (211)

cod (211)
Portuguese-style salt cod bake
149

coffee (211)
Cappuccino cake 159

compôtes
Apple and cinnamon compôte
204
Cranberry, raspberry and apple
compôte 200
Dried fruit compôte with redbush
tea, cinnamon and honey 55
Winter raspberry compôte with
yoghurt and toasted oatmeal
47

coriander (211)
Asian-style chicken broth with
coriander and noodles 109
Fresh coriander chutney 211
Mexican salsa chicken 125
Sweet potato, spinach and
chickpea bake 153

courgettes (211)
Chargrilled chicken, pepper and
herb couscous salad 192
Pizza giardiniera 141
Spaghetti with zucchini and garlic
and lemon breadcrumbs 111
Stir-fried courgettes with dill or
mint 212
Spring vegetable frittata 48

couscous (212)
Chargrilled chicken, pepper and
herb couscous salad 192
Fish couscous 106

crab (212)

cream (212)
A soothing chicken curry 107
Asparagus and barley risotto 120
Cheddar, ham and onion quiche
146
Chestnut and lentil soup 201
Choux puffs with cream and
warm cocoa sauce 180
Danish apple charlotte 157
Hazelnut meringue cake 181
Kidneys with mustard 96
Linguine with Stilton and onion
110
Pea and bacon risotto 121
Pork and prunes 89
Real porridge 44
Salmon fishcakes with lemon
butter 147
Salmon, leek and dill hash 76
Smoked haddock in cream sauce
223
Smoked mackerel and potato

gratin 151
Spiced lentils with tomato and
    cream 116
Summer fruit pavlova 185
Summer pudding 182
Sweet potato, spinach and
    chickpea bake 153

crème fraîche
Mushroom caviar 196

crumbles
Apple, blackberry and nut
    crumble 184

cucumber (212)
Cucumber and herb salad 187
Avocado salsa salad to go with
    tuna or mackerel 69

curry
A soothing chicken curry 107

d

duck (212)
Spiced game pilaf 177
Sweet potato and chicken hash 74

e

eggs (212)
Banana chiffon cake 160
Carrot, oat and cinnamon muffins
    165
Cheddar, ham and onion quiche
    146
Choux puffs with cream and
    warm cocoa sauce 180
Croque monsieur 207
Empress of puddings 156
Egg-fried rice 223
Egg yolks 213
Egg whites 213
Hazelnut meringue cake 181

Lemon drizzle traybake 158
Mayonnaise verte 188
Meringues 213
Portuguese-style salt cod bake 149
Prawn and egg open sandwich 64
Summer fruit pavlova 185
Warm cauliflower, egg and
    anchovy salad 68

f

fat and dripping (213)

fennel (213)
Poached chicken with parsley and
    lemon dumplings 124
Seared tuna with fennel, mint and
    chilli salad 100

fish (213)
Avocado salsa salad to go with
    tuna or mackerel 69
Fish couscous 106
Frugal fish pie 148
Newspaper-wrapped trout with
    lemon butter 103
Prawn and egg open sandwich 64
Poached salmon 186
Pollack, bacon and sweetcorn
    chowder 104
Portuguese-style salt cod bake 149
Roast pollack with tomatoes,
    olives and capers 101
Salmon fishcakes with lemon
    butter 147
Salmon, leek and dill hash 76
Sardine 'rillettes' with lemon and
    parsley 61
Seared salmon with creamed
    leeks and chives 98
Seared tuna with fennel, mint and
    chilli salad 100
Smoked haddock in cream sauce
    223
Smoked haddock, Parmesan and
    chive omelette 50

Smoked mackerel and potato
    gratin 151
Smoked mackerel pâté 197
Warm cauliflower, egg and
    anchovy salad 68

flour (213)
Old-fashioned shortcrust pastry
    214

frittatas
Spring vegetable frittata 48

fruit (214)
An exotic syrup for fruit salads
    182
Apple, blackberry and nut
    crumble 184
Banana chiffon cake 160
Barm brack 161
Cranberry, raspberry and apple
    compôte 200
Fresh fruit muesli with yoghurt
    46
Dried fruits 214
Dried fruit compôte with redbush
    tea, cinnamon and honey 55
Empress of puddings 156
Hazelnut meringue cake 181
Moroccan-style lamb with dates,
    prunes and apricots 190
Peach and blueberry cobbler 154
Spiced game pilaf 177
Strawberry and apricot fruit salad
    with orange and mint 52
Summer fruit pavlova 185
Summer pudding 182
Winter raspberry compôte with
    yoghurt and toasted oatmeal
    47

g

garlic
Breast of lamb with lemon, garlic,
    mint and honey 129

Garlic bread 207
Homemade hummus 152
Salt and pepper wings 126
Slow-roasted shoulder of lamb
    with aromatic herbs 179
Spaghetti with zucchini and garlic
    and lemon breadcrumbs 111
Spiced parsnip soup with garlic
    raita 81

game (214)
Asparagus and barley risotto 120
Rabbit, bacon and perry pie 134
Pot roast pheasant with port 176
Spiced game pilaf 177

gherkins
Sausage, potato and gherkin salad
    72

ginger
A soothing chicken curry 107
Asian-style chicken broth with
    coriander and noodles 109
Hot honey ribs 131
Lemon and ginger flapjacks 166
Spiced lentils with tomato and
    cream 116

goat's cheese
Goat's cheese, beetroot and
    asparagus salad 66

goose (214)

gooseberries
Summer pudding 182

gratins
Smoked mackerel and potato
    gratin 151

greens (215)

gravy (215)
Cream gravy (see Norwegian
    meatballs) 138

Onion gravy 219
Basic gravy from roasting juices
    (see Slow-roast shoulder of
    lamb with aromatic herbs) 179

guineafowl (215)

h

haddock
Fish couscous 106
Smoked haddock, Parmesan and
    chive omelette 50

ham (215)
Cheddar, ham and onion quiche
    146
Croque monsieur 207
Ham, broad bean and herb pasta
    salad 73
Pea and ham soup 79
Potted ham 215
Spring vegetable frittata 48

hashes
Salmon, leek and dill hash 76
Sweet potato and chicken hash
    74

herbs (215)
Basic bolognese 136
Beer-can chicken 189
Chargrilled chicken, pepper and
    herb couscous salad 192
Chicken and mushroom pasta
    bake 112
Cucumber and herb salad 187
Goat's cheese, beetroot and
    asparagus salad 66
Ham, broad bean and herb pasta
    salad 73
Mayonnaise verte 188
Mushrooms a la grecque 218
Persian chicken 191
Pizza giardiniera 141

Red onion, rosemary and Stilton
    tart 144
Salmon, leek and dill hash 76
Sardine 'rillettes' with lemon and
    parsley 61
Seared salmon with creamed
    leeks and chives 98
Seared tuna with fennel, mint and
    chilli salad 100
Sheep's cheese, olive and oregano
    bread 168
Slow-roasted shoulder of lamb
    with aromatic herbs 179
Smoked haddock, Parmesan and
    chive omelette 50
Spiced game pilaf 177
Stalky spinach, pea and mint soup
    179
Stir-fried courgettes with dill or
    mint 212
Strawberry and apricot fruit salad
    with orange and mint 52
Turkey and tarragon terrine 199

honey (216)
Breast of lamb with lemon, garlic,
    mint and honey 129
Carrot, oat and cinnamon muffins
    165
Dried fruit compôte with redbush
    tea, cinnamon and honey 55
Honey-soy marinade 216
Hot honey ribs 131
Sheep's cheese, olive and oregano
    bread 168
Homemade hummus 152

k

kidneys
Kidneys with mustard 96
Lambs kidneys and mushrooms in
    sherry 97

kippers
Smoked mackerel pâté 197

kiwi fruit
Strawberry and apricot fruit salad
  with orange and mint 52

l

lamb (216)
Breast of lamb with lemon, garlic,
  mint and honey 129
Lovely lamb and leek stew 132
Moroccan-style lamb with dates,
  prunes and apricots 190
Slow-roasted shoulder of lamb
  with aromatic herbs 179
Thai beef salad 86

leeks (184)
Chestnut and lentil soup 201
Lovely lamb and leek stew 132
Salmon, leek and dill hash 76
Seared salmon with creamed
  leeks and chives 98
Spring vegetable frittata 48
Two vegetable minestrone 77
Winter sausages with stoemp 91

lemon (216)
Apple lemonade 204
Breast of lamb with lemon, garlic,
  mint and honey 129
Homemade hummus 152
Lemon and ginger flapjacks 166
Lemon drizzle traybake 158
Lemon parsley butter 216
Newspaper-wrapped trout with
  lemon butter 103
Peach and blueberry cobbler 154
Poached chicken with parsley and
  lemon dumplings 124
Salmon fishcakes with lemon
  butter 147
Sardine 'rillettes' with lemon and
  parsley 61
Smoked mackerel pâté 197
Spaghetti with zucchini and garlic

and lemon breadcrumbs 111

lentils (216)
Chestnut and lentil soup 201
Spiced lentils with tomato and
  cream 116

lettuce (217)
Chicken and celery sandwich
  filling 65
Goat's cheese, beetroot and
  asparagus salad 66
Limes 217
Persian chicken 191

liver
Fegato con balsamico 94
Kebda with warm red pepper
  salad 95

m

mackerel
Avocado salsa salad to go with
  tuna or mackerel 69
Mackerel, olive and orange salad
  71
Sardine 'rillettes' with lemon and
  parsley 61
Smoked mackerel and potato
  gratin 151
Smoked mackerel pâté 197

mandarins (219)

mangoes (217)

mayonnaise
Mayonnaise verte 188
Turkey and tarragon terrine 199

meat (217)
See also chicken, duck, game,
  lamb, pork, turkey

melons (217)

muesli
Fresh fruit muesli with yoghurt
  46
Lemon and ginger flapjacks 166

milk (217)
Bread sauce 208
Caramelised cauliflower soup 174
Cardamom rice pudding 217
Empress of puddings 156
Ina Pinkney's buttermilk
  pancakes 56
Quick cheese sauce 217

mince
Basic bolognese 136
Budget meatloaf 140
Norwegian meatballs 138
Thai beef salad 86

mint (218)
Breast of lamb with lemon, garlic,
  mint and honey 129
Seared tuna with fennel, mint and
  chilli salad 100
Stalky spinach, pea and mint soup
  179
Strawberry and apricot fruit salad
  with orange and mint 52

mushrooms (218)
Chicken and mushroom pasta
  bake 112
Italian-style veal stew 133
Grilled mushrooms on toast 60
Lambs kidneys and mushrooms in
  sherry 97
Mushrooms a la grecque 218
Mushroom caviar 196
Rabbit, bacon and perry pie 134
Spiced game pilaf 177
Spicy cashew and mushroom rice
  118
Spinach and Ricotta pasta bake
  113

mustard
Hot honey ribs 131
Kidneys with mustard 96
Salmon fishcakes with lemon
   butter 147
Sausage, potato and gherkin salad
   72
Smoked mackerel and potato
   gratin 151

n

nectarines
Peach and blueberry cobbler 154

nuts (218)
Apple, blackberry and nut
   crumble 184
Banana chiffon cake 160
Chargrilled chicken, pepper and
   herb couscous salad 192
Crunchy peanut cookies 163
Dried fruit compôte with redbush
   tea, cinnamon and honey 55
Goat's cheese, beetroot and
   asparagus salad 66
Hazelnut meringue cake 181
Spiced game pilaf 177
Spicy cashew and mushroom rice
   118
Turkey and tarragon terrine 199

noodles (218)
Asian-style chicken broth with
   coriander and noodles 109

o

oats/oatmeal (219)
Apple and cinnamon porridge 45
Budget meatloaf 140
Carrot, oat and cinnamon muffins
   165
Real Porridge 44
Wholemeal porridge bread 167

Winter raspberry compôte with
   yoghurt and toasted oatmeal
   47

offal
Fegato con balsamico 94
Kebda with warm red pepper
   salad 95
Kidneys with mustard 96

olives (219)
Mackerel, olive and orange salad
   71
Roast pollack with tomatoes,
   olives and capers 101
Sheep's cheese, olive and oregano
   bread 168

omelette
Smoked haddock, Parmesan and
   chive omelette 50

onions (219)
Apple and onion sauce for serving
   with pork or sausages 204
Braised beef short-ribs with red
   wine and polenta 177
Cheddar, ham and onion quiche
   146
Chestnut and lentil soup 201
Linguine with Stilton and onion
   110
Mexican salsa chicken 125
Moroccan-style lamb with dates,
   prunes and apricots 190
Onion gravy 219
Portuguese-style salt cod bake
   149
Pot roast pheasant with port 176
Red onion, rosemary and Stilton
   tart 144
Sweet potato and chicken hash
   74
Sweet potato, spinach and
   chickpea bake 153
Winter sausages with stoemp 91

oranges (219)
Lemon drizzle traybake 158
Mackerel, olive and orange salad
   71
Strawberry and apricot fruit salad
   with orange and mint 52
Moroccan-style spiced carrot
   salad 209

P

pak choi
Asian-style chicken broth with
   coriander and noodles 109

pancakes
Ina Pinkney's buttermilk
   pancakes 56
Spinach and Ricotta pasta bake 113

parsley (220)
Poached chicken with parsley and
   lemon dumplings 124

parsnips (220)
Spiced parsnip soup with garlic
   raita 81

pasta (220)
Asian-style chicken broth with
   coriander and noodles 109
Basic bolognese 136
Chicken and mushroom pasta
   bake 112
Ham, broad bean and herb pasta
   salad 73
Linguine with Stilton and onion
   110
Spaghetti with zucchini and garlic
   and lemon breadcrumbs 111
Spinach and Ricotta pasta bake
   113

pastry
Old-fashioned shortcrust pastry
   214

pâté
Just-like-tuna pâté 82
Smoked mackerel pâté 197

peaches (220)
Hazelnut meringue cake 181
Peach and blueberry cobbler 154
Summer fruit pavlova 185

peanuts
Crunchy peanut cookies 163

pears (220)
Fresh fruit muesli with yoghurt
    46

peas (220)
Pea and bacon risotto 121
Pea and ham soup 79
Spiced game pilaf 177
Stalky spinach, pea and mint soup
    179
Sweet potato and chicken hash
    74

peppers (221)
Avocado salsa salad to go with
    tuna or mackerel 69
Chargrilled chicken, pepper and
    herb couscous salad 192
Chickpeas and chorizo 115
Red onion, rosemary and stilton
    tart 144
Summer sausages with peppers
    and butterbean mash 93
Sweet potato, spinach and
    chickpea bake 153
Tortilla chips and salsa 83
Warm red pepper salad 95

pheasant (221)
Pot roast pheasant with port 176

pies
Frugal fish pie 148
Rabbit, bacon and perry pie 134

pineapple (221)

pinenuts
Chargrilled chicken, pepper and
    herb couscous salad 192
Fresh pesto 206

pizza
Pizza giardiniera 141

plums (221)
Apple, blackberry and nut
    crumble 184
Fresh fruit muesli with yoghurt 46
Peach and blueberry cobbler 154

polenta (221)
Braised beef short-ribs with red
    wine and polenta 177

pollack
Fish couscous 106
Roast pollack with tomatoes,
    olives and capers 101
Pollack, bacon and sweetcorn
    chowder 104

pork (221)
Apple and onion sauce for serving
    with pork or sausages 204
Budget meatloaf 140
Hot honey ribs 131
Italian-style veal stew 133
Moroccan-style lamb with dates,
    prunes and apricots 190
Norwegian meatballs 138
Pork and prunes 89
Roast belly pork with black
    pudding and 'heaven and earth'
    mash 128
Schnitzel 88
Slow-roast shoulder of lamb with
    aromatic herbs 179

porridge
Real Porridge 44

port
Cranberry, raspberry and apple
    compôte 200
Pot roast pheasant with port 176

potatoes (221)
Bubble and squeak 200
German-style potato salad 221
Frugal fish pie 148
Lovely lamb and leek stew 132
Persian chicken 191
Pollack, bacon and sweetcorn
    chowder 104
Portuguese-style salt cod bake
    149
Potato cakes 222
Roast belly pork with black
    pudding and 'heaven and earth'
    mash 128
Salmon fishcakes with lemon
    butter 147
Salmon, leek and dill hash 76
Sausage, potato and gherkin salad
    72
Smoked mackerel and potato
    gratin 151
Stalky spinach, pea and mint soup
    179
Winter sausages with stoemp 91

prawns (222)
Asian-style chicken broth with
    coriander and noodles 109
Fish couscous 106
Frugal fish pie 148
Pollack, bacon and sweetcorn
    chowder 104
Prawn and egg open sandwich 64
Spicy cashew and mushroom rice
    118

prunes
Pork and prunes 89
Spiced game pilaf 177

q

quiche
Cheddar, ham and onion quiche 146

r

rabbit
Rabbit, bacon and perry pie 134

raita
Spiced parsnip soup with garlic raita 81

raspberries (222)
Cranberry, raspberry and apple compôte 200
Empress of puddings 156
Hazelnut meringue cake 181
Winter raspberry compôte with yoghurt and toasted oatmeal 47

rhubarb (222)
Apple, blackberry and nut crumble 184
Danish apple charlotte 157

rice (222)
Asparagus and barley risotto 120
Cardamom rice pudding 217
Egg-fried rice 223
Fish couscous 106
Pea and bacon risotto 121
Spiced game pilaf 177
Spicy cashew and mushroom rice 118

Ricotta
Spinach and Ricotta pasta bake 113

risotto
Asparagus and barley risotto 120
Pea and bacon risotto 121

s

salads (223)
Avocado salsa salad to go with tuna or mackerel 69
Chargrilled chicken, pepper and herb couscous salad 192
Cucumber and herb salad 187
German-style potato salad 221
Ham, broad bean and herb pasta salad 73
Mackerel, olive and orange salad 71
Moroccan-style spiced carrot salad 209
Poached salmon with cucumber salad and herb mayonnaise 186
Sausage, potato and gherkin salad 72
Seared tuna with fennel, mint and chilli salad 100
Strawberry and apricot fruit salad with orange and mint 52
Thai beef salad 86
Warm cauliflower, egg and anchovy salad 68
Warm red pepper salad 95

salmon (223)
Cheddar, ham and onion quiche 146
Poached salmon 186
Salmon fishcakes with lemon butter 147
Salmon, leek and dill hash 76
Seared salmon with creamed leeks and chives 98
Smoked haddock, Parmesan and chive omelette 50

salsas and relishes
Avocado salsa salad to go with tuna or mackerel 69
Mexican salsa chicken 125
Mexican-style guacamole 205
Tortilla chips and salsa 83

sandwiches
Chicken and celery sandwich filling 65
Prawn and egg open sandwich 64

sardines
Just-like-tuna pâté 82
Sardine 'rillettes' with lemon and parsley 61

satsumas (219)

sauces
An exotic syrup for fruit salads 214
Apple and onion sauce for serving with pork or sausages 204
Basic bolognese 136
Bread sauce 208
Choux puffs with cream and warm cocoa sauce 180
Fresh pesto 206
Honey-soy marinade 216
Lemon parsley butter 216
Mayonnaise verte 188
Norwegian meatballs 138
Onion gravy 219
Simple Fresh Tomato Sauce 224
Slow-roast shoulder of lamb with aromatic herbs 179
Smoked haddock in cream sauce 223
Quick cheese sauce 217

sausages
Apple and onion sauce for serving with pork or sausages 204
Budget meatloaf 140
Sausage, potato and gherkin salad 72
Summer sausages with peppers and butterbean mash 93
Winter sausages with stoemp 91

scones, Granny Smith 162

shallots
Bavette aux echalotes 90
Lambs kidneys and mushrooms in
 sherry 97
Mushroom caviar 196
Thai beef salad 86

shellfish
Fish couscous 106
Frugal fish pie 148

sherry
Chestnut and lentil soup 201
Kidneys with mustard 96
Lambs kidneys and mushrooms in
 sherry 97
Turkey and tarragon terrine 199

smoked fish (223)
Frugal fish pie 148
Smoked haddock in cream sauce
 223
Smoked mackerel and potato
 gratin 151
Smoked mackerel pâté 197

soups
Asian-style chicken broth with
 coriander and noodles 109
Caramelised cauliflower soup 174
Chestnut and lentil soup 201
Pea and ham soup 79
Pollack, bacon and sweetcorn
 chowder 104
Stalky spinach, pea and mint soup
 179
Spiced parsnip soup with garlic
 raita 81
Two vegetable minestrone 77

spices
An exotic syrup for fruit salads
 214
Apple and cinnamon compôte 204
Cardamom rice pudding 217
Carrot, oat and cinnamon muffins
 165

Cinnamon toast 207
Dried fruit compôte with redbush
 tea, cinnamon and honey 55
Fish couscous 106
Moroccan-style lamb with dates,
 prunes and apricots 190
Moroccan-style spiced carrot
 salad 209
Norwegian meatballs 138
Roast belly pork with black
 pudding and 'heaven and earth'
 mash 128
Spiced game pilaf 177
Spiced lentils with tomato and
 cream 116
Spiced parsnip soup with garlic
 raita 81
Spicy cashew and mushroom rice
 118
Sweet potato and chicken hash 74
Sweet potato, spinach and
 chickpea bake 153
Kebda with warm red pepper
 salad 95

spinach (223)
Persian chicken 191
Stalky spinach, pea and mint soup
 179
Spinach and Ricotta pasta bake 113
Sweet potato, spinach and
 chickpea bake 153

spring onions
A soothing chicken curry 107
Asparagus and barley risotto 120
Cheddar, ham and onion quiche
 146
Mexican salsa chicken 125
Pea and bacon risotto 121
Pizza giardiniera 141
Spinach and Ricotta pasta bake
 113
Spring vegetable frittata 48
Summer sausages with peppers
 and butterbean mash 93
Sweet potato and chicken hash 74

Warm cauliflower, egg and
 anchovy salad 68

sprouts (224)
Bubble and squeak 200

stews
Italian-style veal stew 133
Lovely lamb and leek stew 132

strawberries (224)
Danish apple charlotte 157
Fresh fruit muesli with yoghurt
 46
Strawberry and apricot fruit salad
 with orange and mint 52
Summer fruit pavlova 185
Summer pudding 182

swede
Pea and ham soup
Winter sausages with stoemp 91

sweetcorn (224)
Chargrilled chicken, pepper and
 herb couscous salad 192
Pollack, bacon and sweetcorn
 chowder 104

sweet potato
Sweet potato and chicken hash
 74
Sweet potato, spinach and
 chickpea bake 153

syrups
An exotic syrup for fruit salads
 214
Lemon and ginger flapjacks 166

t

tarts
Red onion, rosemary and Stilton
 tart 144

tea
Barm brack 161
Dried fruit compôte with redbush tea, cinnamon and honey 55

tomatoes (224)
Avocado salsa salad to go with tuna or mackerel 69
Chargrilled chicken, pepper and herb couscous salad 192
Chickpeas and chorizo 115
Fish couscous 106
Grilled Tomatoes on Toast 63
Hot honey ribs 131
Italian-style veal stew 133
Mexican-style guacamole 205
Pizza giardiniera 141
Prawn and egg open sandwich 64
Roast pollack with tomatoes, olives and capers 101
Simple Fresh Tomato Sauce 224
Slow roast tomatoes 224
Spiced lentils with tomato and cream 116
Spicy cashew and mushroom rice 118
Sweet potato, spinach and chickpea bake 153
Thai beef salad 86
Basic bolognese 136
Tortilla chips and salsa 83
Two vegetable minestrone 77

trout
Newspaper-wrapped trout with lemon butter 103

Tortilla chips and salsa 83

tuna (224)
Avocado salsa salad to go with tuna or mackerel 69
Chicken and celery sandwich filling 65
Mackerel, olive and orange salad 71
Sardine 'rillettes' with lemon and parsley 61
Seared tuna with fennel, mint and chilli salad 100

turkey (224)
Norwegian meatballs 138
Schnitzel 88
Turkey and tarragon terrine 199

turnips
Pea and ham soup 79
Pot roast pheasant with port 176
Winter sausages with stoemp 91

V

veal
Italian-style veal stew 133
Schnitzel 88

vegetables (225)

vegetarian
An exotic syrup for fruit salads 214
Apple and cinnamon compôte 204
Apple and cinnamon porridge 45
Apple, blackberry and nut crumble 184
Apple lemonade 204
Asparagus and barley risotto 120
Banana chiffon cake 160
Barm brack 161
Blue cheese butter 210
Bread sauce 208
Bubble and squeak 200
Cappuccino cake
Caramelised cauliflower soup 174
Cardamom rice pudding 217
Carrot, oat and cinnamon muffins 165
Chestnut and lentil soup 201
Choux puffs with cream and warm cocoa sauce 180
Cinnamon toast 207
Cranberry, raspberry and apple compôte
Cranberry, raspberry and apple compôte 200
Crostini bases 207
Croûtons 207
Crunchy peanut cookies 163
Danish apple charlotte 157
Dried breadcrumbs 208
Dried fruit compôte with redbush tea, cinnamon and honey 55
Easy watercress soup 225
Egg-fried rice 223
Empress of puddings 156
French toast with Polish cherries 53
Fresh coriander chutney 211
Fresh fruit muesli with yoghurt 46
Fresh pesto 206
Fromage fort 210
Garlic bread 207
Goats cheese, beetroot and asparagus salad 66
Granny Smith scones 162
Grilled mushrooms on toast 60
Grilled tomatoes on toast 63
Hazelnut meringue cake 181
Homemade Cheddar straws 195
Homemade hummus 152
Ina Pinkney's buttermilk pancakes 56
Leftover ciabatta and baguettes
Lemon and ginger flapjacks 166
Lemon drizzle traybake 158
Lemon parsley butter 216
Linguine with Stilton and onion 110
Mayonnaise verte 188
Mexican-style guacamole 205
Moroccan-style spiced carrot salad 209
Mushroom caviar 196
Mushrooms a la grecque 218
Old-fashioned shortcrust pastry 214
Onion gravy 219